THE ETERNAL KINGDOM

The

Eternal Kingdom

A HISTORY OF THE CHURCH OF CHRIST

BY

F. W. MATTOX, PH. D
President, Lubbock Christian College
Lubbock, Texas

Revised and With Additional Chapters By

JOHN McRAY
Department of Church History, Harding College
Searcy, Arkansas

"And in the days of these kings shall the God of heaven set up a kingdom which shall never be destroyed, nor shall the sovereignty thereof be left to another people; but it shall break in pieces and consume all these kingdoms, and it shall stand forever." — Daniel 2:44.

GOSPEL LIGHT PUBLISHING COMPANY
DELIGHT, ARKANSAS

PREFACE

The facts of church history are easily obtainable. Even the beginning student may have at his disposal the source material from which the general histories have been written. One may also obtain without difficulty volumes of church history written from many points of view. Why then this volume? To the author's knowledge there is not in existence a general history of the church written to help the reader understand undenominational Christianity. This book is an attempt to fill this need.

All events recorded here are as true to fact as modern scholarship is able to ascertain. The author makes no pretense to the discovery of new materials. Rather he has relied upon specialists in narrow fields of study to supply the needed information, where source materials are not at hand. It is in the realm of selection and interpretation of data that the author hopes a contribution has been made which justifies this publication.

The evils of religious division have caused sincere Christians in every age to try to find a workable basis for unity. These efforts have taken many forms. Since the year 1800, there has emerged with growing clarity the concept that the only solid basis for unity is a return to the undenominationalism of the New Testament.

Ecumenical movements, interdenominationalism, the Open Door church and United Protestant movements all fail to restore the unity due to a necessary watering down of doctrinal teaching. Even the authority of the Scripture is set aside to give freedom to disagree.

The undenominational concept accepts unquestionably the authority of the New Testament. All believers are urged to state their faith in New Testament language. The organization, doctrine, worship and practice of the church is reproduced according to the pattern set forth in the New Testament and any departure from the New Testament pattern is recognized

as a human innovation. The true nature of undenominationalism can be most clearly seen in its historical setting. Since denominational confusion is of recent development and efforts
to unite the various religious groups have resulted in frustra-
tion it is a refreshing experience to view the New Testament
church in its original purity and to realize that the same divine
pattern can be followed with the same results today.

F. W. Mattox
Harding College
Searcy, Arkansas

September, 1955.

(vi)

REVISER'S PREFACE

After THE ETERNAL KINGDOM was written by Dr. Mattox in 1955, it was produced in mimeograph form and used in classwork at Harding College and in church study groups. After five years of such use, the demands that it come out in printed form urged that revisions be made to prepare it for publication.

Chapters nineteen and thirty-three are from the pen of the reviser. It now goes forth with the hope that it may find wide circulation and contribute to a better understanding of the New Testament Church.

It is hoped that the compactness of the book and the refreshing point of view from which Dr. Mattox has written may serve to give it a place in the library of every student of the Bible. Special thanks is due Dr. George S. Benson, President of Harding College, for making the revision and publication of this book possible. It was by his suggestion and liberality that the work was undertaken.

John McRay
Harding College
Searcy, Arkansas

November, 1960

CONTENTS

PART ONE

DIVINE BEGINNINGS

Chapter One

In the Fullness of Time _____ 19
  I. The Roman Government: moral conditions
  II. The Social Order
  III. Moral Conditions
  IV. Religion
  V. The Mystery Religions
  VI. Zorastrianism
  VII. Mithraism
  VIII. Roman Religion
  IX. The Jewish Contribution: The Sadducees; The Pharisees;
       The Essenes; The Zealots
  X. The Greek Heritage

Chapter Two

Historical Evidence Concerning the Life of Jesus _____ 31
  I. Josephus
  II. Tacitus
  III. Suetonius
  IV. Pliny
  V. Conclusions

Chapter Three

The New Testament Church _____ 40
  I. Establishment of the Church
  II. Definition of Terms
  III. The Church in Prophecy
  IV. The Church in Preparation
  V. The Church in Reality
  VI. The Basis of Membership
  VII. Rapid Growth
  VIII. Early Spread
  IX. Organization and Government
  X. Worship of the Church
  XI. Manner of Life

PART TWO

CONTROVERSY AND DEPARTURE 100-312 A.D.

Chapter Four

Uninspired Writings, 100-150 _____ 55
    I. Clement of Rome
   II. Ignatius of Antioch
  III. The Epistle of Barnabas
   IV. The Didache
    V. Papias
   VI. Polycarp
  VII. Shepherd of Hermas
 VIII. Summary

Chapter Five

The Apologists, 185-250 _____ 67
    I. Quadratus
   II. Aristides
  III. Justin Martyr
   IV. Tatian
    V. Melito
   VI. Athenagoras
  VII. Theophilus

The State of the Church
    I. Marcion
   II. Gnosticism
  III. Docetism
   IV. Montanism

Later Apologists
    I. Irenaeus
   II. Clement of Alexandria
  III. Tertullian
   IV. Hippolytus
    V. Origen

Chapter Six

Through Persecution to Victory, 54-313 _____ 88
    I. Chronology of Persecution
   II. Edict of Toleration
  III. Edict of Milan

Chapter Seven

The Development of the Canon _____ 101
    I. The Source of Inspired Writings
   II. Method of Distribution
  III. Early References to New Testament Letters

(x)

IV. Tests Applied to Questioned Books
V. Apocryphal Works

Chapter Eight

Departure From the New Testament Pattern, 100-325 ___ 107
I. Departure in Organization
II. Development of a Priesthood
III. The Growth of Sects
IV. Neoplatonism
V. Manichaeism
VI. The Ebionites
VII. Monarchianism
VIII. Donatists

Further Departure In Doctrine

I. Millennialism
II. Original Sin and Baptism

Departure In Manner O Life

I. Asceticism and Celibacy
II. Easter Celebration
III. Summary of Part Two

PART THREE

THE INCREASE OF ERROR, 313-787 A.D.

Chapter Nine

The Influence of Constantine _____ 125
I. Support of the Church
II. Council of Nicaea

Chapter Ten

The Growth of Episcopacy _____ 134
I. Chronological Development
II. The Battle of the Bishops

Chapter Eleven

The Ecumenical Councils _____ 141
I. Council of Nicaea 325
II. Council of Constantinople 381
III. Council of Ephesus 431
IV. Council of Chalcedon 451
V. Council of Constantinople 553
VI. Council of Constantinople 680
VII. Council of Nicaea 787

Chapter Twelve

The Life, Worship, and Doctrine Under Romanism _____ 149

(xi)

    I. The Establishment of Catholicity
   II. Sacredotalism
  III. Baptism
  IV. The Lord's Supper
   V. Increase of Sacraments
  VI. Instrumental Music Introduced
 VII. Monasticism
VIII. Controversy on the Human Will

Chapter Thirteen
Theory and Organization of Roman Catholicism 160

The Theory of Romanism
    I. The Teaching Ministry of the Church
   II. The Priestly Function of the Church
  III. The Kingly Function of the Church

Organization of the Roman Church
    I. The Regular Priests
   II. The Secular Clergy
  III. Powers of Orders
  IV. Powers of Jurisdiction: (1) Parish Priest; (2) Rural Dean;
        (3) Vicar General; (4) Bishop; (5) Archbishop; (6) Papal
        Legate; (7) The Pope
Chart of Undenominationalism Contrasted with Romanism.

Chapter Fourteen
The Rise of Mohammedanism 169

PART FOUR

THE GROWTH OF PAPAL POWER

Chapter Fifteen
Sources of Support for the Papacy 177
    I. Papal Recognition by Secular Rulers
   II. Papal Support From False Documents
  III. Papal Support From Hierarchy

Chapter Sixteen
The Strong Popes 189
   Gregory I, Nicholas I, Gregory VII, Innocent III, Boniface VIII.

Chapter Seventeen
The Crusades 197

Chapter Eighteen
Opposition to the Papacy 203
    I. Opposition Groups

II. Church Succession Through Opposition Groups
III. The Catharists
IV. Arnold of Brescia
V. Peter of Bruys
VI. Peter Waldo and the Waldenses
VII. The Albigenses
VIII. The Inquisition
IX. The True Church

PART FIVE

REFORMATION BEGINNINGS

Chapter Nineteen

The Need for Reformation 219
I. Celibacy
II. Simony
III. Indulgences
IV. Hagiolatry

Chapter Twenty

Early Reform Movements 223
I. William of Occam
II. John Wycliffe
III. John Huss
IV. Girolamo Savonarola
V. Ximenes

Chapter Twenty-One

Decline of Papal Influence 230
I. The Popes
II. The Renaissance
III. Petrarch

PART SIX

THE PROTESTANT REFORMATION — 1517-1800

Chapter Twenty-Two

The German Reformation 239
I. The Sale of Indulgences
II. Martin Luther
III. Diet of Speier

Chapter Twenty-Three

The Swiss Reformation 254
I. Huldreich Zwingli
II. Marburg

(xiii)

III. John Calvin
IV. Calvinism versus Arminianism

Chapter Twenty-Four

The Spread of Reform Ideas in Europe _____ 262
    I. Anabaptists
    II. Meno Simons

Chapter Twenty-Five

Reformation in England _____ 267
    I. English Humanism
    II. Break With the Pope
    III. Edward VI
    IV. Elizabeth
    V. Bible Translations Into English
    VI. The Rise of Denominations in England
    VII. The Romanists
    VIII. The Dutch Reformed
    IX. The Presbyterians
    X. The Quakers
    XI. The Baptist Church
    XII. John Wesley and the Methodists

Chapter Twenty-Six

Roman Reaction to Reformation _____ 289
    I. Before Trent
    II. The Council of Trent
    III. The Society of Jesus

Chapter Twenty-Seven

The Religious Wars _____ 296

Chapter Twenty-Eight

Denominationalism Transferred to America _____ 303
    I. Roman Catholicism
    II. The Church of England
    III. Puritans, Separatists, Congregationalists
    IV. Presbyterianism
    V. The Methodists
    VI. The Baptists
    VII. Other Religious Bodies
    VIII. Proposed Basis for Unity

PART SEVEN

THE RESTORATION MOVEMENT — 19th Century

Chapter Twenty-Nine

Early Beginnings Toward Undenominationalism _____ 311
    I.   James O'Kelley — Methodist
    II. Abner Jones — Baptist
    III. Barton W. Stone — Presbyterian
    IV. "The Last Will and Testament of the Springfield Pres-
         bytery"
    V. John Wright — Baptist
    VI. Thomas Campbell

Chapter Thirty

Principles of Undenominationalism _____ 320
    "The Declaration and Address"

Chapter Thirty-One

The Restoration Fully Launched _____ 326
    I.   The Brush Run Church
    II. Association With the Baptists
    III. The Campbell-Walker Debate
    IV. The Campbell-McCalla Debate
    V. The Christian Baptist
    VI. Walter Scott
    VII. Extent of Agreement with the Baptists
    VIII. "The Gospel Restored"

Chapter Thirty-Two

Union of Forces: Stone and Campbell _____ 341

Chapter Thirty-Three

The Unfinished Restoration _____ 348

PART I

DIVINE BEGINNINGS

Chapter One

In the Fullness of Time

The death of the Incarnate Son of God on a Roman cross marks the central point in the history of mankind. When He cried out, "It is finished," He marked the completion of a long chain of events that had taken place according to divine guidance. The death of Christ was not accidental nor incidental, but according to God's determinate counsel and foreknowledge (Acts 2:23).

All that had gone on before the death of Christ was preparation for this great event. From the fall of Adam in the Garden of Eden, through the patriarchs and prophets, God's plan began to unfold. We now clearly see how the Law of Moses was a "tutor to bring us to Christ." (Gal. 3:24). However, the revelation of "the mystery of Christ which in other generations was not made known unto the sons of men" (Eph. 3:5) had to wait for this preparation to be completed. "But when the fullness of the time came, God sent forth His Son." (Gal. 4:4).

In order to understand the history of the church we must know the world in which the church had its beginning and in which it moved. The social, philosophical and religious movements of the day affected the church from its beginning. Some of these influences were constructive, while others hindered the spread of the gospel through intellectual attacks and through physical persecution. Let us ascend to the pinnacle of the temple and take a look at the kind of world Christ knew as a boy.

As one climbs to the vantage point of the highest balcony of the temple in Jerusalem, the size of the stones and the skill shown in architectural design make a profound impression. This temple, built by Herod, was smaller than that of Solomon, yet it had been under construction forty years and was considered one of the wonders of the world. It stands as a memorial to God's dealing with the Hebrew race; its very conception being traced back to the tabernacle, which the Divine architect blueprinted and delivered to Moses.

As one looks down upon the crowd he is impressed with the variety of human life. There are the temple priests going and coming with their sacrifices and incense, philosophers of various Greek Schools, Roman soldiers served by slaves taken captive in many battles, but who are superior to the captors in learning and culture. There, too, are the farmers and their donkeys, traders with their goods, women with their water pots, and children; all conversing in a language which is soon to become the language of the Gospels and the letters to the churches. But let us look more minutely at the segments that made up the world that Jesus knew as a boy.

I. THE ROMAN GOVERNMENT

Westward from the temple, forty miles away, is the coast line of the Mediterranean Sea and 1500 miles beyond that in the height of its glory, was what men called the most wonderful city in the world, Rome. It took three months to make a trip to Rome, yet the political genius of the Roman government made itself felt in every hamlet in the most distant province. Palestine was no exception. The presence of the occupation soldiers with the accompanying tax collectors ever reminded the Jews that they were a subject people. Although Augustus Caesar instituted a policy of non-intervention in the interests of the empire, it took very little to stir a spirit of rebellion in the freedom-loving "chosen people of God."

There were obvious benefits, however, from a powerful central government even to a subject people, and many conditions worked together to prepare the world for the coming of the Messiah and make possible the rapid spread of the Gospel to all the world.

At the conclusion of the civil wars, Augustus obtained through the senate autocratic power and restored peace to the Empire. This was felt as an immense boon by the populace, and Augustus himself felt that security was more important than glory won by additional conquest. Such a period of peace was essential for the effective spread of the Gospel.

The opening of the world to trade and travel was another benefit conferred by the empire. Never before in the history of the world had the nations been brought so near to each other. Not only was there universal law, there was also a unity of mankind that had not been known before. Having a common coinage and being encouraged by widely a extended system of free trade, commerce flourished. Excellent roads were built and never until our own generation has travel been so easy or so frequent. The pirates were removed from the Mediterranean, and order and prosperity were found during the first century over the whole Roman world, which included the hinterland lying back of the 6000 miles of Mediterranean coast line. This prosperity, however, could not long continue, for the government had within it the seed of its own destruction. Slavery was the basis of this material and industrial empire. This system of degraded, forced labor, rendered free labor disgraceful and unprofitable. The extravagance of the emperors and of the Imperial Administration wasted the wealth of the world with such rapidity that it resulted in a system of taxation so burdensome, oppressive and finally destructive that it impoverished the most fertile countries, diminished and enslaved the population and made inevitable the ruin of the empire. Taxes were of two kinds. The "annual" tax levied upon the entire community was collected by the city council and constituted a guaranteed annual tax. The city council would use every means to collect these taxes as otherwise they were held responsible. The privilege of collecting the "direct" taxes was sold to the highest bidder, who deposited a large sum with the State as security that the money would reach the state treasury. Such officials must collect these taxes or be financially ruined. These were the publicans. Their profit was the sum raised above the amount required by the state, and they had every reason to oppress the taxpayer. In Palestine they were generally Jews and were looked upon as traitors to their race.

II. THE SOCIAL ORDER

At the top of the stratified Roman society was the Emperor. Then came the Senators, Knights, Citizens, Provincials, free born, slaves and beggars. Besides the general division of society into these classes, there were also subdivisions according to professions and trades. Social inequalities were also fostered by prejudices of race. In the first century it is estimated there were more slaves than freemen in the empire. Of these many were educated and cultured persons holding positions of responsibility. There were also arrangements whereby they could hold back a small part of the value of their services so that eventually they could purchase their freedom. Persons were made slaves in many ways. During the conquests large numbers of captives were subjected to slavery, and children of the slave class remained slaves. Exposed children found and reared for a time by foster parents were also sold into slavery. But the most common cause became debt. Taxes were so oppressive that business reverses or drouth could easily result in a man's being sold with his property to meet his financial obligations. In case a loan could not be met when due, the borrower would be taken into slavery.

The Romans possessed a contempt for trade and the more humble pursuits which give productive occupation to the great bulk of people in a healthy society. There was, as a consequence of this, a large number of persons with no regular means of livelihood. Many of them were attentive to wealthy patrons and by flattery and small services received subsistence in exchange. The poorest class, which was very large in Rome, was provided for by a daily dole of bread by the state.

Knowledge of these extremes in social and economic conditions clarifies the fact that "not many noble, not many mighty were called," but that "the poor heard Him gladly."

III.   MORAL CONDITIONS

The depraved condition of mankind pictured by the Apostle Paul in the first chapter of Romans is verified by all secular history. As a result of Roman conquests, wealth and luxury were made possible for the upper classes. Through the wide extension of slavery a wave of corruption swept over the empire that completed the dissolution of morals and offered a period unparalleled in history for debauchery and wickedness. Pagan religion readily adapted itself to the propagation of vice and the temples of Isis were constantly used for the vilest purposes. Women became even more depraved than the men and from the court to the beggar the whole society was corrupted. The great towns such as Antioch, Alexandria, Corinth and Ephesus were imitators of Rome in its worst excesses.

The first marriage was usually arranged by the parents with the young people unacquainted. The marriage was a civil contract and could be dissolved at the pleasure of either party. Divorce became so commonplace that Seneca referred to women who counted their age by the change of husbands, and Juvenal mentions one woman who married eight husbands in five years. Divorce was resolved upon the slightest pretext, and many separated merely from the love of change.

The idea of life being sacred in itself was quite foreign to the Roman mind. Abortion was not discouraged by law and was very extensively practiced. It was apparently well understood and a regular part of the physician's practice. The destruction of a new born infant was common. A sickly or deformed child was drowned at birth, and the fate of the normal child was solely in the hands of the father. The exposure of girl babies was common enough that there were professionalists who gathered them up and reared them until they could be sold into slavery.

Suicide was considered an open door through which a man might escape the woes of life at any time and that he had a perfect right to avail himself of it. Pliny looked upon death as one of the best gifts given to men by which a man could remove himself from the miseries of life, and Seneca congratulates the human race on this "liberty" which is in the reach of all.

This may explain somewhat the lack of abhorrence felt concerning the tremendous loss of life suffered in the gladiatorial combats in the name of sport. At Rome one of the main amusements was the spectacle of human bloodshed.

The combat of armed men was varied by every kind of fantastic device designed to appeal to the spectators love of novelty and constant craving for some new excitement. The life of the vanquished gladiator depended upon the wishes of the spectators. The number of participants were greatly increased until in the reign of Trajan, 10,000 gladiators were used in one "game." Such morbid craving for bloodshed was unopposed by pagan religion, and Stoicism with its emphasis upon a brotherhood of man seemed unaware of any opposition to its philosophy by wanton destruction of human life. It took the moral power of the Gospel of Christ to check such inhumanity. After hearing the ideals of the Christ, the contrast was so great that many immediately recognized a fulfillment of inward desires for a better day, and accepted the new faith.

IV. RELIGION

The religions of the Roman Empire were exceedingly varied. As the masses of the population were illiterate, the imaginations of pagan superstition and idolatry were generally accepted. After Alexander had united the East and the West, the free flow of ideas brought into the Western world the ancient religions of Persia and Egypt. These "mystery" religions were readily accepted, and when added to the Greek mythology and the Roman deification of the state, presented a wide choice of religious experiences. Unlike religions of today, these cults were not mutually exclusive, and adherence to one did not imply hostility to the others.

V. THE MYSTERY RELIGIONS

During the first century many Romans, due to the pessimism, despair and insecurity of existence, felt that the world was essentially evil and that real life was possible beyond death if the right secret could be found. The mystery religions claimed to provide this secret. They claimed a person could gain salvation and access to God through certain secret ceremonies and mysterious rites. The candidates were prepared psychologically to feel emotional excitement which was interpreted to be a transformation or realization of achievement. These experiences were very similar to emotional experiences that certain religious bodies today attribute to the Holy Spirit. On the exact method of initiation very little seems to be clear. We know it took many forms and consisted of various ascetic practices, and often these ceremonies required some time to be completed. The outward ceremonies consisted of bathing, fasting, animal sacrifices and midnight processions designed to produce a state of excitement and ecstasy. Even drugs, intoxicants and whirling dances were employed at times to induce the soul to leave the body and to temporarily unite with the universal spirit.

VI. ZOROASTRIANISM

The religion of Zoroaster goes back 500 years before Christ to the land of Persia. It encompasses the idea of an all wise god with angelic beings associated with him. In opposition to this good god was a devil or evil spirit who carried on a ceaseless war against the god of light and goodness. Some have supposed that this Persian concept of God and the Devil was transformed into the God and Devil of the Bible. No doubt just the reverse is nearer the truth, for contacts had been made with the Jews long before the Babylonian captivity. Jehovah, the God of the Jews, was well known to this part of the world before the Medes conquered the Babylonian Kingdom.

Zoroastrianism also presented a system of good and evil, of guilt and merit. Man would be held accountable for his sins and blessed for his goodness. In support of this there is an inscription of Darius the Mede, giving Ahuramazda, the Zoroastrian god, credit for bringing him help "because I have ruled according to righteousness." It was believed men would be punished after death for their sins, and there was also an idea that there would be a series of three saviors one thousand years apart, each born of a virgin.

VII. MITHRAISM

Out of Zoroastrianism grew Mithraism, which became for a time a rival of Christianity. Mithra, the god of light, through death and a resurrection, was supposed to be able to cleanse the sinner and support the weak. The moral system included the chief features of Zoroastrianism and was the most honorable of the pagan cults. The system maintained places of worship and a priesthood. The rites included sacrificial meals, and its mythology included a miraculously born savior.

VIII. ROMAN RELIGION

An obvious characteristic of Roman life was that pagan superstition and idolatry pervaded all conduct. Yet, the worship of the gods could not bring personal satisfaction or moral improvement. The average Roman looked for some deliverer to bring peace and happiness. After Augustus, the Emperor was looked upon as this deliverer, and the State was expected to deliver all from physical evil. Every person was expected to take part in the religion of the State, although this did not exclude one from activity in other religions. The leading officials on special occasions acted the part of priests, and the temples were the finest buildings in each community. The regular priesthood was supported by the state, and the priests forced their idolatry into every aspect of life.

In general it may be said that outside of Judaism there was

no conscious relationship of religion and morality. A person could be very religious and very immoral at the same time, for the pagan religions did nothing to promote personal purity or social improvement.

Outside of Judaism there was no voice raised against the mass slaughter of gladiators in the name of sport or against the exposure of infants, or slavery, or abortion, or brothels and public immorality in the name of pagan gods.

For those who are interested in the theory that Christianity was an evolutionary development from these pagan religions, it should be pointed out that:

1. Christianity is a religion based on historical fact. The pagans had their myths, but the Christians had their facts. The miracles and resurrection of Christ were first preached and had their greatest influence in the very location where they took place. The truth of Christianity does not rest upon its philosophical aspects; but rather upon the death and resurrection of Christ, and these facts were open to public investigation.

2. The pagans had no concept of guilt in the Christian sense or of God's forgiving and cleansing sin through a divine sacrifice. Since these ideas constitute the very heart of Christianity, the pagan religions cannot be said to have produced it.

3. Christians were not only conscious of a great difference between themselves and others, but also stood against all other religions with an uncompromising opposition. This very exclusiveness was the cause of persecution. Since the pagan ideas were readily accepted in Roman society, it is not conceivable to think that Christianity was the offspring of paganism and yet refused to recognize the relationship.

4. If Christianity was the offspring of Pagan religions, how does one account for its strength under persecution and its final victory over the pagan cults?

5. No Christian ever referred to paganism as the source of his ideas. Christ crucified was to the pagans, foolishness, but to the Christian the hope of glory. Between the atoning death of Christ, His bodily resurrection and ascension on one hand and the pagan superstitious idolatry on the other, is a gulf fixed that no man can cross.

IX. THE JEWISH CONTRIBUTION

The Christian religion is the culmination of God's plan to save the world through Christ. Before the world would be ready to accept Christ as a savior a long period of spiritual preparation was necessary.

Through Abraham, God began to reveal Himself and His purposes. These purposes became clearer through the law revealed at Mt. Sinai, but it requires a backward look, with the fulfillment of the prophecies in mind, to understand and see how the hand of God was in it all.

The law revealed sin to be sin and showed that every individual fell short of the required standard of conduct. Through the law God made the Jews conscious of their shortcomings and through the required sacrifices God emphasized the seriousness of their sin. The entire dispensation, with the prophets, priests, ceremonies and sacrifices, forced upon the Jewish mind the reality of God's presence and the inability of man to save himself through his own effort. This impression was consciously made according to God's plan so that the world would feel its need of a savior and accept the Messiah when He came.

As the years passed the Jews modified and annulled the high purposes of God through their traditions. When Jesus came into the world this Jewish tradition was of greater importance than the original commandment of God. No doubt many Jews were seriously endeavoring to do God's will, yet they were affected by traditional interpretations and separated into denominational groups with quite different emphasis.

The Sadducees

The origin of the term Sadducee is not known. Their leading tenets were a belief in free will and the rejection of the traditional interpretation of the Mosaic Law. They denied that there would be a resurrection or future rewards and punishments. The Sadducees were aristocratic, and after the crystalization of their party, constituted a conservative element in Judaism inasmuch as they were opposed to additional innovation. This conservatism often caused them to be intolerant and severe toward others. It was a Sadducean high priest who condemned Christ, and it was the Sadducees who first began to persecute the church. They primarily opposed the church's doctrine of the resurrection of Christ from the dead.

The Pharisees

The Pharisaic party was the representative of a noble attempt to reform Judaism. Its members were the puritans of the day and based their reforms on a traditional treatment of Scripture. They held that the Law of Moses was supplemented by a great amount of oral tradition which they believed was given by God at the same time as the giving of the Law. This fostered a tendency to put legal purity above morality. They declared that the law lacked some things that were desirable and tended to place their learned men above the priest. The Pharisees were very devout in outward manifestation of prayer, and the doctrine of the resurrection was an important part of their faith. Their conflict with Jesus was primarily over the interpretation of the Law of Moses.

Essenes

The Essenes were distinguished as an exclusive sect of Phariseeism. They were characterized by a craving for moral purity as the result of a mixture of foreign customs borrowed from the religions of the East. They opposed marriage and objected to the slaughter of animals and the use of animals as food. They lived in communities regulated by ascetic discipline and refused to take part in the simple worship because animals were slain in the sacrifice. The Dead Sea Scrolls have shed a great deal of light on the sect since their discovery in 1947. It is now generally agreed that the members of the monastery near the Dead Sea were Essenes.

The Zealots

The Zealots were also an off-shoot from the Pharisees, becoming a fanatical movement that refused to recognize any legal authority. Their watch word was "No King but the Lord." It was the fanaticism of the Zealots that ultimately led to the ruin of the Jewish nation in the destruction of Jerusalem. At least one of the twelve apostles had been a member of this party — Simon the Zealot (Acts 1:13).

Although Judaism was greatly divided at the time Christ came into the world, there was a sense of great expectation in their looking for the coming Messiah. In their use of the Scripture and their contact with God the Jews created an influence in society by uniting religion and morality. Their emphasis on the one true God and the revelation of Himself to man in the giving of the Law had prepared a people in expectation of God's revelation of additional truth and a readiness to accept the Messiah. It was because of this readiness that Christ sent the disciples to the Jew first in the proclamation of the gospel story. Evidently it was to these Jews that John the Baptist came as the forerunner of Christ, boldly announcing that the kingdom of heaven was at hand. He set forth the coming spiritual kingdom and emphasized that in order to enter it there must be first a genuine repentance, telling the people to clean up their lives in order to participate in the great coming kingdom. Through the dispersion of the Jewish race the idea of one God, who was altogether good and loving, had become known in many countries outside of Palestine. In this way the spiritual preparation for the coming Christ was ready throughout the entire Roman world.

X.   THE GREEK HERITAGE

The average man at the time Christ walked the earth was without formal education in the classics, yet his entire life was influenced by the contributions of Greek culture. In Palestine the Jews retained a native Hebrew tongue called Aramaic, yet they conversed familiarly in the more widely used Hellenistic Greek. This common language is known as Koine, which means "common" or "general." The difference in this language of the market place and the classical Greek is about the same as one finds today between our everyday language and that of the universities.

There is no language known to men that could be better used to convey a divine message. Over the entire Roman world this Greek possessed a uniformity that made it possible to convey a fine distinction of thought and be accurately understood. The language itself possesses tenses and moods that enable an exactness of expression not possible in English.

XI.   SUMMARY

It is no accident that we find the world so completely prepared for the coming of Christ. A period of peace, good roads, extensive travel and commerce, an exact language known and used throughout the empire, were certainly a great help in the spread of the gospel. The social conditions with slavery, immorality, a disregard for human life, debasement of womanhood, the frequency of divorce and suicide, created a desire for improvement and prepared minds for the ready acceptance of the purity of Christianity.

The pagan religions were unable to relate morality to religion and with all their variety their superstitious idolatry had nothing to satisfy the eternal longing of the human race or save man from sin. Man was looking for a solution, and by allowing the pagans to attempt every possible means they could invent for their salvation, God showed the world that man left to himself could not provide for his salvation. By giving the Jews a revealed code of morals and sacrifices for sin God showed that man could not earn salvation by his own merit, but that he needed a savior.

So, through the Gentiles God showed the world that man's efforts to provide his own salvation ends in failure. Through the Jews God showed that man could not keep a revealed religion based upon human effort, and, accordingly, both Jews and Gentiles needed a savior. This accomplished, it was time for the "Word" to become flesh (Jno. 1:14).

Chapter Two

Historical Evidence Concerning
The Life of Jesus

Having seen the world into which Christ came, it is appropriate for us to examine briefly the historical evidence presented by Pagans and Jews as to the historicity of Jesus. If the stories of Jesus are simply myths without historical basis; if He was not born of a virgin; if He performed no miracles; if He was not raised from the dead, we would be, as Paul said, of all men most pitiable. However, the historical evidence confirming the Christian's faith is overwhelming. At one time it was necessary to write books to prove that Jesus was an historical person. Today no person of learning doubts that He lived. The facts of the life of Christ are confirmed both by pagans and unbelieving Jews. Let us look at their testimony.

I. JOSEPHUS

One of the most brilliant writers of the first century was a Jew named Josephus, the son of Matthias. He took the name of Flavius in honor of the Flavian emperors. He was born in 37 or 38 A.D. When twenty-six years old, he visited Rome and was so impressed he spent the rest of his life trying to bring about better relations between the Jews and the Romans. He was so highly respected by the Romans that he was with Titus when Jerusalem was destroyed in A.D. 70. Later, he wrote the history of the event in seven books entitled, *History of the Jewish War*. He also wrote *Jewish Antiquities* and his autobiography.

Concerning Jesus, Josephus says, "At that time lived Jesus, a wise man, if he may be called a man; for he performed many wonderful works. He was a teacher of such men as received the truth with pleasure. He drew over to him many Jews and Gentiles. This was the Christ. And when Pilate, at the instigation of the chief men among us, had condemned him to the cross, they who before had conceived an affection for him did not cease to adhere to him. For on the third day he appeared to them alive again, the divine prophets having foretold these and many other wonderful things concerning him. And the sect of the Christians, so called from him, subsists at this time."[1]

This passage has been rejected by some scholars as an interpolation on the grounds that it does not sound like an unbelieving Jew such as Josephus. It is also said to be out of place in the context, for here Josephus was discussing seditions. In defense of the passage it may be said that it appears in every copy of Josephus that has come down to us and was quoted twice by Eusebius as early as 315 A.D. In a North Slavic manuscript of Josephus there is the description of a tumult made on account of Jesus and the statement reads, "At that time a man appeared, if he can be called a man. His nature and his body were human, but his appearance was more than human. He performed miracles through some invisible power. Some said of him that he was our first Law giver, Moses, risen from the dead, and making himself known by many healings and magic works; others thought that he was sent by God. I, personally in view of his whole life, should not call him a messenger of God." More likely the original statement of Josephus and its setting is in harmony with the context.

From these accounts it seems clear that in this place Josephus did make reference to Jesus but that some person very early tried to improve his statements. However, in another passage that has been less questioned as authentic, Josephus refers to Jesus when he is describing the death of James. He said, "But this younger Ananus who took the high priesthood, was a bold man in his temper, and very insolent, when therefore he thought he now had a proper opportunity to exercise his authority he assembled the Sanhedrin and brought before them the brother of Jesus who was called Christ, whose name was James and some other when he had formed an accusation against them he delivered them to be stoned."[2]

In referring to John the Baptist, Josephus says, "But some of the Jews were of opinion that God had suffered Herod's whole army to be destroyed as a just punishment on him for the death of John, called the Baptist. For Herod had killed him,

1. Antiquities, Book 18, Chapter iii, Section 1.
2. Antiquities, Book 20, Chapter ix, Section 1.

who was a just man, and had called upon the Jews to be baptized, and to practice virtue, exercising both justice toward men and piety toward God. For so would baptism be acceptable to God, if they made use of it, not for the expiation of their sins, but for the purity of the body, the mind being first purified by righteousness. And many coming to him, (for they were wonderfully taken with his discourses), Herod was seized with apprehensions, lest his authority should be led into sedition against him; for they seemed capable of undertaking anything by his direction. Herod therefore thought it better to take him off before any disturbance happened, than to run the risk of affairs, and of repenting when it should be too late to remedy disorders. Being taken up upon this suspicion of Herod, and being sent bound to the castle of Macherus, just mentioned, he was slain there. The Jews were of opinion that the destruction of Herod's army was punishment upon him for that action, God being displeased with him."[3]

This passage has been accepted as genuine even by the most critical. It is quoted by Origen, Eusebius and Jerome. In this context Josephus corroborates many facts recorded in our gospel accounts.

II.   TACITUS

Carius Cornelius Tacitus who wrote about the year 100 had a strong dislike for the Christians. This, however, makes his testimony even stronger. In discussing the life of Nero and the accusation that he burned the city and blamed it on the Christians, Tacitus says, "But neither all human help nor the liberality of the Emperor, nor all the atonements presented to the gods, availed to abate the infamy he lay under of having ordered the city to be set on fire. To suppress, therefore, this common rumor, Nero procured others to be accused, and inflicted exquisite punishment upon those people, who were in abhorrence for their crimes, and were commonly known by the name of Christians. They had their denomination from Christus, who in the reign of Tibertius was put to death as a criminal by the procurator Pontius Pilate. This pernicious superstition, though checked for awhile, broke out again and spread not only over Judea, the source of this evil, but reached the city also; whither flow from all quarters all things vile and shameful, and

3. **Antiquities**, Book 18, Chapter v, Section 1.

where they find shelter and encouragement. At first they were only apprehended who confessed themselves of that sect; afterwards a vast multitude discovered by them, all of which were condemned, not so much for the crime of burning the city, as for their enmity to mankind. Their executions were so contrived as to expose them to derision and contempt. Some were covered with the skins of wild beasts, and torn to pieces by dogs; some were crucified; others having been daubed over with combustible materials, were set up as lights in the night time, and thus burned to death. Nero made use of his own gardens as a theater upon this occasion, and also exhibited the diversions of the Circus, sometimes standing in the crowd as a spectator, in the habit of a charioteer, at other times driving a chariot himself; till at length these men, though really criminal, and deserving exemplary punishment, began to be commiserated, as people who were destroyed, not out of regard to the public welfare, but only to gratify the cruelty of one man."[4]

This testimony which is unchallenged historically states that: (1) Christ is the founder of the "denomination" of Christians. (2) Christ was put to death as a criminal by Pontius Pilate. (3) His death took place while Tiberius was Emperor; therefore He must have been born under the reign of Augustus. (4) Christianity, this "pernicious superstition," began in Judea and was suppressed for a time, then broke out again and reached Rome before Tacitus wrote his *Annals*. (5) Christians were persecuted in Rome as early as A.D. 64. (6) "Vast multitudes" were executed to gratify the "cruelty of one man," Nero. (7) Tacitus recognized they were innocent of the crimes charged against them.

This testimony confirms the facts of the gospels; and, since there were large numbers of Christians scattered all over the empire as early as 30 years after the death of Christ, the book of Acts is also vindicated, and the theories that Christianity was a synthesis of the mystery religions or the result of a growth of myths must be of necessity forever rejected.

III. SUETONIUS

Suetonius, who was born about the year 88 and was a friend of Pliny the younger, wrote *The Twelve Caesars*. In his

---

4. Tacitus, Annals, 15, 44. in Henry Bettenson, ed. Documents of the Christian Church (New York: Oxford University Press, 1957) pp. 3-5.

"Life of Claudius" he says, "Because the Jews at Rome caused continuous disturbances at the instigation of Chrestus, he expelled them from the City."[5] This passage undoubtedly confirms Acts 18:2 that Claudius had commanded all Jews to depart from Rome. This included Priscilla and Aquila and proves that there were Christians in Rome as early as Claudius.

In the "Life of Nero," whose reign began in 54 and ended in 68, Suetonius says, "Punishments were also inflicted on the Christians, a sect professing a new and mischievous religious belief."[6] By referring to Christianity as "new" Suetonius confirms our faith that the Christian religion did arise in the time and place set forth in the New Testament.

IV. PLINY

Pliny the younger, born in 61, was sent by the Emperor Trajan to Bithynia in 112 as propraetor. Finding many Christians there he wrote back to Trajan to get information on how to deal with them. He tells of the moral integrity of the Christians and gives historical evidence concerning Christ. The entire letter is worthy of careful study. Pliny says, "It is my rule, Sire, to refer to you in matters where I am uncertain. For who can better direct my hesitation or instruct my ignorance? I was never present at any trial of Christians; therefore I do not know what are the customary penalties or investigations, and what limits are observed. (2) I have hesitated a great deal on the question whether there should be any distinction of ages; whether the weak should have the same treatment as the more robust; whether those who recant should be pardoned, or whether a man who has ever been a Christian should gain nothing by ceasing to be such; whether the name itself, even if innocent of crime, should be punished, or only the crimes attaching to that name.

"Meanwhile, this is the course that I have adopted in the case of those brought before me as Christians. (3) I ask them if they are Christians. If they admit it I repeat the question a second and a third time, threatening capital punishment; if they persist I sentence them to death. For I do not doubt that, whatever crime it may be to which they have confessed, their

5. Suetonius, The Twelve Caesars, trans. Robert Graves, Penguin Classics. (Baltimore: Penguin Books, Inc., 1957), p. 197.
6. Ibid., p. 217

pertinacity and inflexible obstinacy should certainly be punished. (4) There were others who displayed a like madness and
whom I reserved to be sent to Rome, since they were Roman
citizens.

"Thereupon the usual result followed; the very fact of my
dealing with the question led to a wider spread of the charge,
and a great variety of cases were brought before me. (5) An
anonymous pamphlet was issued, containing many names. All
who denied that they were or had been Christians I considered
should be discharged, because they called upon the gods at my
dictation and did reverence, with incense and wine, to your
image which I had ordered to be brought forward for this purpose, together with the statues of the deities; and especially because they cursed Christ, a thing which, it is said, genuine
Christians cannot be induced to do. (6) Others named by the
informer first said that they were Christians and then denied it;
declaring that they had been but were so no longer, some having recanted three years or more before and one or two as long
as twenty years. They all worshipped your image and the statues of the gods and cursed Christ. (7) But they declared that
the sum of their guilt or error had amounted only to this, that
on an appointed day they had been accustomed to meet before
daybreak, and to recite a hymn antiphonally to Christ, as to a
god, and to bind themselves by an oath, not for the commission
of any crime but to abstain from theft, robbery, adultery, and
breach of faith, and not to deny a deposit when it was claimed.
After the conclusion of this ceremony it was their custom to
depart and meet again to take food; but it was ordinary and
harmless food, and they had ceased this practice after my edict
in which, accordance with your orders, I had forbidden secret
societies. (8) I thought it the more necessary, therefore, to find
out what truth was in this by applying torture to two maid-
servants, who were called deaconnesses. But I found nothing
but a depraved and extravagant superstition, and I therefore
postponed my examination and had recourse to you for con-
sultation.

"(9) The matter seemed to me to justify my consulting
you, especially on account of the number of those imperiled;
for many persons of all ages and classes and of both sexes are
being put in peril by accusation, and this will go on. The con-

tagion of this superstition has spread not only in the cities, but in the villages and rural districts as well; yet it seems capable of being checked and set right. (10) There is no shadow of doubt that the temples, which have been almost deserted, are beginning to be frequented once more, that the sacred rites which have been long neglected are being renewed, and that sacrificial victims are for sale everywhere, whereas, till recently, a buyer was rarely to be found. From this it is easy to imagine what a host of men could be set right, were they given a chance of recantation."[7]

So writes Pliny. We are now to observe the Emperor's reply. "You have taken the right line, my dear Pliny, in examining the cases of those denounced to you as Christians, for no hard and fast rule can be laid down, of universal application. (2) They are not to be sought out; if they are informed against, and the charge is proved, they are to be punished, with this reservation — that if anyone denies that he is a Christian, and actually proves it, that is by worshiping our gods, he shall be pardoned as a result of his recantation, however suspect he may have been with respect to the past. Pamphlets published anonymously should carry no weight in any charge whatsoever. They constitute a very bad precedent, and are also out of keeping with this age."[8]

V. CONCLUSIONS

From such irrefutable evidence we learn that within one man's life time the church had spread from its beginning in Jerusalem to the entire Roman Empire. So successful were the evangelists that in some places the heathen temples were being neglected. The best explanation for this phenominal growth is that Jesus was the divine personage set forth in the Gospels. The reader is urged to go to the New Testament itself for information on the life of Jesus. Here we will make but brief comments on his divine personage.

The New Testament states clearly that Jesus was not an ordinary man. He refers to Himself as having "come down out of heaven" (Jno. 6:51) and again, "I am come from God" (Jno. 8:42). As to His existence He said, "Before Abraham was born, I am." (Jno. 8:58). Paul speaks of Him as "the

7. Bettenson, pp. 5-7
8. Bettenson, p. 7

image of the invisible God, the first born of all creation. . . .
he is before all things and in him all things consist." (Col. 1:
15-17). Moses quotes God as saying, "I will put my words in
his mouth, and he shall speak unto them all that I shall command him. And it shall come to pass, that whosoever will not
harken unto my words which he shall speak in my name, I will
require it of him." (Deut. 18:18-19). In keeping with this and
emphasizing the divine quality of His teaching, Jesus said that
the words He spoke were not His own, but were given Him of
His Father.

To perpetuate the divine message Jesus selected and taught
the Apostles for three and one-half years. During this time the
many miracles observed by the Apostles caused them to know
that Jesus was not an ordinary man. Yet it took the appearance
of Christ after the resurrection to confirm their faith beyond the
point of wavering. After this preparation the Apostles were
given the Holy Spirit to guide them into all truth and bring
to their memory all Jesus had said to them (Jno. 14:26; 16:
13).

Christianity is not only a religion of ideas. It also combines
ideas with facts and the facts are subject to historical investigation. The teaching of Christ is important, but the heart of the
Christian religion is not in what Christ said. It is in what He
did. The sermon on the mount is a beautiful and valid moral
philosophy. It is the most important proclamation of truth the
world has ever received, yet if Christianity had stopped there it
would have made a very small ripple on the sea of Roman
thought. It was what Christ did that revolutionized the world.
Christ brought a cure for man's guilt and sin and made a new
vocabulary necessary. The words propitiation, atonement,
justification, redemption and sanctification are the characteristic words of Christianity and they all have their meaning in
the cross of Christ.

The historicity of the death of Jesus, as we have seen, makes
the prophecy of Isaiah more sure that "He hath borne our
griefs, and carried our sorrows . . . he was bruised for our
iniquities . . . and with his stripes we are healed." (Isa. 53:4-
5). This is the message that turned men from idols to serve the
living God and created in them a strength to take the gospel to
all men and even die for their faith.

The atoning death and bodily resurrection of Christ were not isolated historical events. Miracles characterized His entire ministry and were attested to by historical developments. On Pentecost Peter boldly declared to a great multitude in Jerusalem that the mighty works, wonders and signs done by Jesus in their midst declared Him to be the Son of God, "even as ye yourselves know." (Acts 2:22). This statement was a challenge to the inhabitants of Palestine to examine the evidence upon which Christ was declared to be divine. Such evidence was abundant in that very audience. It is also significant to know that the preaching of the resurrection of Christ had its greatest result in the very locality where it took place and immediately after it happened. If any people in the world's history could have examined the evidence, that audience could and no doubt did. The result was the baptism of the 3000 the first time the gospel was presented (Acts 2:41).

The historical evidence concerning the life of Christ and His message gives us every reason to accept the gospel accounts of His miraculous life without question. The incarnation and virgin birth of Jesus are in perfect harmony with His being the revelation of God to man. The gospel accounts set forth clearly that Jesus had no earthly father. Since the writers are accurate in all reference to contemporary personages and events, and since they were dealing with a divine personage, they set forth this portion of their history without any special emphasis and passed on to other phases of His life which are equally miraculous.

It is this manifestation of the supernatural that became the foundation of Christian faith and that has led God's people to suffer martyrdom, oppose heresy, evangelize the world and earnestly wait for the second coming of Christ.

Chapter Three

The New Testament Church

I. ESTABLISHMENT OF THE CHURCH

The church of Christ began on the first Pentecost after the resurrection of Jesus in the city of Jerusalem. On this day the Holy Spirit fell upon the Apostles and the gospel in its completeness was preached for the first time. The 3000 buried with Christ in baptism on that day became the first fruits of the harvest of souls. This great occasion culminated the work God had accomplished through prophecy, the preparatory work of John the Baptist and the miraculous life of Jesus.

II. DEFINITION OF TERMS

The word church in the New Testament translates a Greek word that literally means "called out." The term carries the idea of separation or being set apart for a given purpose. This word is first used in the New Testament in Matthew 16: 18 when Jesus said, "Upon this rock I will build my church." The same Greek word, however, in Acts 19:41, is translated "assembly." In the first passage Jesus is referring to those He would call unto Himself. They would be spiritually separated from the world and sustain a new relationship to God signfied as being a "peculiar people" not of this world. In this way they are called out and set apart. The second passage refers to a mob in Ephesus who had assembled to defend Diana, the Ephesian idol. These are referred to by the Greek word for church because they were separated from the rest of the Ephesians and were set apart in defense of Diana.

This Greek word was commonly used to signify any separated group and was not invented by Jesus to describe His people. Since this is true, one would expect to find this word used in a general way and such is the case. In Acts 7:38, Stephen referred to Moses and the "church" in the wilderness. The word church is used here to signify those who had come out of Egyptian bondage and were gathered together in the wilderness. Therefore, the term does not always signify the church of Christ.

(40)

The word church, signifying the "called out" aspect of the nature of God's people, is only one of several terms to designate them. In Matthew 16:18 after using the word church, Jesus used the expression "kingdom of heaven" to refer to the same group (vs. 19). This expression describes the position of people under the reign of God. The expressions "Kingdom of Heaven" and "Kingdom of God" are used interchangeably and always refer to the sovereignty of God, generally meaning the same as that signified by the word church, but not always so. The context must be relied upon to ascertain that part of mankind referred to as being under the sovereignty of God. In the parables of the dragnet and tares the entire human race, the evil and the good, is being considered as under the sovereignty of God and the world is called "kingdom of heaven."

Attempts have been made to designate the "Kingdom of Heaven" as the church in the world before Christ comes again, and the "Kingdom of God" as the calling together of all the elect when Christ comes again. That this is an arbitrary distinction is seen in the records of Matthew and Luke. Quoting Jesus in the sermon on the mount, Matthew says, "Blessed are the poor in spirit for theirs is the 'kingdom of heaven'," and Luke says "kingdom of God." They, of course, were referring to the same thing.

III. THE CHURCH IN PROPHECY

The Apostle Paul says the mystery of Christ was not made known to other generations (Eph. 3:5), but rather it was hidden in God and was to be revealed according to His eternal purpose (Eph. 3:11). Yet in prophecy revelations were given about the coming kingdom. Daniel shows that it would be set up in the days of the kings of the Roman Empire (2:44) and that it was to be an eternal kingdom. Isaiah states that when the word of Jehovah would go forth from Jerusalem, Jehovah's house was to be established and all nations would flow into it (Isa. 2:2-3). He further states that a virgin would bear a son who would be called Immanuel (God with us) (7:14), and that His soul would be made an offering for sin. He would bear our iniquities and be cut off from the land of the living for the transgression of the people to whom the stroke was due (ch. 53).

David, with true prophetic spirit, puts the crucifixion in the present and crys out, "My God, my God, why hast thou forsaken me" and in vivid description of the suffering on the cross says, "they pierced my hands and my feet." (Ps. 22).

In looking back upon such prophecy we see clearly God's plan to send His own Son into the world as a sacrifice for sin that the church might be purchased by His own blood (Acts 20:28).

IV. THE CHURCH IN PREPARATION

Matthew states that John the Baptist came in fulfillment of God's plan to "make ready the way for the Lord." (Matt. 3:3). His message was designed to prepare a people in heart and mind to receive the Christ as the Son of God. As he convicted multitudes of their sin, preaching "Repent ye for the kingdom of heaven is at hand," he was telling people to clean up their lives and get ready to participate in the greatest event in the world's history. His message was so effective that all Jerusalem and Judea and the region round about the Jordan came out to be baptized in the river Jordan, confessing their sins (Matt. 3: 5-6).

John told the people plainly that he was not the Christ, but that he had come before Him, and after Jesus began His ministry, John said that Christ must increase and he would decrease. The Apostle Paul, looking back upon the work of John, said that he preached a "baptism of repentance saying unto the people that they should believe on him that was to come after him, that is on Jesus." (Acts 19:4). It is clear that John's work was only preparatory. The statement so characteristic of his preaching, "The kingdom of heaven is at hand," means the kingdom or church was not yet in existence, but was to be soon. John's work was done under the dispensation of the Law of Moses.

When God gave the Law at Mt. Sinai, He was working out His eternal purpose. Before people would feel a need for a savior they must first be made conscious of sin. This was accomplished by the Law. It showed sin to be sin, and by requiring righteousness on the basis of merit it showed that all people were sinners. The Law then became a schoolmaster to bring the world to Christ (Gal. 3:24). This Law was not abolished until Christ died on the cross, and since two laws or covenants cannot exist at the same time any more than a wife can have two husbands at once (Rom. 7:1-7), we know that the kingdom under Christ did not become a reality until after the crucifixion.

While John was telling of the coming kingdom, Jesus began to preach the same message, and to say, "Repent ye for the kingdom of heaven is at hand." (Matt. 4:17). As He began to gather His disciples He "went about Galilee, teaching in their synagogues and preaching the gospel of the kingdom." (Matt. 4:23). This expression "gospel of the kingdom" means good news of the approaching kingdom. It is used again in Matthew 9:35, "and Jesus went about all the cities and villages, teaching in their synagogues and preaching the gospel of the kingdom." This is followed by a record of Jesus' choosing the twelve and sending them out with the instruction, "as ye go, preach, saying, the kingdom of heaven is at hand." (Matt. 10:7). The two expressions, "gospel of the kingdom" and "kingdom of heaven is at hand," mean the same.

That the kingdom, or church, was not in its completed form during the personal ministry of Christ is seen in the fact that Jesus kept the Law and told His disciples to do so (Matt. 23:2-3). In reference to the establishment of the church He put it in the future when He said, "Upon this rock I will build my church." This expression means "to found — to cause to come into existence," and shows that the church in its fullness had not yet come into existence. The other references Jesus made to the church were in the form of instruction to be followed after it came in its fullness.

V. The Church in Reality

Pentecost was the birthday of the church. Jesus had told the Apostles, after His resurrection, to remain in Jerusalem and wait for the coming of the Holy Spirit (Lk. 24:49). This promise had been given to the Apostles earlier. Jesus had said that the Holy Spirit would come upon them to teach them all things and bring to their remembrance all that Jesus had said to them (Jno. 14:26). The Holy Spirit would also guide them into all truth, revealing the message that he would receive from heaven and in doing so would also reveal things that were to come (Jno. 16:13).

Jerusalem had been chosen as the place of beginning. Here was the center of the Jewish world and the only logical place for the establishment of the church. It had been prophesied that the church would begin here (Isa. 2:14). Since Christianity was the ultimate development of God's plan to save man, and God had protected the Messianic seed line from Abraham through David and had given to them the Law and the prophets, it was appropriate that "repentance and remission of sins should be preached in his name to all the nations beginning from Jerusalem." (Lk. 24:47).

The promise of Christ that the Apostles would be filled with the Holy Spirit was fulfilled on Pentecost. Under His guidance the Apostles began to preach in languages they had never studied. This miracle had a varying effect on the audience. Some mocked and accused them of being drunk, but Peter explained that they were not. He then preached the death, burial and resurrection of Christ (Acts 2). He told the audience that the Jesus they crucified was the working out of God's plan to save mankind, that He had been set forth on the cross according to God's determinate council and foreknowledge and that they should know assuredly that He was both Lord and Christ.

The effect of the sermon was momentous. No doubt there were many in the audience who had been healed of diseases by the power of Jesus as He walked their streets. Lazarus of Bethany had been raised from the dead about a mile from where Peter stood. It was with the knowledge that such remarkable proofs of divinity were readily available as unimpeachable evidence that Peter boldly declared Christ raised from the dead and exalted at the right hand of God.

VI. THE BASIS OF MEMBERSHIP

The audience was also conscious of the truth of Peter's statements and being convicted of sin cried out, "What shall we do?" Jesus had prepared the Apostles for their answer to such a question in His last instruction to them, referred to as the great commission. Matthew, Mark and Luke each refer to this statement and when their reports are combined we know that Jesus said, "Go into all the world and preach the gospel of my death and resurrection to all mankind. They who believe, repent and are baptized in the name of the Father, Son and Holy Spirit shall be saved and those who disbelieve shall be condemned."

With this commission brought to Peter's memory by the Holy Spirit, he gave instructions for the first time as to how men who were believers could obtain remission of sin. His reply to their question was, "Repent ye and be baptized, every one of you in the name of Jesus Christ unto the remission of your sins; and ye shall receive the gift of the Holy Spirit." (Acts 2: 38).

The area used as the place of assembly was called Solomon's Porch. It consisted of the Eastern side of the temple area and was 912 feet long. The size of the audience Peter addressed is unknown,[1] but the scripture says "about 3000" responded to this first sermon and were baptized that day. In reconstructing this great event from Scripture, history and Bible geography we thrill at the sight of 3000 penitent believers as they leave the temple and are led by the Apostles to Solomon's pools to receive baptism into Christ. The one baptism of believers in the New Testament was clearly immersion. The Greek word itself means to dip, submerge or immerse. The language of the New Testament shows there was "one baptism" (Eph. 4:4) and that it was a burial and resurrection (Rom. 6:3-4) by which the penitent believer reinacted the death, burial and resurrection of Christ (Col. 2:12). The sinner was thus related to Christ in the likeness of His death that he might also be in the likeness of His resurrection.

The idea that the baptism of the 3000 could not have been immersion because of the time required can be answered by simple mathematics. One man can baptize by immersion sixty people in one hour. Twelve men could baptize 3000 in less than four and one half hours. To contend there was not sufficient water available is to ignore the presence of Solomon's pools that had been constructed as the city water supply and were ideal for such a purpose. There is unanimous consent of early church historians that baptism in the early church was only immersion.

VII. Rapid Growth

So powerfully did the Apostles impress the people with

1. That the temple area accommodated large crowds of people is attested to by Eusebius who refers to a riot in the Temple in which 30,000 Jews perished by trampling on each other. Eusebius, **Ecclesiastical History** 2:19:1, (any of the standard editions.)

their miracles and preaching, and so dedicated were the new converts, that they "had favor with all the people" and soon "the number of men came to be 5000." (Acts 4:4).

This number apparently refers to men only to signify the strength of the church. When the women and young people are estimated, there was perhaps in Jerusalem a congregation of 15,000. The number then continued to grow and "believers were the more added to the Lord, multitudes both of men and women." (Acts 5:14). This growth is what we would expect in the miraculous beginning of the true church. The Apostles were true to their charge, "and every day, in the temple and at home, they ceased not to teach and to preach Jesus as the Christ." (Acts 5:42). Under such activity "the Word of God increased; and the number of disciples multiplied in Jerusalem exceedingly, and a great company of the priests were obedient to the faith." (Acts 6:7).

VII. EARLY SPREAD

According to God's plan the gospel was to go to "the Jew first and also to the Greek." (Rom. 1:16). Jesus told the Apostles they should be His "witnesses both in Jerusalem and in all Judea and Samaria, and unto the uttermost part of the earth." (Acts 1:8). Through the first part of the book of Acts this pattern was followed by the early church. The gospel was taken from Jerusalem by Christian Jews throughout Judea and Samaria. When the first persecution began and the church was scattered abroad, they went every where preaching the word. The Apostles remained at Jerusalem for a time, but soon they were making evangelistic tours.

Philip went to Samaria and baptized people into Christ (Acts 8). He was filled with the Holy Spirit and performed miracles, but because he was not an Apostle he did not have the power to impart the Holy Spirit through the laying on of hands to others. Since the instructions for the church (the New Testament) had not been written, it was necessary for each new congregation to have spiritual guidance. Accordingly, word reached the Apostles of the success in Samaria, and they sent Peter and John who laid hands on certain of them and they received the Holy Spirit.

The gospel was having its effect in every quarter. Philip

converted the Ethiopian nobleman who took the gospel to Ethiopia and the court of Queen Candace (Acts 8). Peter baptized the household of Cornelius, the first Gentile converts (Acts 10). Saul of Tarsus, who became the Apostle Paul, having seen the Lord, came penitently to Ananias and was told to "arise and be baptized and wash thy sins away, calling on the name of the Lord." (Acts 22:16).

Such success was sure to arouse the Jewish leaders to form an organized opposition movement. This was done. Stephen was arrested, and after a brilliant defense of Christianity as the ultimate plan God had in mind while preserving their Jewish fathers, the Jews would hear no more, and Stephen gave his life in defense of his faith, the first recorded Christian martyr.

The gospel was taking root, however, in many places. Barnabas found the Apostle Paul and took him to Antioch of Syria where a strong church had already developed. From Antioch as headquarters Paul made three missionary journeys and later as a prisoner was taken to Rome and over a period of two years was allowed to preach to all who came to him. Tradition tells enough of the work of the early evangelists that it is rather certain that they deliberately went to various parts of the world to establish congregations. From such tradition we read that Thaddaeus went to Edessa where he healed Abgar, the king, of a serious disease and converted most of the city. Mark went to Alexandria and established the church and founded a school. Bartholomew preached in India and left the new converts a copy of Matthew in the Hebrew language. John, after being exiled on Patmos was released following the death of Domitian and went to Ephesus where he labored to the age of 90. Matthias preached in Ethiopia, Thomas in Parthia and India, Andrew in the Near East, and James the less in Egypt. A detailed account of the death of James, the brother of Christ, tells how the Scribes and Pharisees stood him on the pinnacle of the temple and required that he denounce Christ to the crowd below. When he exalted Christ instead, they threw him to the ground, and as he was not killed they began to stone him, and a laundryman took the club he used to beat out the clothes and ended his life. The same tradition says that James spent so much time in prayer that his knees had grown hard like a camel's.

IX. ORGANIZATION AND GOVERNMENT

No question concerning the New Testament church has had more differing opinions than the question of its organization and government. Most solutions offered have come out of humanity's trying to solve its problems out of a background of human government rather than a careful study of Scripture. There are many advocating the idea that Christ gave no pattern of government, and accordingly, any form that works is acceptable to God. This puts the matter in the hands of man and such a view is responsible for church governments varying from congregational independence to universal dictatorship. Some have gone so far as to contend that in the New Testament different types of church organization can be found. This claim is entirely without foundation. It is very likely that many have overlooked the organization set forth in the New Testament because of its simplicity.

As long as the Apostles lived the highest authority rested in them as they spoke under the guidance of the Holy Spirit. The Apostles, however, soon appointed elders and deacons in each congregation. The elders were to "exercise the oversight" or rule the church. As long as Apostles were available the elders and Apostles worked together. In Jerusalem it was the Apostles and elders (Acts 15:2-6) who met to consider the influence of the Judaizers. The letter written back to counteract their influence was from the Apostles and elders. But even before the persecution scattered the church from Jerusalem, the elders had begun the oversight of the congregation (Acts 11: 30). As Paul and Barnabas completed their first missionary journey, they retraced their steps, "and when they had appointed for them elders in every church, and had prayed with fasting, they commended them to the Lord on whom they had believed." (Acts 14:23).

It is significant that in each congregation there was appointed a plurality of elders. This pattern was followed universally throughout the lives of the Apostles and for many years after the last Apostle died. Paul left Titus in Crete to "set in order the things that were wanting, and appoint elders in every city." (Titus 1:5). From Miletus Paul "sent to Ephesus and called to him the elders of the church," (Acts 20:7) to give them final instructions.

In order to fully understand the pattern of government in the New Testament one must realize that these called "elders" are also called "bishops" or "overseers." This is seen in Acts 20 where the elders (vs. 17) are called bishops in verse 28. The elders of Titus 1:5 were called bishops in verse 7. The qualifications and work of elders in Titus are the same as those of bishops in 1 Timothy 3. Bishops and elders are never mentioned together as two different orders of officers. Paul wrote to the saints at Philippi "with the bishops and deacons" (Phil. 1:1), not bishops, elders and deacons. Paul gives Timothy instructions for appointing bishops, lists their qualifications and then proceeds directly to give instructions for deacons (1 Tim. 3). If elders were different from bishops Paul gave Timothy no instructions as to their qualifications. Yet this does not constitute an oversight, for Paul goes on to mention that elders who rule well are to be counted as worthy of double honor (1 Tim. 5:17). There is no doubt that the bishops of chapter three are the elders of chapter five.

The idea that James was the monarchal bishop of Jerusalem in the sense that later developed is entirely without foundation. His authority was that of an Apostle. Unwarrantable attempts have also been made to establish Timothy in Ephesus and Titus in Crete as bishops over a diocese. It is certain the Scripture gives them no such position and there is nothing in the writing of the first two centuries that refers to their having had such a position or that either of them bore the name "bishop." These men were evangelists, traveling companions and assistants of the Apostles, who were sent to set the various churches in order and appoint elders to take over the rule of the churches. The "angels" of the churches mentioned in the letters to the seven churches of Asia (Rev. chap. 2 and 3) are also used in the attempt to find a third century bishop in the New Testament. This argument is based upon very thin supposition. The Greek word translated "angel" is the equivalent to a Hebrew word used commonly in the Old Testament to designate a prophet. In this sense the "angel" of the church would be the leading teacher. This leading teacher has been compared to the superintendent who directed the worship in the Jewish synagogue. The word "angel" probably referred to the elder or bishop who presided over the order of worship in the church.[2]

The congregations of the Apostolic period were independent, autonomous groups. Each group with its elders was independent from any other authority because each followed the same God-given instructions. The "conference" in Jerusalem described in the 15th chapter of Acts was not an ecumenical council. The church at Antioch was making great progress, and a large number of Greeks were converted (Acts 11:21). When the church at Jerusalem heard of this success, they sent Barnabas who found large numbers of people turning to the Lord. Seeing great opportunity, Barnabas went to Tarsus and brought Paul to assist in the work. For a year they worked together, and soon we find three other men working with Paul and Barnabas as ministers and teachers. Antioch had thus become one of the strongest congregations of the first century with Jews and Gentiles working together for the spread of the gospel.

Into such a situation came men from Judea teaching that the Gentiles could not be saved unless they received circumcision and kept the Law of Moses (Acts 15:1). This teaching was contrary to revelations received by the inspired men at Antioch. Paul and Barnabas contended that what they taught was not the will of God. Since the confusion was caused by men from Judea, it was necessary to send Paul and Barnabas to Jerusalem to bring back assurance that such men were not sent by the authority of the Apostles and that this requirement was not being made by the brethren. The discussion that followed revealed that there was a segment of the Jerusalem church, made up of former Pharisees, which was contending that the Gentiles must receive circumcision and keep the law of Moses (Acts 15:5) in order to be Christians. After each had expressed himself on this subject, it was clear that all of the Apostles and elders were of one accord. The Jerusalem church had not sent out the Judaizers, and the Gentiles were under no instruction from God to receive circumcision or keep the Law. In order to inform the church of the true state of affairs a letter was sent back by Paul and Barnabas. The Holy Spirit had guided the entire discussion. Peter reminded them that God had led him to preach to the Gentiles; James quoted prophecy

---

2. See L. Coleman, A Manual on Prelacy and Ritualism, p. 146-150 for a full discussion of the matter.

showing that the Gentiles might come in; and Paul reported on the mighty work of God being performed among the Gentiles.

The fact that this conference was not of the modern council or synod type is seen in the fact that the Jerusalem church had not sent out invitations and that, at the most, representatives from only one other congregation were present. Further, Paul later pointed out that he had not received any instruction from those of Jerusalem different to what was revealed to him (Gal. 2:6; 1:8). It should also be noted that there was no surrender of independent congregational government.

Although congregations were complete and independent in their government, this did not preclude their cooperating in Christian service or in the spread of the gospel. The details are not given, but relief was sent from Antioch to Judea during the famine under Claudius (Acts 11:28-30). The congregations of Macedonia had fellowship in ministering to the saints (2 Cor. 8:1-4). The congregations of Galatia and Achaia also cooperated in sending relief to Jerusalem (1 Cor. 16:1-3).

X. WORSHIP OF THE CHURCH

The New Testament Church met on the first day of the week for public worship. The assemblies were in general held in private houses. The service was informal, but characterized by great sincerity and devotion. It consisted of songs, prayer, reading of the Scripture and partaking of the Lord's Supper. There was no set formality or ritual and the order of service varied from one congregation to another, but in the essentials there was general agreement. Simplicity and fervency characterized all that was done. Prayer was the sincere expression of the heart, making wants known to God and expressing gratitude for blessings received. Earnest devotion and praise to God were expressed in song. Although some have supposed the Greek word "psallo" (used in Eph. 5:19) to indicate the use of instrumental music in early church worship, it is generally admitted by the scholars of ancient church history that the first century Christians used no instrumental music in their worship services. The general practice was congregational a cappella singing.

XI. MANNER OF LIFE

It was customary for the early Christians to share their faith and hope and also their possessions. In the Jerusalem church, before the persecution began, it was customary for the Christians to have their regular meals together. As the number was large and included many poor it was necessary for those with possessions to care for those who were without. This situation became complicated because of the large number of persons away from home. They had come from great distances to worship at the Temple. After the establishment of the church and their conversion, it was natural for them to desire to remain in Jerusalem to learn from the Apostles and participate in the activities of the church. Soon their money was gone, work was unavailable and, accordingly, the number dependent upon the daily ministration of food increased. With this situation local Christians sold their possessions and gave the money to the Apostles to be used as there was need.

Some have used this situation to support the contentions of Socialists and Communists in their effort to establish a system of community of goods or state ownership of property. Nothing is farther from the truth. When the early Christians brought money to the Apostles it was a voluntary sharing. The Apostles did not divide every one's property so that they all had an equal amount, neither did they hold the property of all to be used by all. They used what was voluntarily given to meet the needs of those who had nothing. Distribution was made according as any one had need, but the system is clearly that of private ownership of property.

Out of the early custom of eating together grew the love feasts. This term applied to the meal that was eaten preceding the Lord's Supper. The entire congregation brought their food to the place of worship and ate together a common meal. This custom varied and in some places the love feast followed the worship. The poor of the community were invited to share in the meal.

PART TWO

CONTROVERSY AND DEPARTURE
100 - 312 A.D.

Chapter Four

Uninspired Writings -- 100 - 150 A.D.

The purity of the New Testament Church was soon lost. The Holy Spirit revealed to the Apostles that there would shortly be a departure from the divine pattern, and they in turn prepared the bishops of the church for the coming departure. While the Apostle Paul was visiting the elders of the church at Ephesus, in the town of Miletus, he told them to take heed unto themselves and to the church for after his departing grevious wolves would enter in among them not sparing the flock, and that from among themselves men would arise speaking perverse things and draw away the disciples after them (Acts 20:28-30). To the church of Thessalonica he stated that Christ would not return until the falling away came first, but hurried on to state that the mystery of lawlessness was already working in his day (2 Thess. 2:3-7). The safeguard against the falling away set forth by Paul was close adherence to the Word of God. Jesus had emphasized to the disciples that in His kingdom there would not be men exercising authority as was the custom among Gentiles. He taught that true greatness came through the road of service (Matt. 20:25-28). It was not long, however, until the warning given through the Holy Spirit against departure through the exaltation of men became a reality. The Apostle John referred to Diotrephes who loved to have the preeminence among the brethren and said that he worked with such high handed methods that he would not even receive the Apostle John (3 Jno. 3).

The student of church history is immediately impressed with the growth of heresy during the second century. For here we see the departure from the New Testament pattern gaining momentum. There are stalwart Christians defending the truth with great success, and for a period of time the departure is a very slow movement.

The uninspired writers who did their work from the year 100 to 150 are generally referred to as the Apostolic Fathers.

These are the men who knew the Apostles or knew people who had known them and had received their teaching in this direct manner.

The study of early church history consists largely of a study of the valiant fight made by the church in defending itself against inroads from every side. After leaving the inspired writings of the apostolic period, there is a growing avalanche of uninspired writings portraying this struggle. We must select from this large amount of literature that which seems to depict most accurately the turn of events. Until recently much that took place during the first fifty years following the death of the last Apostle was clouded with obscurity. Recent scholarship, however, has cleared away much of the mist, and we are now able to see with a great degree of certainty the life and work of the church. During this period the church was faced with growing heresies from within and developing persecution from without. Greek philosophy was making inroads into the thinking of leaders of the church while at the same time the Judaizers were carrying on their work of requiring Christians to keep the Law of Moses. These developments will be seen more clearly as we study the lives and writings of the first uninspired writers.

I. CLEMENT OF ROME

Following the death of the Apostles, each church was governed by a plurality of elders. No distinction was made between an elder and a bishop as both of these terms were used interchangeably, having reference to the same individual. The church at Rome had as it elders, men by the name of Linus, Anacletus and Clement. There is a tradition to the effect that each of these men was appointed by either the Apostle Paul or Peter.

Although we know nothing of the early life and work of Clement, there is no reason to doubt but that his life did overlap the period of the Apostles. In the past, students of church history thought that this was the Clement mentioned by the Apostle Paul in his letter to the Philippians, but later scholarship has rejected this conclusion. Clement was probably a Jew or a proselyte; however, even this has no conclusive evidence in its favor.

About the year 96, there developed in the church at Corinth a rebellion of young men against the elders. To encourage the Corinthian church to settle its difficulties, the church at Rome wrote a general letter which modern scholars believe came from the pen of Clement. The epistle was written in Greek and is believed to be the earliest writing after the inspired work of the Apostles. It was read publicly in the church at Corinth. Copies were sent to other congregations and it was soon found in the canon of inspired works. A number of writers refer to this epistle as inspired. Clement, however, made a distinction between inspired writing and his own. He appealed to "the blessed epistle of Paul the Apostle" as authority and considers his own as a work of admonition. The letter is of great importance to those who are interested in knowing the life, worship and organization of the church immediately following the Apostolic period. The epistle contains one hundred and fifty quotations from the Old Testament as well as numerous references to the New Testament writings. The church at Corinth is pictured as being in a state of confusion even worse than when the Apostle Paul had written to it earlier. Accordingly, the Corinthian Christians were admonished to have love, patience and humility. Examples of disobedience in the Old Testament are appealed to, and the coming resurrection is pictured to prove motivation for submission and purity in the Corinthian church. The epistle shows clearly that the church was governed by elders, that there was no distinction between bishops and elders and that the eldership was to continue in the churches. Clement states "the apostles . . . appointed their first fruits (having proved them by the Spirit) to be bishops and deacons of them that should believe."[1] This statement significantly sets forth the order of officers in the church. Although a later distinction arose between elders and bishops, at the time of Clement such a development was yet in the future. Clement goes on to say:

> Our apostles knew through our Lord Jesus Christ that there would be strife on account of the office of the episcopate. For this cause, therefore, in as much as they had obtained a perfect knowledge of this, he appointed those already mentioned and afterwards gave instruction that when they should

1. "I Clement" 42:4, Edgar J. Goodspeed (ed.), The Apostolic Fathers (New York: Harper & Bros., 1950).

fall asleep other approved men should succeed them in their ministry.[2]

In Clement's day there were elders who had been appointed by the Apostles, and he considered the elders of each congregation to be the proper successors of the Apostles. There is no doubt but that when Clement wrote, the oversight of the churches in Rome and Corinth was in the hands of a plurality of elders. Clement also sets forth the idea that obedience to the elders was a basis for unity in the church. The idea of submission to the elders as a basis for unity later prepared the way for obedience to "the" bishop, which was advocated by Ignatius and came to be a reality after the year 150.

In looking back upon the times of Clement the student should be very careful to understand the use of terms in his day. Later writers have thought that Clement perhaps was even in the position that the Pope of Rome now occupies. Such ideas are entirely foreign to the true situation. After a distinction between elders and bishops had developed, later writers tried to work out a succession of bishops in the Roman church in the sense of the Monarchial Episcopacy. Such attempts have always resulted in confusion of thought.

Irenaeus says that Linus was the first bishop following Peter and Paul and that Anacletus followed Linus and Clement was third in the succession. Augustine follows Irenaeus in this attempt stating that Linus was first after Peter. Tertullian, however, states that Clement was the first bishop after Peter, and Jerome agrees with Tertullian in this order. Various attempts have been made to harmonize these statments and work out what was believed to be the true line of the episcopal order. Since the tradition is held by some that Peter ordained Clement as a bishop in the Roman church, it has been supposed that Linus and Anacletus died or resigned very early even before the death of Peter so it would be possible for Peter to also ordain Clement as the third in line following Peter. Such confusion of thought continues until the student realizes that in the church at Rome no one of these men was *the* bishop, but each an elder, contemporary with the others. It is clearly set forth in Clement's own writing, as stated above, that the churches were governed by elders. There was no distinction between elders

2. "I Clement," 44:1-2.

and bishops. This should always be kept in mind, for to fail to do so will continue to propagate a false conception of conditions; we cannot put third century ideas into second century terminology. The above is in harmony with scriptural statements and makes more meaningful Peter's statement that he was a "fellow elder." (1 Pet. 5:1).

II.   IGNATIUS OF ANTIOCH

In the writings ascribed to Ignatius of Antioch there seems to appear glaring exception to all that is said concerning the church in the writings of Clement. In recent years it has become more apparent that the statements attributed to Ignatius cannot be taken as the true picture of conditions in the church, but rather represent what he wanted them to be. It is traditionally believed that Ignatius was ordained by the Apostle Peter and for a time served as chairman of the elders in the church at Antioch. He was arrested during a persecution under Trajan and was escorted to Rome in the care of ten soldiers to be thrown to the wild beasts in the amphitheater. On the way to Rome he was allowed to visit with the brethren, carry on long discourses and dictate letters to various churches. The kindness of treatment on the way to Rome has led many students of church history to doubt the authenticity of the letters. It is thought that his permission to talk with Polycarp and dictate to secretaries do not harmonize with true conditions during the period of persecution. Furthermore, in a letter to the church at Rome he pleads passionately with the brethren there to make no effort to prevent his martyrdom, which also seems absurd since it is not likely that the church at Rome had enough influence to have prevented his martyrdom even if they had tried. His desire for martyrdom and his attitude toward the elders of the church has led many to believe that he had a "neurotic will to power," and that this explains his statements that elders should be in subjection to their bishops. A consideration of external conditions surrounding the writing of these letters and the statements made in the letters themselves has caused able scholars of the past to doubt their genuineness. The other writers of this early period all agree that the churches were governed by a plurality of elders and there was no congregation which had a monarchial bishop as Ignatius advocates.

This evidence has been used to corroborate the idea that later writers interpolated his work. In spite of this it is now generally believed by modern scholars of early Christian literature that the work is geniune. Ignatius believed that the church could be protected from heresy and could be unified only by one individual in each congregation assuming a position of authority. This position would naturally fall to the chairman of the group of elders. Since the word bishop originally meant overseer it is logical to believe that what Ignatius meant by his statement was that the chairman of the meeting of the elders should make decisions and set the standard for orthodoxy and unity, and that the other elders and deacons should be in submission to the chairman, whom he calls "Bishop." It seems clear that Ignatius felt the need for a strongly organized system in the church to meet the conditions of his day. The chief ideas set forth by Ignatius may be seen in the following quotation:

> "Follow the bishop as Jesus Christ . . . the presbytery as the the Apostles; and respect the deacons . . . Let no man perform anything pertaining to the church without the bishop. Let that be considered a valid eucharist over which the bishop presides . . . It is not permitted either to baptize or to hold a love feast apart from the bishop."[3] "For since you are subject to the presbytery as to the apostles of Jesus Christ."[4]

When Ignatius wrote these words, there was rapid development of heresy within the church, and the chief desire of Ignatius was to maintain unity in the congregation and provide protection against such heresy. He believed that unity would be maintained through a continuity of bishops and complete submission to them. Accordingly, he showed a clear distinction between elders and bishops. However, in the writings of Ignatius there is no indication that a bishop's authority goes beyond that of the one congregation in which he worships, and there is no indication of rank among the bishops and no suggestion of the idea that a bishop of Rome has any more authority than a bishop in any other congregation. The very fact that Ignatius labors at length to bring the "elders" into submission to the "bishops" indicates that such a distinction did not exist at the time he wrote but that he was working to bring it about. His writing and thinking, however, was generally accepted later

3. Epistle to the Smyrnaeans. Sec. VIII
4. Epistle to the Trallians, Sec. II:2

and became the basis for the departure from the New Testament pattern into a succession of bishops. The fact that his ideas did not constitute the general practice of the church of his day will be clearly seen by the following evidence from the other writers of the period which followed the work of Ignatius.

A student of church history needs to be reminded that radical changes can come about in religious movements in a very brief period of time. The student should also begin very early in his thinking to be critical of his sources. It may be suggested that the extreme position set forth by Ignatius should be considered in the light of the development of Diotrephes, described in the third Epistle of John. In all of the writings of this early period, however, the student can see a very close relationship to developments in the Apostolic period. Ignatius was strongly opposed to the doctrine of Docetism. This doctrine stated that Christ's sufferings were not real but it was only a semblance of actual suffering, that Christ only seemed to suffer. Ignatius was very strong in combating such an idea insisting that the suffering of Christ was real. This reminds one of the writings of the Apostle John, showing that Christ came in the flesh. (cf. 1 Jno.).

III. THE EPISTLE OF BARNABAS

In the New Testament there is clear evidence of the struggle the church was having to establish itself as a separate institution from traditional Judaism. Since it is clear that God has had one plan for man, and His purpose in giving the Law of Moses was to prepare the world for the coming of Christ, it is rather natural that men would want to hold on to the old forms rather than accept the new. The books of Romans, Galatians and Hebrews deal specifically with this problem. In an early writing known as the *Epistle of Barnabas* this same question is further discussed. Early apologists and historians thought the Epistle was written by Barnabas who was a companion of the Apostle Paul on his first missionary journey. It is found as a part of *Codex Sinaiticus* which is one of the oldest copies of the Bible now in existence. More careful research, however, has shown conclusively that this epistle was written by some other than Paul's traveling companion. This epistle answers the Judaizers who say that the law is still in force. By showing that the death

of Christ is sufficient for salvation, the epistle argues that the
Law has been abolished and is no longer binding on Christians.
The method of discussion is highly allegorical and even clear
passages of Scripture are so used as to destroy their evident
meaning. The argumentation is a mixture of Greek philosophy
with Christian Scripture. It is likely that this letter set a pattern
for the allegorical use of scripture that followed later. It is in
this epistle that the word "gnosis" is used to signify "knowledge" or spiritual insight. This term is used later by many of the
early writers, and the student should discern between the early
use of the word and its latter use after the development of
gnosticism. In this early period the term signifies the true Christian who is following the spiritual guidance of Christ. This
epistle is also interesting from the viewpoint of moral exhortation which signifies that at the time it was written there was a
need for strong encouragement in regard to purity of life.

IV. THE DIDACHE (130-150)

Another very interesting document of this period from an
unknown author is that generally referred to as the *Didache* or
the *Teaching of the Twelve Apostles*. The exact date of this
composition is unknown and scholars have differed very widely
as to its probable date. It was quoted as early as the year 200
which is positive evidence that it was in existence at this date.
Evidence as to the time of writing is taken largely from the
contents. Some date it as early as the year 90, but the more
conservative scholars of early Christian literature believe it to
have been composed about the year 150. Those who give it the
early date do so on the basis that it referred to congregations
governed by bishops and deacons. The statement reads "Elect
therefore for yourselves, bishops and deacons worthy of the
Lord, men that are gentle and not covetous, true men and approved."[5] It is definitely established that during the period from
100 to nearly 150 the church was governed by elders and deacons without a distinction between elders and bishops. This
reasoning is used to date the composition in the early period.
However, there is a statement concerning baptism that indicates it was not close to the Apostolic period. This statement
reads "baptize in this way . . . in the name of the Father, Son

5. The Didache, Sec. 15.

and Holy Ghost, in living water, but if you have not living water, baptize in other water. And if thou canst not in cold, in warm, if you have neither, pour water thrice on the head . . ."[6] This is perhaps the earliest statement found in Christian literature indicating that even in emergency conditions any other baptism than immersion might be acceptable to God. Throughout the entire New Testament period, baptism was practiced only by immersion and this composition indicates that immersion was the regular form in use.

This instruction of the *Didache,* however, keeps us from believing the writings to be as early as the year 100. The writing consists of general instruction in regard to morality and Christian life. It sets forth two ways, the way of life and the way of death, and exhorts Christians to follow the way of life. The worship of the church is discussed and Christians are encouraged to assemble on the Lord's day and break bread. It also warns concerning the second coming of Christ and gives regulations concerning the ministry. It is a valuable find to help us understand the conduct of the church during the second century.

V. PAPIAS (125-150)

Papias lived in Hierapolis in Phrygia where he served as bishop of the church. We cannot establish dates for him, but he wrote about the year 140. Although his work has disappeared, Irenaeus and Eusebius quote from it sufficiently for us to know that he gathered up all the oral statements of the Apostles he could hear and put them in writing. Irenaeus says he was a disciple of John, but Eusebius doubts that he was.[7] He says that Mark wrote his gospel while being with Peter and it is an exposition of Peter's preaching. He also states that the gospel of Matthew was written in Hebrew. Papias refers to the officers of the church as presbyters, even calling the Apostles presbyters. Eusebius gives him credit for starting the millennial views, saying he received:

> "strange parables and mythical accounts. Among them he says that there will be millennium after the resurrection of the dead, when the kingdom of Christ will be set up in material form on this earth. I suppose that he got these notions by

6. The Didache, Sec. 7.
7. Eusebius, Ecclesiastical History III:39.

perverse reading of the apostolic accounts, not realizing that
they had spoken mystically and symbolically. For he was a
man of very little intelligence, as is clear from his books. But
he is responsible for the fact that so many Christian writers
after him held the same opinion, relying on his antiquity, for
instance Irenaeus and whoever else appears to have held the
same views."[8]

VI. POLYCARP (115-156)

Polycarp is best known as the aged bishop of Smyrna who
was martyred for his faith. The story of his death was one of
the first to be recorded and circulated among the churches. He
was killed February 22, 156,[9] at eighty-six years of age after
he had served as an elder of the church for forty or fifty years.

About the year 115 Polycarp wrote a letter to the church
at Philippi. The letter begins, "Polycarp and the elders with
him." It continues with admonition to godliness, consisting
mainly of Bible quotations. He quotes at least sixty passages
from the New Testament and presents no idea foreign to its
teaching. As to the government of the church he mentions no
distinction in bishop and elder, but admonishes the church "to
be subject to the presbyters and deacons." "Let the presbyters
also be compassionate, merciful to all, bringing back those that
have wandered," etc. The idea is the same that the Apostle Paul
used when he wrote to this same church with its "bishops and
deacons." (Phil. 1:1).

Irenaeus says that Polycarp was a companion of the Apostles and was appointed bishop by "eye witnesses and ministers
of the Lord." He says that as a child he saw Polycarp and that
he constantly taught those things he had learned from the
Apostles. He reports a tradition from the lips of Polycarp.
"John the disciple of the Lord going to bathe at Ephesus and
perceiving Cerinthus within, rushed out of the bath-house without bathing, exclaiming, 'Let us fly, lest even the bath-house
fall down because Cerinthus, the enemy of the truth, is within'."[10] This Cerinthus advocated a material reign of Christ on
earth.

8. Ibid.
9. Goodspeed, The Apostolic Fathers, p. 245. The date is disputed by
many, however. Kirsopp Lake suggests Feb. 23, 155.
10. Irenaeus, "Against Heresies" III:3:4, The Ante-Nicene Fathers, Grand
Rapids: ed. Alexander Roberts and James Donaldson. (Grand Rapids: Wm. B.
Eerdmans, 1956) I, p. 416.

The church at Smyrna wrote a statement for the brethren in general, telling of those who had died at Smyrna for their faith and there is every reason to believe this record is true. It tells of the arrest of Polycarp and how, because of his age, the officers tried to persuade him to say "Lord Caesar," and to sacrifice to the gods that he might be spared. He refused to do so and when brought before the Pro-Consul his freedom was offered if he would revile Christ. To this Polycarp said, "For eighty and six years have I been his servant, and he has done me no wrong, and how can I blaspheme my King who saved me?"[11] After further threatening with wild beasts and fire Polycarp said, "You threaten with the fire that burns for a time, and is quickly quenched, for you do not know the fire which awaits the wicked in the judgment to come and in everlasting punishment."[12] With this he was bound and burned. Eleven from Smyrna had been martyred before Polycarp.

VII. SHEPHERD OF HERMAS (140-150)

An interesting composition called the Shepherd of Hermas was written about the year 150. Its author is supposed to have been Hermas, a brother of Pius who was bishop of Rome from 140 to 155. Hermas was a slave of Rhoda, a wealthy woman of Rome, who became a Christian and freed him. He then became a well to do farmer and turned to a life of sin. His children also became corrupt. When misfortune took his money he considered his situation and turned to God.

The chief problem with which the composition deals is whether there is forgiveness for sin committed after baptism. There was an idea prevalent that a Christian could lead a sinless life and that if sin was committed after baptism there could be no forgiveness for it. The *Shepherd of Hermas* was written to correct this idea and show that there was forgiveness for the erring Christian who repented.

The composition takes the form of visions similar to the book of Revelation. The chief character is the angel of repentance in the form of a shepherd and the book develops in detail the doctrine of repentance. This is the earliest indication of the idea of penance as it later developed into a sacrament.

In regard to the organization of the church it is clear that

11. The Martyrdom of Polycarp. 9:3
12. Ibid. 11:2

66 THE ETERNAL KINGDOM

no distinction existed between elders and bishops for the book was to "the elders who are in charge of the church."[13] In regard to baptism it says, "we went down into the water and received remission of our former sins."[14] And in another place, "They go down into the water dead and come up alive."[15]

VIII. SUMMARY

The best information on the church of the first fifty years after the death of the last Apostle (100-150) is found in the works of the writers just discussed. They are ordinarily referred to as the "Apostolic Fathers" because they lived so near the Apostolic age and some of them knew the Apostles personally. Through their writing we find that the actual practices of the church had changed little from that set forth in the New Testament. There is however, the beginning of a departure. Many have thought Ignatius shows a change in elders and bishops in actual practice and that his use of the term bishop refers to a monarchial bishop. Since the evidence of all the other writers is contrary to this view, it is likely that Ignatius used the word bishop to refer to the chairman of the elders and that his exhortation for the elders to be subject to the bishop was more an attempt to create such a situation than a factual report of what was actually being practiced.

These writers give evidence of the independence of each congregation, and there is no reference to the church at Rome having any pre-eminence. Peter is neither mentioned as bishop of Rome nor is there any evidence of his having been in Rome. These writers can be studied with great profit in regard to the history of doctrinal changes. In their works there is no indication of the doctrine of original sin, but contraiwise, clear evidence of the freedom of the human will. Baptism is referred to by all as immersion for the remission of sin.

13. Shepherd, "Vision" 2:4:3.
14. Shepherd, "Mandate" 4:3:1
15. Shepherd, "Parable" 9:16:4

Chapter Five

The Apologists -- 185 - 250 A. D.

At the beginning of the gospel the church was tolerated by the government as a sect of the Jews. The Roman government required that each religion be duly authorized and "licensed" before it had a right to function in the empire. Since the Jewish religion was the ancient religion of Palestine, it was permitted to function unmolested as long as the Jews were submissive to Roman rule. The early disciples used the temple and then synagogues as places of worship until after the opposition of Jewish leaders developed and Gentiles came into the church. There was at the same time an attempt of Jewish Christians to keep the church as a Jewish development and to require Gentiles to become proselyted Jews before granting them church membership. This, however, was contrary to God's plan and the church successfully resisted any encroachment upon its independent status. As Roman officials became aware of this quality of distinctiveness, they began to regard the church as an illegal religion. This did not cool the zeal of the early Christians for they continued to preach the gospel and worship God even though their religion was not recognized as legal by the government.

After the persecution under Nero began, the Christians in many places had to worship in secret. This brought upon them all manner of false accusations. Since Jesus had said symbolically that Christians must "eat his flesh and drink his blood," and since the Lord's Supper is a communion of His body and His blood, it was very easy for the rumor to spread that the Christians were cannibals. Such false rumors began to grow, and with the charge that Christians were responsible for burning the city of Rome, both the officials and the population at large began to turn against the church.

The Christians knew that their lives were purer, their worship more noble and their religion more suited to improving the Roman world than anything the pagan religions had to offer. They accordingly began to defend themselves by writing what are known as Apologies. These writings explained the origin, doctrine and worship of the new religion and are very valuable as sources of information on this early period. Since the student of church history should be acquainted with their work, brief sketches will follow. Dates, in most cases, are approximations.

I. QUADRATUS (125-129)

One of the first to write a defense of Christianity was Quadratus. His composition was addressed to Hadrian the emperor and presented to him when he visited Athens about 129. All of the information we have about this is taken from the church history of Eusebius which was written about 326. At that time there were many copies of the Apology of Quadratus in circulation, but none of them are known to have survived to our day. Eusebius quotes one selection from his work that is as follows:

> "But the works of our Saviour were always present, for they were genuine; those who had been cured, those who had risen from the dead, who were seen not only when they were cured and raised, but on all occasions when they were present; and not only while the Saviour was on earth, but also after his departure, they were alive for some time, so that some of them lived even to our day."[1]

II. ARISTIDES (138-147)

The Apology of Aristides gives us the first complete document in defense of Christianity. Eusebius was familiar with it, and it was in common circulation in his day. Recent discovery has brought it to light either in part or the whole in Armenian, Syriac and Greek.

In contrasting Christian worship, morals and practices with that of human religions he refers to Christian books and shows familiarity with the four Gospels, Acts, Romans and 1 Peter. His closing chapters contain valuable information concerning the practices of the church in the middle of the second century.

III. JUSTIN MARTYR (103-165)

When we come to the life and work of Justin we emerge into an era of greater certainty in historical information. Justin was a native of ancient Shechem in Palestine. Having a very in-

1. Eusebius, Ecclesiastical History IV 3:2

quisitive mind he visited the various philosophical schools in an attempt to find satisfactory explanation to the serious questions of life. He received no satisfaction until he met an aged Christian at Ephesus about 133 and became a Christian. He then began to teach his new faith to others and in time visited Rome where he did extensive writing. Eusebius mentions eight different works, but only two have been preserved for us. These are his *Apology* addressed to Antonius, 150 A.D., and a *Dialogue with Trypho,* the Jew.

In the *Apology* Justin urges the emperor to investigate Christianity and learn the truth about the Christians. He then goes on to inform him that they are not atheists, or idolaters or immoral, but that Christianity is more noble than the pagan religions and that Christ was described in prophecy.

In regard to worship in the second century Justin gives a detailed account as follows:

> "But we, after we have thus washed him who has been convinced and has assented to our teaching, bring him to the place where those who are called brethren are assembled, in order that we may offer hearty prayers in common for ourselves and for the baptized (illuminated) person, and for all others in every place, that we may be counted worthy, now that we have learned the truth, by our works also to be found good citizens and keepers of the commandments, so that we may be saved with an everlasting salvation. Having ended the prayers, we salute one another with a kiss. There is then brought to the president of the brethren bread and a cup of wine mixed with water; and he taking them, gives praise and glory to the Father of the universe, through the name of the Son and of the Holy Ghost, and offers thanks at considerable length for our being counted worthy to receive these things at his hands. And when he has concluded the prayers and thanksgivings, all the people present express their assent by saying Amen. This word Amen answers in the Hebrew language to genoito (so be it). And when the president has given thanks, and all the people have expressed their assent, those who are called by us deacons give to each of those present to partake of the bread and wine mixed with water over which the thanksgiving was pronounced, and to those who are absent they carry away a portion.
>
> "And this food is called among us Eucharistia (the Eucharist), of which no one is allowed to partake but the man who believes that the things which we teach are true, and who has been washed with the washing that is for the remission of sins,

and unto regeneration, and who is so living as Christ has enjoined.

"And we afterwards continually remind each other of these things. And the wealthy among us help the needy; and we always keep together; and for all things wherewith we are supplied, we bless the Maker of all through His Son Jesus Christ and through the Holy Ghost. And on the day called Sunday, all who live in cities or in the country gather together to one place, and the memoirs of the apostles or the writings of the prophets are read, as long as time permits; then, when the reader has ceased, the president verbally instructs, and exhorts to the imitation of these good things. Then we all rise together and pray, and, as we before said, when our prayer is ended, bread and wine and water are brought, and the president in like manner offers prayers and thanksgivings, according to his ability, and the people assent, saying Amen; and there is a distribution to each, and a participation of that over which thanks have been given, and to those who are absent a portion is sent by the deacons. And they who are well to do, and willing, give what each thinks fit; and what is collected is deposited with the president, who succours the orphans and widows, and those who, through sickness or any other cause, are in want, and those who are in bonds, and the strangers sojourning among us, and in a word takes care of all who are in need. But Sunday is the day on which we all hold our common assembly, because it is the first day on which God having wrought a change in the darkness and matter, made the world; and Jesus Christ our Saviour on the same day rose from the dead. For He was crucified on the day before that of Saturn (Saturday); and on the day after that of Saturn, which is the day off the Sun, having appeared to His apostles and disciples, He taught them these things, which we have submitted to you also for your consideration."[2]

Justin's description makes it clear that Christians met on the first day of the week, or Sunday for their worship. In the *Didache* it was stated, "on the Lord's own day gather together and break bread and give thanks."[3] Justin makes it clear that the "Lord's Day" was Sunday. Baptism is referred to as a washing by Justin because immersion was the common form. He also shows that it was "for remission of sins and unto regeneration." One should also notice that Justin refers to the bishop in charge of the assembly as "the president."

The other work of Justin, *Dialogue with Trypho*, is the

2. Justin Martyr, "Apology," Chapters 65-67, Ante-Nicene Fathers, Vol. I, pp. 185-186.
3. "Didache" 14:1 Goodspeed, Apostolic Fathers, p. 17.

longest book written up to its time. It presents the Christian views in their relationship to the Law of Moses and as a development from prophecy. Justin shows that the prophecies of the Old Testament are fulfilled in Jesus as the Messiah, and that the God of the Old Testament is the God of the Christians.

Justin used Greek philosophy and the allegorical method of interpreting the Bible to defend the truths of Christianity which led him into fantastic interpretations of Scripture. It is apparent that he quoted from memory and accordingly was not accurate in his Scriptural quotations. There is every reason to believe, however, that when he is describing what the Christians of his day did or believed, that we can accept his statements as accurate. In addition to that already stated Justin believed that all Christians were priests. He set forth Christ as the Logos who had existed as God's faculty of reason and that He by voluntary process was caused to be generated as the Christ.

IV.   TATIAN (125-200)

Tatian was an individual who had traveled widely over Greece studying Greek philosophy. Not being satisfied he visited Rome and met Justin who converted him to Christ before the middle of the second century. On returning to Greece about 152-155 he wrote an "Address to the Greeks" in which he ridiculed their pretention to superiority and shows that Christianity holds the higher position. He said Greek immorality was shown by their sculpture and art, in their sports and also in their religion. He argues that Moses was more ancient than Homer, living even before the Trojan wars and that Christianity as a religion (through prophecy) was older than Greek religions.

Tatian later returned to Rome and for a time worked with Justin. It may have been here that he completed his greatest work called *Diatessaron*. This is an account of the life and work of Jesus. In it Tatian takes the four Gospels and interweaves them all into one continuous story. It was written in Greek, but was almost immediately translated into the Syriac and became very popular among the Syriac-speaking Christians.

After the death of Justin, Tatian became over-exalted in his own eyes and left the Scripture, becoming a Gnostic. He then began to teach that the Old Testament was not from God, that Adam was lost beyond salvation through Christ, and that marriage was sinful. He had taught Clement of Alexandria who turned away from him, calling him a heretic.

V.   MELITO (169-190)

Melito was bishop of Sardis, one of the churches mentioned in the book of Revelation. According to Eusebius, he produced eighteen or twenty compositions. Among them, one "On the Lord's Day," and one "On Baptism." His "Apology" was written about 170. In it he shows the emperor that the church is a positive force for good in the empire; and that, instead of persecuting it, the emperor would do well to defend it and use its influences. He defended Christianity as the final revelation of God to man which had been fore-shadowed in the Old Testament. The sacrifices were all typical of the sacrifice of Christ, and the Law was a forerunner of the gospel. He was a forceful preacher, and, although a tedious writer to modern readers, he strongly influenced the Apologists who followed him.

VI.   ATHENAGORAS (177-180)

One of the earliest examples of a person's being converted to Christ from a personal reading of the Scripture is Athenagoras, who was a teacher in Athens. He was very familiar with the writings of the Greek philosophers and quoted them freely in defense of certain Christian principles. In his "Supplication for the Christians," written about 180, he refutes the charges made against the Christians and shows that the pagan gods are human inventions since they have the same weaknesses as men. He also wrote a treatise "On the Resurrection of the Dead" which sets forth the reasons for believing in the resurrection. He states that the resurrection of the dead is not only a reality, but that it is also a necessity.

VII.   THEOPHILUS (190)

According to Eusebius, Theophilus was the sixth bishop of Antioch. He also became a Christian as a result of his own study of the Scripture. He wrote many things, but only his defense of Christianity has come down to us. It was written about 190 and addressed to Autolycus, a learned pagan official, whom Theophilus hoped to convert. The first part deals with the existence of God, absurdities of pagan gods and idolatry and discusses the fact of the resurrection. The second part contrasts the defense Greeks made of their gods and religion with that set forth in the Old Testament. The third part shows that Christianity is a true development of God's plan of which Judaism was the first phase, that Christianity is superior to paganism and that pagans are wrong in the attacks they make on the Christians. Theophilus quoted freely from both the Old and the New Testaments and said they were both "inspired by one spirit of God."

THE STATE OF THE CHURCH

Before going further with our sketches of the Apologists we must broaden our perspective, for we can understand the position of these later Apologists only in the light of developments affecting the state of the church.

The last half of the second century was characterized by persecution from without and heresy within. It is in this period that schismatic movement developed very rapidly. The canon of Scripture was not yet established. Christian doctrine was being handed down orally, and this gave opportunity for personal views to be added to uninspired gospels, Acts and Revelation. Some of these are as old as the New Testament writings. Most of them are anonymous or pseudonymous, and for some time they were confused with the inspired writings and are responsible for the rapid spread of false ideas. Movements that deserve our special attention at this time are Docetic, Gnostic, Marcionite and the Montanistic.

I. MARCION

Marcion was born in 85 A.D. the son of Sinope, an elder of the church in Pontus. He also later became an elder, but at the same time he became a wealthy ship owner. He came to Rome from Asia Minor in 138. He was rich, intelligent, zealous and a skillful organizer. In Rome he made a great impression and won the hearts of many by his generous gifts. He is said to have given ten thousand dollars to benevolent work at the Roman Church. He soon gained considerable influence. Marcion felt that the church was drifting into a cold legalism. He was probably at least partially justified in his criticism of the church. In periods when the church enjoyed peace and freedom from bitter persecution it probably gained some adherents who were not fully converted, who were poorly taught and imperfectly understood the teaching of the Lord. There was a growing tendency in the church to turn the gospel into law. There was an ever present temptation to exalt the letter above, and to the neglect of, the spirit. In their arguments the Christians fell back into the kind of casuistry they had practiced as Jews.

Marcion was at heart a reformer. He saw in the Law the greatest enemy of the liberty and grace of the Gospel. He wanted to throw the Old Testament away completely. He even went so far as to assert that the God of the Old Testament was a different being from the God of Jesus: that the God of the Old Testament was a God of justice; the God of Jesus was a God of love and mercy; these two opposed each other; Paul was the only Apostle who really understood the gospel; the others had fallen into the errors of Judaism. He was what we today would call a "modernist" or "liberalist," for he rejected the commandments of Christ, thinking they were no part of faith.

The church in Rome was forced to withdraw from Marcion in 144 because of the extremes to which he went. But when he had withdrawn he formed a Marcionite church. In controversy he went to extremes that he probably never intended at the beginning. To support his position he gathered up what he called the inspired books of the Apostles. He accepted only the epistles of Paul and the Gospel of Luke. It seems he even cut from these all passages that seemed too favorable to the Law. About 150 he wrote a treatise called "Antitheses" or "Contradictions."

Marcion drew away many followers from the church. His movement showed great missionary zeal and spread extensively. It survived into the fifth century.

II. Gnosticism

The word Gnostic comes from a Greek word meaning "to know." For a time the Christians referred to themselves as "true Gnostics" with the implication that through Christ they had learned the true wisdom. This term, however, is generally used to refer to those who reject the revelation of God and relied upon human wisdom. They were the religious rationalists who, through their own mental gymnastics, solved problems according to their own speculative philosophical bent. They became to the early church what the Christian Scientists are today. Salvation was to be obtained through intellectual means.

Basically, Gnosticism is a dualism that pronounces the material world evil and the spiritual good. In order for man to get above the material and reach the spiritual he must go through a hierarchy of intermediate beings of which Christ is only one. The angels are also an important part, and accordingly, they are to be worshipped. Man is to buffet his body through asceticism and by special knowedge rise above the sinful world of material things. God is spirit and therefore could not have made a material world. This great God, however, breathed out emanations that resulted in the formation of a lesser God who is the Jehovah of the Old Testament.

The Gnostics had most fertile imaginations and were very prolific in theories. There were many schools of Gnostics. They mixed up a little Christianity, a little Judaism, a little philosophy, some from the mystery religions and other pagan religions and a lot of wild dreaming. The incarnation was just a temporary union between the divine and human person. They held that there was an essential antagonism between body and spirit. The spirit was imprisoned in the body. Their goal was to free the spirit that it might ascend back to God. They divided men into three classes: animal or material men predestined to destruction (non-Christians); psychic men who could attain salvation with the help of ordinary Christians; and the spiritual men who were destined to eternal life. They put great stress on secret knowledge and traditions which they claimed were handed down by Jesus and the apostles. They wrote numerous books which they ascribed to inspired apostles.

Many people were led astray by the Gnostics. Their ideas exerted great influence in the church. In meeting the threat of Gnosticism the Christians of that day had to distinguish very carefully between the genuinely inspired books and the forged works. They had to inquire searchingly which books really came from Apostles and men associated with Apostles and which books were later in origin and from uninspired men. Another weapon that was used with telling effect against the

Gnostics was an appeal to the bishops of the churches. If Jesus had handed down a secret doctrine he would have given it to His Apostles. The Apostles would have given it to the elders or bishops. There were a few churches who could trace the succession of their bishops back to the time of the Apostles. Since the bishops of these churches knew nothing of the secret traditions of the Gnostics, their teaching was exposed.

Some of the Gnostics went to wild and fantastic extremes like the Ophites who claimed that the Old Testament was the perversion of the devil. The God of the Old Testament was really the devil. The Serpent in the Garden was the true God who was trying to liberate Adam and Eve who had been imprisoned by the evil God. The Serpent suggested eating the fruit that would give the knowledge of Gnosis necessary to free them. The Ophites stressed the healing effects of the brazen serpent of Moses. They sanctified the elements used in the Lord's Supper by having snakes crawl over the bread and in the wine. This shows how far men can wander from the truth.

Gnosticism reached its greatest height about 150 and resulted in a large number of divergent theories. Some of them believed the material body should be turned over to the fulfillment of all fleshly desires and in this way destroy its desires. Gnosticism had in it conclusions that were very contrary to truth. The idea of two or more gods made the God of the Bible inferior. Since he created matter which is evil within itself, and since he favored the Jews, the Gnostics became anti-Semetic and began to deny the reality of Christ's fleshly nature and the resurrection of the body. This depreciation of the physical body led some to celibacy and monasticism. In spite of these general differences many Christians who were influenced by Gnosticism remained in the church until about 200 A.D. After this, they withdrew to form their own societies or associations.

III. DOCETISM

Docetism is the belief that Christ did not really suffer on the cross, but rather that He just "seemed" to suffer. The word docetic comes from a Greek word which means "to seem." The theory is based upon the conception that matter is essentially evil; therefore, Christ was not corrupted with anything of the material world. Neither the incarnation nor the crucifixion were actual facts, but only the semblance of reality. Ignatius describes Docetic teaching and insists that the sufferings of Christ were real. It was this threat to true Christianity that led Ignatius to feel that the church could be protected from such error by exalting the chairman of the elders to a permanent position of authority.

IV. MONTANISM

As Marcion reacted to legalism in the church, Montanus reacted to a growing formalism and reliance upon human leadership in the church. He was opposed to the growing importance of bishops in each congregation and instead of going to the inspired writings of the Apostles for his authority he said that the Holy Spirit was still guiding the church in a direct way. He took the promises of the Holy Spirit Jesus had made to the Apostles and said they applied to him. He even claimed that he was the first to receive the Holy Spirit in its completeness.

From many quarters in the second century we find complaints of growing worldliness, coldness and legalism in the church. There was a certain sadness and uneasiness that came from the fading away of the spiritual gifts. Men were reluctant to give up miracles. There was always a great temptation to claim spiritual gifts that one did not have. In the time of the *Didache* the church was greatly troubled by false prophets who claimed to have the Spirit. Some probably wanted these gifts so badly that they deceived themselves into thinking they had them. Out of this unrest came the Montanist movement.

Montanus lived in Arboda, a town in Mysia, where Jerome says he was a priest in a pagan temple of Cybele. Just after his conversion to Christianity he continued to practice emotionalism that was customary with the worship of Cybele. He would go into a great trance and begin to rave and utter strange sounds. He claimed that while in such a trance Christ spoke to him and through him. He converted two women, Priscilla and Maximilla, who also began to prophesy and lead the true believers astray. Their chief work was done in Pepuza, a town of Phrygia. The chief point of their prophecy was that Christ would shortly return and set up His headquarters for an earthly reign of one thousand years in Pepuza. But the Montanist movement with its emphasis on strict Christian living and on spirituality spread to many lands. Even the brilliant Tertullian was carried away by it. They made the possession of spiritual gifts the test of a true Christian and insisted upon a practice of strict asceticism. They taught that marriage was permissible but that it was a lower state of existence than celibacy. Under no condition, however, could a person be married a second time after the first companion died. If a person fell into sin after once being a Christian there was no possibility for forgiveness or fellowship in the church. All worldly enjoyments were forbidden and a strict asceticism enforced. Montanus considered himself greater than the Apostles and his visions more important than their writings. This was too much for the church to accept. He made the fatal mistake of setting a date for Jesus to return. His followers gave away all of their goods and when Jesus did not return at that time, the poor Montanists had to pillage neighboring farms for goods until they were scattered by the police — and unenviable position for Spirit filled people.

Montanists were soon excommunicated in Asia Minor and then rejected in nearly every region. They maintained their own churches for a time and divided into many differing groups before they finally were absorbed into the Novatianists in the third century.

With the above brief sketch of Marcionism, Gnosticism, Docetism and Montanism added to our background we can better understand the writings and work of the Apologists of the latter half of the second century, for these influences will appear many times in the course of church history.

LATER APOLOGISTS

I. IRENAEUS (130-200)

Irenaeus was born in Asia Minor about 130 A.D. He states that as a youth he heard Polycarp preach and became a Christian and his disciple. From his writing we know he was very learned. He quoted from nearly every Christian writer before his time. He also traveled widely, but he settled at Lyons in Gayl where he became bishop in 177. About 185 he wrote five books *Against Heresies*. In them he gives the best description we have of Gnosticism. He is careful in organization and presents a systemized statement of faith. He insists that plain

Scripture should not be made ambiguous and that ambiguous passages or parables should not be made the source of doctrine. He shows that Matthew, Mark, Luke and John are the only inspired Gospels and appeals to the Bible to prove the gnostic theory false. The supposed antagonism between Paul and the other Apostles, which some were advocating, is strongly denied, and the inspiration of Scripture in general is defended. It is interesting to know that in his day some were translating Isaiah 7:14 to read "young women." He rejected that rendering and insisted that "virgin" was intended. The virgin birth of Christ was defended, and he proved that Christ recognized only one God and Father who is the Jehovah of the Old Testament. He established a continuation of God's plan from the Old Testament into the New and believed the sacrifices were continued in the Lord's Supper. The resurrection of Christ was emphasized to refute the dualistic idea that the material body is itself sinful.

Irenaeus was disturbed by the many warring sects that had grown up within Christianity. He attempted to oppose their errors and to present a plan to unify and secure the perpetuation of a standard type of Christianity. In order to do this the scattered churches would have to be organized and placed under authority. He appealed to the fact that some of the churches were established by Apostles and had a continuous succession of officers down to his day. These he believed to be the least affected by heresy. It was in opposing the heretics that he traced the bishops from the beginning down to his day and used this chain of succession to prove that the right doctrine had been preserved — a practice hardly necessary in our age.

He first appealed to the Scripture, but the heretics attacked the Scripture as incomplete, saying that the truth had not been handed down in writing but by oral traditions. Irenaeus then turned to tradition and traced the bishops back to the beginning to prove that his doctrine had the sanction of oral tradition as well as Scripture. As an example he appeals to the church at Rome. He says it "was founded and set up by the two most glorious Apostles, Peter and Paul . . . the blessed bishop. . . . He was succeeded by Anacletus, after whom Clement was appointed to the bishopric."[4] He then mentions bishops in

4. Irenaeus, "Against Heresies," 3:3:2-3, A.N.F., 1, 415-416.

order down to Eleutherus who was the Roman bishop of his
time.

It should be noticed that Irenaeus was using the succession
of bishops only as a proof of orthodoxy to confirm the truth of
Scripture. For this he relies upon tradition which had reached
him. Some of this tradition is obviously in error. He refers repeatedly to the church in Rome being established by "Paul and
Peter" when the New Testament shows that the church was a
thriving congregation before Paul ever reached Rome (Acts
28:15; Rom. 15:24; 1:11). There is no sure tradition that
Peter was ever in Rome.

The story of Peter spending time in Rome comes from a
highly imaginative writing called the "Acts of Peter"[5] written
between 200 and 220. This is a compilation of imaginary
legends. It tells that Jesus would not allow the Apostles to leave
Jerusalem until twelve years after Pentecost, but as soon as this
time had passed Peter went to Rome where he performed all
kinds of miracles such as sending a message to Simon Magus
by a talking dog, putting a dried fish in water and bringing it to
life, making a seven-month old baby talk, using holy water, etc.
The story tells how the people were charged admission to enter
the forum to see a contest of power between Peter and Simon
Magus. Simon kills a boy with a word and Peter restores his
life. Simon then flies over the city and Peter has him fall and
break his leg in three places. It is also in this document that we
have the now popularized story of "Quo Vadis." The story says
Peter taught that wives should leave their husbands and that
the husbands persecuted him. The story then says that Peter
was leaving Rome to avoid this persecution when Jesus meets
him going into Rome. Peter recognized Jesus and said "Lord,
where are you going?" (Domine quo Vadis?) Jesus answers
that He is going into Rome to be crucified again. This makes
Peter ashamed, and he returned to Rome to face the persecutors and was crucified at his request with his head down.

The foregoing account is obviously inaccurate throughout.
The New Testament tells of Peter's work in Caesarea and that
he was in Jerusalem when Paul and Barnabas went up to see if
the Jerusalem church had sent the Judaizers to Antioch (Acts

5. M. R. James (ed.), Apocryphal New Testament (Oxford: Clarendon
Press, 1955), pp. 300 ff. (Chicago: University of Chicago Press, 1947) pp. 111-
118.

15). Peter's work was clearly to be with the Jews (Gal. 2:8), and he writes to the "Dispersion in Pontus, Galatia, Cappadocia, Asia and Bithynia (1 Pet. 1:1) as though he had labored among them. When Paul writes his letter to the church at Rome, Peter obviously was not there or he would have sent him greetings along with the twenty-seven other brethren. After his third missionary journey, Paul was taken as a prisoner to Rome where he wrote letters back to the churches. He sent greetings from brethren in Rome, but never once does he mention Peter's being there. In the last letter written, he said "all have forsaken me." (2 Tim. 4:10). If Peter *was* there, he had forsaken Paul. It cannot be established historically, however, that Peter was ever in Rome or that he was martryed there.

Irenaeus is the first to give a list of bishops of the church at Rome. It is of interest that he does not mention Peter as the first of the Roman bishops. No writer as early as Irenaeus attempts to claim Peter was the first bishop of Rome. This began about the middle of the third century. The congregations, according to Irenaeus, were still independent, and there was no organization outside of the local congregation. Centralization of authority and submission to Rome was yet in the future.

II. CLEMENT OF ALEXANDRIA (150-215)

Titus Flavius Clement, a native of Athens, became known as Clement of Alexandria because of his writings while connected with the famous Alexandrian Bible School. This school had an old history when Clement came as a student in 180 to study under Pantaenus, its famous teacher. Eusebius says that "Pantaenus had charge of the life of the faithful in Alexandria, for from ancient custom a school of sacred learning existed among them."[6] We are not able to establish the date this school began, but Eusebius repeats the tradition that Mark was the first bishop of Alexandria, and it has been thought that the school goes back in operation for some time before Pantaenus took charge of it.

Clement started out as many of his day, to visit the various schools of philosophy in search of knowledge. After studying with a number of teachers he found Pantaenus "hiding in Egypt." He pays tribute to his ability saying, "he drew honey

6. Eusebius, Ecclesiastical History. 5:10:1

from the flowers in the meadow of the Apostles and prophets, and implanted in the souls of his pupils pure knowledge."

Clement succeeded his teacher as head of the school in 190. He was thoroughly familiar with Greek philosophy, and as the Gnostics had used it to further their theories, Clement used it to oppose them and to defend the Scripture. Of his writing that has come down to us we have his instruction for the unconverted in a work called, *A Hortatory Word to Gentiles*. This is generally referred to as the *Address*. To the newly converted he wrote *The Instructor* to develop in them a life of godliness. To the mature Christians he wrote a treatise called "Clothes-bags." The Greek word he used for this title referred to a long bag of striped canvas in which bed clothes were kept rolled up. We would refer to it as a scrap-bag into which would be stored odds and ends. In this Clement preserved ideas that he thought should be passed on to the Christian or "true Gnostic." This work is also called *Miscellanies* because of its miscellaneous nature.

Clement is a good example of the intellectual Christian of his day. The majority of the Christians were afraid of Greek philosophy because it was used by the Gnostics to lead men away from the truth. These Christians thought that as soon as a person became a believer he should keep his mind free of philosophy lest he be led astray. Clement, however, accepted the idea of Philo that philosophy was the handmaid of theology. He accordingly studied philosophy and showed that the Greeks had taken their ideas from Moses and, accordingly, there was some truth in their writings. He thought, and no doubt rightly so, that this attitude was the only approach to use in getting an educated Greek to accept Christ.

III.   Tertullian (155-223)

The church was established in north Africa very early, and it is believed that the Bible was first translated into Latin in the region of Carthage. It was here that Tertullian was born about 155 A.D. During his early years he was interested in becoming a lawyer, and later, while practicing law and teaching in the city of Rome, he was taught the Christian religion and was baptized in 195. He then returned to Cathage to help spread the gospel in his native province. He was zealous and possessed the qualities that placed him in the leadership of the brethren. Not being satisfied with oral teaching his fiery nature led him to write on all the issues facing the church. Twelve Christians had been martyred in Carthage under Commodus in 180, and when in 197 the Christians refused to celebrate the victory of Septimius Severus, they again were persecuted. At that time Tertullian wrote a defense appealing for justice. He called attention to the injustice of condemning Christians without first examining their belief and their conduct. He mentions the common charges of incest, infanticide, cannibalism and disloyalty to the government and shows these charges were not true. In later writings to Roman governors he deals at length with the charge of disloyalty. He shows that, although the Christians cannot call the Emperor, God, they do respect him and are good loyal citizens. Tertullian further argues that persecution would never destroy the church, but rather increase it. In this connection he made the famous statement, "We multiply whenever we are mown down by you; the blood of Christians is seed."

To those Christians in prison Tertullian wrote to strengthen their faith and give them encouragement in time of torture. In opposition to error he wrote on many Biblical subjects, and to help new Christians he went into great detail on such things as the adornment of women, modesty, attending amusement, etc.[7] His known works number forty-three.

Tertullian's life as a Christian is divided into two parts. At first he was a staunch defender of the strong organization idea that was being advocated in his day. Under this influence he wrote in his *On Prescription of Heretics,* "What we hold is the belief of the church, handed down from the Apostles, from bishop to bishop, in all the historic centers of Christianity, so it must be true, and there is no more to be said." He did not believe any one church established by Apostles was more a depository of truth than another, but since the nearest "historic center" to Carthage was Rome, he used it as an example and accepts the tradition that had built up around the Apostles' having suffered martyrdom there. He wrote, "How happy is its church, upon which Apostles poured forth all their doctrine

7. For a discussion of his writings see Goodspeed, Early Christian Literature, pp. 210-226.

along with their blood. Where Peter endures a passion like his Lord's! Where Paul wins his crown in a death like John's! Where the Apostle John was first plunged unhurt into boiling oil and then returned to his island exile!"

Without realizing it Tertullian was building a tradition around the church at Rome, following a pattern set by Irenaeus, which was later to lead to Rome's exaltation above all other churches. Tertullian referred to Rome as he did to other historic Apostolic churches as added proof of the truth of Christianity. They could trace their teaching back to the Apostles through oral tradition, but to him the Scripture was final authority. He stated in his *Prescription* that the church at Rome also relied upon Scripture: "The Law and the prophets she unites with the writings of evangelist and Apostles, from which she drinks in her faith."

By 202 Tertullian began to react against the movement toward centralization and authority. The spiritual emphasis had been reduced and laxity increased. The movement toward legalism caused Tertullian to move in the opposite extreme toward Montanism.

This shift from one extreme to another will be seen repeated throughout the history of the church. It is also very apparent in our generation. When the outward form is stressed the spirit seems to be lost. Then when the reaction comes and the spirit is emphasized the form becomes of no importance regardless of what the Scriptures say. The "either-or" fallacy has caused many to miss the true way. Tertullian was justified in his opposition to the growing organization, and whether he accepted fully the extremes of Montanism is doubtful. He did accept the Montanists' views on an earthly millennium and he became ascetic. He then wrote an "Exhortation of Chastity" and a work "On Fasting."

In 202 Tertullian left the traditional church and worked with the Montanists until 222. By this time, however, he reacted to their extremes and organized a congregation on what, to him, represented the true Christian teaching. This independent movement may have been close to the New Testament pattern, but information on it is too brief for us to pass judgment. This movement lasted two hundred years as an independent church in Carthage but then entered the Catholic church through the persuasion of Augustine.

IV. HIPPOLYTUS (170-236)

Hippolytus was born about 170 A.D. He studied under Irenaeus in Gaul, but spent his mature life in Rome. Origen tells of visiting Rome and hearing him preach about 215 A.D. He was a fiery preacher and a puritan in morals. At that time the Roman church had a Bishop Zephrinus who cared more for himself than the church, and Hippolytus opposed his laxity. The church divided, and one part chose Hippolytus as their bishop. The other part had a succession of bishops, Calixtus, who was appointed at the same time as Hippolytus, and then Urganus and Pontianus. These three are now considered by the Roman Catholics to have been popes. Pontianus and Hippolytus were both seized in 235 during the persecution under Maximin and sent to the Sardinian mines together. It seems that the division in the church was healed during this persecution. At least the Roman Christians erected in 236 or 237 a marble statue of Hippolytus seated in a chair and engraved on it a list of his principle writings. Most of his writings have disappeared, but what we have show that he was a strong opponent of the trend the Roman church was taking. He recognized a distinction between bishops and elders, but he would not bow to popish tendencies and was unafraid to oppose and criticize his three successive contemporaries in the other congregations in Rome who were later looked back upon as popes.

His writing consisted of Biblical interpretation, opposition to laxity in the church and especially opposition to heresy. He believed that heresy had its origin in Greek philosophy and paganism; therefore, he surveyed philosophy, the mystery religions, and astrology and magic in order to better contrast them with pure Christianity. He was the last writer in Rome who wrote in the Greek language as Latin had by then become the language in use in the Roman church.

V. ORIGEN (185-254)

Origen was born into a pagan family of Alexandria in 185 A.D. When he was eight years old, his father and mother were converted to Christ and became very steadfast Christians. Origen then attended the Bible school of Alexandria and studied under its famous teacher, Clement. In 202 when Origen was only seventeen his father, Leonidas, was caught during a wave of persecution and was to be killed. A touching story has reached us to the effect that Origen decided to give himself up and die with his father, but his mother hid his clothes and persuaded him not to do so. He then wrote his father in prison to encourage him to steadfastness.[8]

The following year, 203, Origen was placed in charge of the school to train new converts. He taught for twelve years, until another wave of persecution began, at which time he fled to Rome. He then went to Palestine and preached in Caesarea and Jerusalem with such success that Demetrius, the bishop of Alexandria, called him back to continue his work at the school, which he did for another thirteen years.

During this second period of teaching he converted Ambrose from Gnosticism and obtained a wealthy patron who both urged him to put his thoughts into writing and supported him in carrying on an extensive publishing house.

Origen dictated to seven secretaries, who replaced each other as they tired. He also had seven scribes and a number of young lady assistants whom he kept busy making copies of his work. He produced so rapidly that he did not take time to re-read his work before the process of re-copying began.

His great work was in producing an Old Testament in six languages in parallel columns (9,000 pages) and in writing a commentary on each book in the Bible (291 scrolls).

Origen was a brilliant man and he believed the Scripture to be inspired of God, but he thought he knew the truth on every question when much of the time it was really his own speculation. He was visionary and so allegorical in his interpretation that instead of explaining a Scripture he exploited it to fit his theory. He put ideas into passages that the writer never had in mind and that could not be explained literally. In fact, Origen looked with scorn upon any who took a Scripture at its literal meaning. He relied upon living tradition that had been handed down from one Christian to another. He thought he knew, in this way, what the will of the Lord was and relied on this in preference to the obvious meaning of Scripture.

As philosophy was popular and Christianity persecuted,

8. Eusebius, Ecclesiastical History. 6:2:5-6.

Origen tried to show that Christianity was essentially a philosophy and accordingly should receive equal respect. He propounded a philosophical interpretation of Christianity and linked Christian teaching to Greek philosophy. This tendency toward philosophy may account for Origen's theory of the pre-existence of souls and the final salvation of all men perhaps including the devil. In regard to this he speculated that God made in the beginning all of the souls who were ever to be in the universe. Part of these souls turned to righteousness and became the angels. Part of them turned entirely to evil and became the devil and evil spirits. Part of them sinned, but to a lesser degree and these are the men of earth. All men are therefore sinners because their soul sinned is their pre-existent state. Since there is salvation for sinful men, he thought there would be salvation for the evil spirits and perhaps the devil himself. This was possible because both men and evil spirits had freedom of choice and could improve their lot. This tendency to speculate has caused the serious minded of every age to look with question upon his work and because of it the influence of a brilliant mind has been lessened or nullified.

Origen was not dogmatic in regard to that which we call speculation. To him it fit his philosophical theories. In regard to fundamentals his work can be read with great profit today. His "Exhortation to Martyrdom" written to Ambrose who was in prison as a Christian shows great faith in God and confidence in the truth of Scripture. His treatise "On Prayer" reveals a rich understanding of Scripture and complete trust in the providence of God.[9]

9. For the text of these writings and excellent introductions, see **Alexandrian Christianity**, Vol. II. "The Library of Christian Classics," Henry Chadwick (ed.) (Phila.: The Westminister Press, 1955).

Chapter Six

Through Persecution to Victory
54 - 325 A.D.

Long before the coming of Christ the people of Rome worked out a close relationship between the Roman government and Roman religion. Religion was supported by the government which allied it with patriotism.

Foreign religions were looked upon with suspicion as subversive to the State and a source of conspiracy against Roman rule. This had been especially true in regard to the relationship of the Romans with the Jews. At first Judaism in Palestine was unmolested by the Roman conquerors, but the Jewish leaders were not content to remain under Roman rule. A strong nationalism had been a part of Jewish life, and this burning desire for independence resulted in intermittent rebellion against Rome. Christianity had its background in the law and the prophets. Jesus was a Jew, the gospel was first preached among the Jews and the synagogues were first used as places of worship. It is to be expected that under these circumstances the Christians would share the suspicions and contempt held by Romans for the Jews.

The Christians, however, worked to free themselves from association with Jewish activities. They took no part in independence movements, and when the Roman army marched against Jerusalem in A.D. 70, they had deserted the city. They did not want to be found opposing the Roman government. In spite of this, throughout the second century the Christians shared the general dislike the Romans held toward the Jews.

The teaching that Christ is King of kings and that Christians share in His kingdom and are sealed as members of a new covenant all seemed to the Romans to be leading to rebellion. The very existence of the Christians was considered a threat to the peace and security of the State and accordingly it was felt that they should be eliminated.

From the beginning Christianity had no legal status. It was an illegal religion and until it could be licensed by the Senate it was destined to exist as best it could. During times of opposition the meetings had to be conducted in secret and under such conditions it was natural for all kinds of suspicions to develop.

Christians began to be accused of most absurd crimes. These accusations included incest, cannibalism, the drinking of blood, infanticide and plotting to overthrow the government.

There were two chief reasons why these accusations were made. One is the development of an extreme gnosticism and the other the existence of illegal pagan societies that had actually practiced in secret the things Christians were accused of. These were the Roman Druids and the Bacchanalia.

The Druids carried on human sacrifices in their rites and practiced magic. The Bacchants considered nothing to be immoral. They held secret meetings at night where they bound themselves to practice all kinds of crime. If we can believe the description they committed murder, forged wills and took oaths to oppose law and order. Under influence of drink they practiced cannibalism and engaged in all kinds of immoral conduct. Although these groups were outlawed they persisted to such a degree as to cast suspicion upon all secret meetings.

The reproach brought upon the church through the Gnostic influence was based upon the conduct of extremists. Gnosticism developed two extremes. One was asceticism and the other debauchery. Both extremes grew out of a false notion of the material world. It was believed that matter itself was evil. This included the human body. One group believed the evil of the material body should be overcome by depriving it of its desires. This resulted in asceticism. The other extreme group believed that the body should be destroyed by indulging its desires until they were all satisfied. They believed the body would thus burn itself out and when it ceased to desire, the soul could overcome its hindrance. This theory was actually practiced and no doubt the stories that Christians were people of lust and incest resulted from these sources. The Apologists explained that they could not justify such conduct and that this type of life did not represent the true Christian. They also explained that the Christian was a good citizen. Regardless of explanations, however, the average Roman believed that immorality and conspiracy was a necessary part of a foreign religion.

The Christians could not take part in the worship of the

public gods and for this reason they were called "Atheists," "godless" and disloyal. Since the Christians could not take part in the idolatry of public worship when all citizens were called upon to sacrifice, they were made conspicuous to their neighbors by their absence and this aggrevated the rumors about them.

Christ had been crucified during the reign of Tiberius in A.D. 33. During the following seven years of his reign the church began its rapid spread over the Empire. This spread was accelerated by the jealousy of the Jews and their persecution which began with the martyrdom of Stephen and the scattering of the church. Christians, however, were not officially persecuted by the Romans at this time.

I. Chronology of Persecution

Under the reign of Gaius, commonly called Caligula, (37-41), there was no official persecution, but ground work was laid that later brought on persecution. Caligula's sister, Drusilla, died the year after he became emperor, and as he was fond of her she was deified among the Roman gods as the universal goddess. Caligula next reasoned that if she was the universal goddess he must himself be the universal god. Accordingly he required all official oaths be taken in his name and he be considered a deity.

The Jews, of course, could not accept such claims to deity and refused to worship him. In retaliation the Romans set up images of him in Jewish synagogues and erected a large image of him in Jerusalem that was to be moved into the temple. This was delayed due to strong Jewish opposition and at Caligula's murder in 41 A.D. the attempt was abandoned. During the reign of Caligula, however, "the church throughout all Judea and Galilee and Samaria had peace, being edified; and, walking in the fear of the Lord and in the comfort of the Holy Spirit, was multiplied." (Acts 9:31).

When Claudius became emperor (41-54) the Jews were immediately released from the obligation to recognize the emperor as deity. Claudius then gave Judea to Herod Agrippa who was a native and sympathetic to the Jewish feeling. The Jews took advantage of their favorable position and turned Herod against the Christians. We read how he "killed James the brother of John with the sword." (Acts 12:2). This opposition to the Christians also reached Rome. Riots of some nature broke out and Suetonius said: "Because the Jews at Rome caused continuous disturbances at the instigation of Christus (*i.e.* Christ, J.M.) he expelled them from the city."[1] We know it was at this time that Aquila and Priscilla had to depart from Rome (Acts 18:2), but it is almost certain that they were not Christians until Paul came to Corinth to work with them as a tentmaker.

When Nero came to power in 54 A.D. the church had made remarkable growth. The toleration that had permitted this growth, however, was about to end. In Palestine there had been revolutionary efforts by Theudas in 44 A.D. (Acts 5:36) and by "the Egyptian" (Acts 21:38) in 53 A.D. These movements had been crushed with great blood shed, and the Jews were eager to blame such riots on the Christians. It may be that certain of the un-taught Christians had taken part in efforts to throw off the Roman yoke. The fact that Christians became associated with revolutionary movements in the minds of the rulers proved injurious to the Christian cause.

It was during the time of Nero and between governors in Palestine that Ananias the high priest moved with indignation against the Christians called James — the brother of Jesus — before the Sanhedrin and obtained a conviction against him. He and certain others were then stoned to death. These were the first martyrs during the reign of Nero.

On the night of July 18, 64 A.D. fire broke out in the city of Rome. It burned fiercely for six days and slowly for three more. Before it was quenched it had destroyed three-fourths of the city. As Nero desired to rebuild the city around his palace and had been making plans to obtain ground, suspicion rested upon him for having caused the fire. In order to remove this suspicion he blamed it on the Christians and began a very cruel persecution.

The description of this as given by Tacitus has already been related in chapter two. It is significant that Tacitus refers to Christians as being in "abhorrence for their crimes" and possessing "enmity to mankind." He also refers to Christianity as a "pernicious superstition." This indicates that he accepted the

1. Suetonius, **The Twelve Caesars**, 197.

general rumors and agreed that Christians were deserving of punishment. He does not, however, approve of the treatment they received under Nero, and indicates that he knew they were innocent of the crime. Nero also knew that the Christians were accused of all manner of crimes against mankind and that ingenius public torture would divert the minds of the populace from him. Accordingly, he ordered that Christians in large numbers be killed. Nero's use of the Christians as a scape-goat made them odious to the public and set a precedent for future official persecution. This persecution was the first to be instigated by government officials and although it was severe it was local in nature.

The stories which tell of Peter's being martyred in Rome at this time are based on late tradition. Although Eusebius refers repeatedly to Peter's stay in Rome, he relies upon the unhistorical "Acts of Peter" as his chief source. When he quotes Justin or Irenaeus in this regard he is quoting sections of their writing where they, too, rely on this same unrealistic source. Eusebius also believed Peter's reference to "Babylon" (1 Pet. 5:13) to be a reference to Rome. While there is no evidence that this was so, there is good reason to believe that Peter was working among the large Jewish population of historical Babylon when this letter was written.[2]

The tradition that Paul suffered martyrdom under Nero is quite different from that concerning Peter. There is evidence to the effect that Paul was released from the imprisonment he endured as mentioned in the close of the book of Acts. After this he visited the churches in Crete and Asia Minor and then went to Spain. Here he was seized in 67 or 68 A.D. and returned to Rome as a prisoner where, after writing 2 Timothy, he was beheaded.

Under the rule of Vespasian (69-79) there is no record of Christians suffering for their faith. When Jerusalem was overthrown in A.D. 70 the Christians all withdrew from the city before the seige began. Tradition states that this withdrawal was in obedience to the instruction Jesus left in Matthew 24:15-16, saying that when they saw the "abomination of desolation" (the Roman Army), they were to "flee into the mountains."

2. Guy N. Woods, A Commentary on the New Testament Epistles of Peter, John and Jude. (Nashville: Gospel Advocate Co., 1954), p. 135.

Domitian (81-96), the son of Vespasian, on becoming emperor began to think of himself as divine. Eusebius said, "He was the second to promote persecution against us." It was during his reign that the Apostle John was banished to the Island of Patmos and wrote the *Book of Revelation*. Eusebius seems to agree with Irenaeus that Domitian was the beast to whom John gave the number 666.

Eusebius says that Domitian "put to death without any reasonable trial no small number of men distinguished at Rome by family and career, and had punished without a cause myriads of other notable men by banishment and confiscation of their property. He finally showed himself the successor of Nero's campaign of hostility to God."[3]

From the reign of Nero through that of Domitian the government looked upon Christianity as a sect of Judaism. Beginning with Trajan (98-117) a clear distinction was made and Christians were punished for no other "crime" than that of being a Christian. Under him the existing laws which made Christianity illegal were interpreted in such a way as to make possible the destruction of the Christian religion.

The Romans looked upon the deification of the emperor as necessary to the existence of the state. The populace would recogize the authority of a god in human form and be loyal citizens. Any opposition to this idea was counted as conspiracy against the government. From this point of view we can readily understand why Christians had to be eliminated from the empire.

Trajan had a loyal group of assistants in Pliny, Tacitus and Suetonius who left instruction as to the procedure that should be followed in dealing with Christians. The most detailed account is that given in the Pliny-Trajan letters referred to in an earlier chapter. These are very important documents and should be carefully studied.

Throughout this period Christianity is referred to as superstition. Tacitus calls it "detestible superstition;" Pliny terms it "vicious and immoderate" and Suetonius calls it, "new and harmful superstition." It was made clear to all Roman governors that Christians who would not deny Christ had to be eliminated. By nature, however, Trajan was benevolent. He

3. Eusebius, Ecclesiastical History, 3:17

was desirous of personal glory and so long as he was not opposed he showed no inhuman cruelty. Accordingly, Trajan issued the statement that Christians should not be sought for. Christians who were Roman citizens were to be sent to Rome for trial. We have a record of Ignatius and others from Antioch being taken to Rome to die in the Amphitheater. Eusebius tells of several being martyred in Jerusalem at this time. One of them was Symeon who was one-hundred and twenty years old.

Under Hadrian (117-138) there was no severe persecution of Christians. The laws of Trajan were not repealed, and we know of martyrdom during Hadrian's reign, but this was a period of comparative peace for the church.

During the long reign of Antoninus Pius, Christians were subject to persecution, but we have no account of actual cases. He received a written defense of Christianity which might have influenced him toward a lenient policy, for he wrote letters of instruction that violent measures should not be taken against the Christians. This policy was opposed by certain influential subordinates, and when Marcus Aurelius became emperor in 161 A.D., he fell in with the view that Christians were dangerous to the State.

Under Marcus Aurelius (161-180) persecution broke out in various parts of the empire. Justin and a group of Christians were beheaded in Rome in 166. Polycarp and eleven others were killed in various ways in Smyrna. Persecutions were also carried out in Thyatira and Laodicea. After the death of Polycarp the church at Smyrna wrote an account of the recent persecution. This is the earliest known contemporary account of Christian martyrdom. Its genuineness is unquestioned. The letter begins, "We write to you, brethren, the story of the martyrs and of the blessed Polycarp." It then tells of the suffering and torture endured by the saints until the multitudes began to cry out for Polycarp. He had gone into the country where he moved from one farm house to another. When the police found him he requested an hour of undisturbed prayer and asked his host to serve supper to the officers. On the way to the city the police tried to persuade him to say "Lord Caesar" and to save himself. He replied, "I am not going to do what you counsel me." When he entered the arena there was a great uproar. Here let us quote the original description.

Therefore when he was brought forward the Pro-Consul asked him if he were Polycarp, and when he admitted it he tried to persuade him to deny, saying, "Respect your age," and so forth, as they are accustomed to say: "Swear by the genius of Caesar, repent, say: 'Away with the Atheists'" but Polycarp, with a stern countenance looked on all the crowd of lawless heathen in the arena, and waving his hand at them, he groaned and looked up to heaven and said; "Away with the Atheists." But when the Pro-Consul pressed him and said; "Take the oath and I let you go, revile Christ," Polycarp said, "For eighty and six years have I been His servant, and He has done me no wrong, and how can I blaspheme my King who saved me?"

But when he persisted again, and said, "Swear by the genius of Caesar," he answered him, "If you vainly suppose that I will swear by the genius of Caesar, as you say, and pretend that you are ignorant who I am, listen plainly: I am a Christian. And if you wish to learn the doctrine of Christianity fix a day and listen." The Pro-Consul said, "Persuade the people." And Polycarp said, "You I should have held worthy of discussion, for we have been taught to render honour, as is meet, if it hurt us not, to princes and authorities appointed by God. But as for those, I do not count them worthy that a defense should be made to them."

And the Pro-Consul said: "I have wild beasts, I will deliver you to them, unless you repent." And he said: "Call for them, for repentance from better to worse is not allowed us; but it is good to change from evil to righteousness." And he said again to him: "I will cause you to be consumed by fire, if you despise the beasts, unless you repent." But Polycarp said: "You threaten with the fire that burns for a time, and is quickly quenched, for you do not know the fire which awaits the wicked in the judgment to come and in everlasting punishment. But why are you waiting? Come, do what you will."[4]

After saying this the Pro-Consul ordered him to be burned, and the Jews worked zealously to gather the wood. At Polycarp's request he was fastened without being nailed and during fervent prayer he gave his life for his faith.

During this persecution informers began to accuse Christians in order to obtain their property. This became so common that Melito, bishop of Sardis, wrote to Marcus Aurelius asking for an investigation of the murders and robberies being carried out in the name of loyalty.

4. "Martyrdom of Polycarp," **Apostolic Fathers**, trans. Kirsopp Lake, Loeb Classical Library, T. E. Page et. al (ed.). (Cambridge: Harvard Univ. Press, 1948), II, pp. 325-26.

He goes on to explain that the church is not deserving of punishment, and that if an examination were made the emperor would remove the persecution. The emperor, however, was biased against the Christians and was inclined to blame all of the calamities of his reign to the growth of Christianity. In order to have an easy test to distinguish true Christians a type of "loyalty oath" was devised.

Sporadic persecution continued until the reign of Decius. From the reign of Trajan no additional law was passed against Christians until the Emperor Severus (193-211) forbade conversion to Christianity in 201. The Christians continued their evangelistic efforts in spite of the Emperor's legislation. The example of the Apostles was no doubt an encouragement to them. Christ had said the gospel was to be preached to every creature, and when rulers had forbidden the Apostles to preach or teach in the name of Christ, they replied, "We must obey God rather than man."

It was 203 before the government took rigorous action against the Christians. The information we have shows most of the activity centering in Africa and Alexandria. Tertullian wrote a lengthy defense of Christianity and sent it to the various governors. He also is believed to be the author of the "Martyrdom of Perpetua and Felicity."

Perpetua was a twenty-two-year-old and the mother of an infant child. In prison as a Christian her aged father visited her and pled for her to renounce Christianity. She pointed to a pitcher and said she could no more deny that she was a Christian than to deny the pitcher being what it was. Her father used every appeal he knew to change her mind, but without success. At her trial he carried in her child and pled that she renounce Christ and save the life of her child. The judge supported the father's plea and said, "Spare thy father's grey hairs; spare the tender age of thy child. Sacrifice for the welfare of the emperor." She replied, "I cannot do that." The judge then asked, "Are you a Christian?" and she answered, "I am a Christian." She was then condemned to the beasts. Felicity, another young married woman who was about to have a baby, and who stood up courageously under trial, and three young men who were devout Christians were put into the arena together.

Under Decius (249-251) a plan was devised to reveal the

identity of all Christians. The emperor was determined to eliminate all Christians who would not give up their faith. To this end Decius issued an edict that at least once a year a sacrificial offering must be made to the Roman gods and the genius of the emperor.[5]

At the time the sacrifice was made a certificate was issued, and by demanding to see this certificate the officials would be able to detect the Christians. This plan would have been disastrous to the church, but the following year Decius died and the persecution was dropped. Two years later Valerian (253-260) continued the policies of Decius, and Christians were again persecuted with systematic measures.

From 260 to 303 there was no persecution by authority of the state. During this period the church grew rapidly, and many large church buildings were erected. In 284 Diocletian (284-305) assumed dictatorial powers and abolished the senate that had shared authority with the emperor since Augustus Caesar in 27 B.C. With despotic authority, Diocletian began to unify the empire. Under such conditions it was certain that persecutions would again face the church.

Christians had continually spoken out against the idolatry of Roman religion. It was not enough for them to sit by and fail to participate in the public worship. Christianity has in it a militant quality that urges each Christian to share his knowledge and faith with all others. Christians could not, therefore, submit to Roman religion, but had to speak out against government pressure to make them conform.

It was March, 303, before Diocletian got around to suppressing all religion contrary to that authorized by the government. When the decree came, it was complete. Christians could no longer hold meetings, all church buildings were to be destroyed, leaders were to be imprisoned and all Christians were to turn in their copies of Scripture to be burned.[6] As this edict did not bring the desired results, in April, 304, a second decree was issued which required that all people without exception should sacrifice to the idols.[7] Any who refused would be killed. Eusebius described the terrible torture that followed: Christians were caused to suffer in every conceivable way. The

5. Bettenson, p. 19
6. Bettenson, p 21
7. Ibid.

prisons ran over, and slave labor camps were set up in which Christians were worked to death in the mines.

Fortunately for the church, Diocletian abdicated in 305, and the furry of persecution was gradually dissipated.

Additional efforts were made against Christians, but this was the last organized attempt to eliminate Christianity from the empire. Galerius had been associated with Diocletian in persecuting the Christians. After seeing that the persecution accomplished nothing, he issued a toleration edict in 311[8] that gave security to Christians so long as they did not oppose the peace of the empire. All persecution, however, did not cease until Constantine issued the Edict of Milan in 313,[9] which granted toleration to all religions in the empire.

Throughout the period of persecution the church continued to grow. It is estimated that by 250 A.D. ten percent of the people of the Roman empire were Christians. The persecution in many respects had served a good purpose. As people called Christians were in danger of death all who were insincere were deterred from becoming Christians. The church was able to remain comparatively pure and the courage with which the truly converted confessed their faith in time of trial made a profound effect upon the non-Christian.

The Christians had persistently claimed that they were good citizens and obedient to the government in all things except in matters pertaining to God. In matters where God had spoken they must obey God rather than man.

II. Edict of Toleration

The persistence with which Christians refused to obey the government and worship the idols had finally won toleration for their convictions. There had been a great deal of misunderstanding. The church would have been a blessing to the empire, and the rulers should have recognized that the God of the Christians required obedience to civil law. It was not reason on the part of Galerius, however, that led to toleration of Christianity. It was rather a feeling of shame and inhumanity with a knowledge of the fact that additional persecution would serve no purpose that moved Galerius on his death bed to issue the

8. Ibid, p. 22
9. Ibid.

Edict of Toleration. After admitting the futility of persecution he says:

> Nevertheless, since many still persist in their opinions, and since we have observed that they now neither show due reverence to the gods nor worship their own God, we therefore, without our wonted clemency in extending pardon to all, are pleased to grant indulgence to these men, allowing Christians the right to exist again and to set up their places of worship; provided always that they do not offend against public order. We will in further instruction explain to the magistrates how they should conduct themselves in this matter. In return for this indulgence, it will be the duty of Christians to pray to God for our recovery and for the public weal and for their own; that the state may be perserved from danger on every side, and that they themselves may dwell safely in their homes.[10]

III.   EDICT OF MILAN

The Edict of Milan issued by Constantine in 313 not only granted Christians the right to exist, but they are now to be encouraged. He says:

> We therefore, announce that, notwithstanding any provisions concerning the Christians in our former instructions, all who choose that religion are to be permitted to continue therein, without any let or hindrance, and are not to be in any way troubled or molested. . . . Moreover, concerning the Christians, we before gave orders with respect to the places set apart for their worship. It is now our pleasure that all who have bought such places should restore them to the Christians, without any demand for payment. . . .[11]

He then stated that former places of worship that were in the hands of non-Christians should be returned to the Christians without cost and the owners should make application to the government for their compensation.

This is the first government action which was favorable to the church and represents a complete reversal of policy. Instead of confiscation there is restoration of property. The future of the church looked bright. Actually there was great danger ahead. With the removal of persecution and a growing popularity, the church was to be perverted and polluted with growing heresy.

10. Ibid. p. 22
11. Ibid. p. 23

The reason for the victory of the Christians rests primarily in the fact that God was with them. The Eternal Kingdom could not be exterminated from the earth. The part the Christians had in winning the victory is set forth pointedly by Gibbon when he attributes this success to the pure morals of the Christians, their inflexible zeal in missionary work, the unity of the congregations, the miraculous powers shown by the Apostles and the Christian hope of eternal life.

Chapter Seven

The Development of the Canon

I. THE SOURCE OF INSPIRED WRITINGS

Christianity is a revealed religion. When Jesus came to earth, He began to speak the things given Him by His Father. After teaching the Apostles three and a half years He told them that they should not preach until the Holy Spirit came to bring to their memory all that He had said. The Holy Spirit was also to "teach them all things, guide them into all truth and reveal things to come." (Jno. 14:26; 16:13). The Hebrew letter says that this great salvation was "at the first spoken through the Lord and confirmed unto us by them that heard him; God also bearing witness with them, both by signs and wonders and by manifold powers and gifts of the Holy Spirit according to his own will." (Heb. 2:3-4).

Paul said the gospel he preached was not received from man, but that it came through revelation of Jesus Christ (Gal. 1:12). To the Ephesians he said that he had received the gospel by revelation and had written it down, and when they would read it they could understand the mystery concerning Christ (Eph. 3:3-4).

There was a time, however, before the whole gospel message was put in writing, when the Apostles had to give the church the instruction needed orally. They were empowered to impart the Holy Spirit in miraculous measures through the "laying on of hands." In this way each new congregation had spiritual teachers who could give needed instruction through divine guidance. This miraculous age, however, was soon to cease for Paul said to the church at Corinth, in which there was jealousy over spiritual gifts, that they should "Take knowledge of the things which I write unto you, that *they* are the commandment of the Lord." (1 Cor. 14:37). In this it is clear that the inspired written word of the Apostles was to take precedence over the spoken word, and should be considered a stan-

(101)

dard by which the spoken word of public teachers should be judged (cf. 1 Jno. 4:1 also).

Since there was a period of time required to get the completed written Word into the hands of all the churches, it is natural that oral tradition should be highly regarded. Also since uninspired writings began to appear as early as some of the inspired, it was natural that oral tradition was relied upon to test the teaching of such uninspired writers. There was from the beginning a difference in inspired and uninspired writings. The church in many places, however, did not know how to distinguish between them. *At times uninspired works were accepted as inspired and inspired were rejected as uninspired.* Those finally accepted were called canonical, those rejected, apocryphal.

The church did not give the world the Bible. It was the Bible in "oral form" that produced the church (Acts 2). God selected men in the church to serve as instruments through whom the Bible was to be written. The organization known as "the church" did not pass judgment upon the truth to be included in the Bible. The Holy Spirit did that. All the church could do was to apply tests to ascertain whether or not a letter was from God.

II. METHOD OF DISTRIBUTION

Under these conditions the inspired writings soon began to be collected by the churches. There is no historical evidence in regard to the distribution of inspired letters, but the pattern set a little later in regard to uninspired letters seems to be the logical manner in which the inspired ones were copied and circulated.

We have evidence in regard to the letters of Ignatius to the effect that the church in Philippi heard that Polycarp had letters from Ignatius. They wrote asking for copies of the letters and Polycarp gladly complied with this request. He wrote the Philippian church himself as he sent copies of the letters they requested.

In this way we believe the letters of the Apostles were circulated. Each congregation would hear that a letter was received by a certain church and they in turn would ask for a copy. After receiving it, they in turn would send copies to others who requested them. There is no reason to doubt that this applied to all of the books of the New Testament.

The churches faced a real problem, however, in determining just what letters were inspired. Many men who had known the Apostles also wrote and as they were highly respected their writings began to be read in the churches and given Apostolic authority. On this basis some of the early church leaders had what to them was a New Testament which contained many more books than we today accept as inspired.

III.   EARLY REFERENCES TO NEW TESTAMENT LETTERS

In the letters of Clement to the church at Corinth, previously referred to, written between 90-100, there are references to many of the New Testament books. Clement respected such books as inspired and commonly used such expressions as "The Holy Witness." Clement does not give the location of any of his quotations except in regard to First Corinthians. Here he says, "Take up the letter of blessed Paul, the Apostle; what did he first write you, at the beginning of the gospel preaching?" He then refers to 1 Corinthians 1:1-12. He doesn't quote word for word but rather quotes from memory and discusses ideas. In this way he refers to a number of quotations taken from the teaching of Christ from both the Sermon on the Mount and later teachings. Since he does not tell which gospel he uses, we cannot determine which one, but it is sure he was familiar with one of the gospels and he may have had them all.

Clement quotes many passages from the Old Testament. From the New Testament he uses passages taken from the Gospels, Romans, First and Second Corinthians, Ephesians, Hebrews, Titus, James, First Peter and Revelation.

Concerning the gospels, Eusebius quotes Papias as saying that John the Presbyter taught that Mark became Peter's interpreter and that he wrote accurately what Peter remembered of the things said and done by Christ.[1] Papias went on quoting John to say that Mark did not give a chronological order, but that he wrote as Peter taught and he was careful to make no false statements.[2] Papias also said that Matthew wrote in Hebrew.[3] Eusebius later says that Pantaenus, a teacher from

1. Eusebius, III: 39:15
2. Ibid.
3. Ibid. 39:16

Alexandria, went to the Indians (Arabia) and found that Bartholomew had preached to them and left them a copy of Matthew written in Hebrew.[4] Eusebius says further that Matthew had first preached to Hebrews, and before leaving them he transmitted the gospel to them in their native tongue.[5] He further says that Mark and Luke had already published their gospels before Matthew wrote.[6]

Concerning the Gospel of John, Eusebius says that John had used the gospel in oral form, but in addition he had copies of the other three by Matthew, Mark and Luke as they "were distributed to all." John welcomed these gospels and testified to their truth, but as they emphasized the things of Jesus after the imprisonment of John the Baptist, he wrote chiefly of things before this event and touched on things said and done which the other evangelists did not cover.[7]

Eusebius then lists the books he said had been traditionally accepted without question as inspired. After the gospels came Acts of the Apostles, then the epistles of Paul, First John, First Peter and perhaps Revelation. He then listed as disputed books, James, Jude, Second Peter, Second and Third John. The book of Hebrews was also a disputed book.

The fact that the early church questioned some of these books indicates the seriousness with which this question was considered. After the death of the Apostles the church soon began to rely upon their written records for guidance and one of the chief tests for the inspiration of a book was whether or not it could be traced to an Apostle. Why then was Hebrews questioned? Because its author is not stated. The tendency of the early Christians in general was to be very careful to accept only books as inspired that were without question. All of the books we have in the New Testament were known and used in the early church. Some books that we do not accept as genuine were also used (1 Clement, Barnabas, Shepherd of Hermas).

IV. TESTS APPLIED TO QUESTIONED BOOKS

Gradually tests were applied to eliminate the uninspired and include all of the inspired books in a definite form for use

4. Ibid. V:10:3
5. Ibid. III:24:5-7
6. Ibid.
7. Ibid.

in the churches. These tests include such questions as: (1) Does the book claim inspiration? 1 Clement, for example, does not. (2) Is it written by an Apostle? (3) If not, is its content in keeping with Apostolic teaching — whether orally or in books already written by Apostles? (4) Is it accepted by loyal churches (*i.e.,* loyal to Apostolic teaching) and read in their worship services? (5) Last, but not least, does it have the "ring of genuineness"?

It remained for later "Church Councils" only to "officially" recognize the canon of books that had already been formed and accepted by churches throughout the empire. They did not "determine" which books would be accepted and which rejected by the churches. Edward Young correctly points out that "men recognize the word of God, because God has told them what his word is . . . He has identified it for them. Of great importance, therefore, . . . is the doctrine of the inward testimony of the Holy Spirit."[8]

These questions could be answered by historical evidence that had surrounded the various writings. By 175 at least twenty of the New Testament books were generally accepted as inspired.[9] The others were used but not with the same authority. By the time of Origen (250) the twenty-seven books we have were accepted, and to them he added Barnabas and the Shepherd of Hermas. These two, however, did not stand on the test. Eusebius (326) held to the twenty-seven books, and from Athanasius (367) on there was little controversy. Later, church councils also passed on the books which should be counted as inspired, but these were mere expressions of what the sincere Christians had held to years before.

V. APOCRYPHAL BOOKS

There were many books in circulation from the beginning of the second century that various groups accepted, which were not inspired. These are called apocryphal (*i.e.,* "doubtful"). From the year 150 on many sects developed. Each set forth certain writings which to them were important. Marcion (about 140 A.D.) set forth his own canon of Scripture, rejected

---

8. Edward J. Young, An Introduction to the Old Testament (Grand Rapids: Wm. B. Eerdman's, 1954), p. 38
9. J. C. Ayer, A Source Book for Ancient Church History (New York: Charles Scribner's Sons, 1941), pp. 117-120. There are twenty specifically named in the muratorian Fragment of about 175 A.D. and others implied. This is the earliest list.

the Old Testament and all of the New Testament that contained any idea of "Law" in it. He accepted only Paul's writing and not all of it. Luke was accepted because he felt it was similar to Paul's teaching and because traditionally Luke learned about the life of Christ from Paul. Eusebius mentions a number of these rejected works. Among those he names, are Acts of Paul, Shepherd of Hermas, Apocalypse of Peter, Barnabas, the Teaching of the Twelve Apostles, the Gospel of Peter, Thomas and Matthias and the Acts of Andrew, John, Peter and other Apostles. Of these Eusebius says, "the type of phraseology differs from Apostolic style, and the opinion and tendency of their contents is widely dissonant from true orthodoxy and clearly shows that they are forgeries of heretics."

These forgeries, however, did great harm in the church and some of the imaginary stories they told of the Apostles were accepted as true and are yet being repeated in popular literature. Even the theological system that depends upon Peter's alleged work in Rome, is built upon these forgeries. Occasionally references are made to "New Testament" books not now in use but it should be understood that all such references are to those "apocryphal" books which were rejected with good cause by the early churches.

Chapter Eight

Departure From
The New Testament Pattern
100 - 325 A.D.

During the first fifty years after the death of the Apostle John, the church struggled to maintain Apostolic purity. The literature of this period, written by men who are commonly called the "Apostolic Fathers" and "Apologists," shows clearly the efforts made to maintain the New Testament pattern and the trends that later brought on apostasy. The forces that began to distract the church were from many sides.

Externally, Greek philosophy made its impression on the minds of Christian thinkers, and before long Christians found themselves using philosophical terminology to explain Christian concepts. This continued until revealed truth lost its unique position, and instead of Christianity's being understood and defended upon the basis of miracle, revelation and inspiration, it was watered down with human rationalism.

Internally, the church was torn by various interpretations of its relationship to Judaism. These concepts should have been settled forever by the epistles of Paul in which he showed the place of the Law of Moses in regard to Christianity. These ideas, however, were re-emphasized to such an extent that much time had to be devoted to them.

Problems originating from the pride of men also led to new interpretations and changes in the organization of the church as ambitious men led off groups of disciples. The Apostles had warned the church that departure would come through drifting away from the original teaching (Heb. 2:1). To safeguard against such departure, adherence to the "Word of his grace," was encouraged. (Acts 20:32). We are on safe ground when we say that any change in doctrine or organization from that

(107)

found in the New Testament is a departure. This is the only test needed. Any claim to undenominationalism rests solely upon this principle. If the church under Apostolic guidance taught or practiced a certain thing the adherence to this same teaching or practice today cannot be said to be denominational. Any departure from such teaching and practice, however, is denominational and cannot be said to be a characteristic of the Eternal Kingdom. In order to remain undenominational we must adhere to the New Testament pattern. A study of how departures came about and the forms they took will be very helpful in safe-guarding the church today.

I.   DEPARTURE IN ORGANIZATION

One of the most striking departures from Apostolic practice and teaching was the rise of the monarchal episcopate. This refers to congregational rule by one man, as a distinction arose between the terms bishop and presbyter. Some local churches came to be ruled by one "bishop" with a group of presbyters and deacons under him. Ignatius of Antioch was the champion of this departure. One by one churches adopted the practice. Rome seems to have been one of the last to acquire a monarchal bishop.

The rise of such "Bishops" was an early process, but not as early as the New Testament. All scholars, Roman Catholic, Protestant and liberal, agree that in the New Testament there is only a dual order: bishops (or presbyters) and deacons. The distinction between bishops and presbyters was the first change in organization.

Reference is sometimes made to the *Didache* and the letters of Ignatius to prove that there was a diversity of organization in churches during the first century. However it is likely that Ignatius was attempting to *create* a situation rather than represent the *existing* one. There can be no doubt that the organization of the New Testament church consisted of a plurality of elders (or bishops) in each church or that these terms were used interchangeable. (See Titus 1:5, 7; Acts 20:17, 28).

Although the words elder and bishop are used interchangeable in Scripture there is a difference in their meanings. Elder has reference to age or maturity and bishop to oversight or guardianship. This difference of meaning is important to an understanding of the change that developed. In the early church all elders were bishops or overseers, and each congregation had a plurality of them. However, as the elders had their meetings to discuss the work of the church some one had to be chairman of the meeting. This chairmanship apparently became a permanent position and the word bishop was reserved for the one who occupied the position. He was sometimes called the "president" of the church and gradually assumed the responsibilities that had originally rested upon all the elders. This position, by the year 150, had developed into the monarchal bishop arrangement.

For another hundred years there was no authority above the monarchal bishop, and he had no authority outside of one local congregation. The office of elder was continued, but the eldership was subordinate to the bishopric. Generally the congregations had a voice in determining who the bishop should be. Jerome tells us that in the church at Alexandria, until 233 A.D., the presbyters always chose one of their own and styled him "bishop."[1]

There were certain circumstances that tended to favor the development of the monarchal bishop and the subsequent hierarchy. The bishop, as chairman of the elders, took the lead in combating heresy, and in time of danger or calamity was expected to take charge. By the close of the third century these bishops were regarded as successors to the Apostles.

As the office became general it was natural for the bishop of the large city churches to assist in starting new congregations. These also came under his authority and soon there were bishops who looked after a rather large territory.

After the year 150, synods began to be called. The large city bishops were the men of greatest influence and in these meetings their prominence was increased. It was not long before the city bishops began to oversee the work of the country bishops who in turn began to disappear.

By the time of Irenaeus (185) there was some interest in trying to establish a succession of bishops back to the Apostles. Eusebius dedicates a part of his church history to this effort. Many of the men so listed in the early period were nothing more than elders in the New Testament sense. They may, how-

1. Letter 146: To Evangelus "Library of Christian Classics" V, p. 387.

ever, have served as the chairman during the elders' meetings. The Catholic church officials have in recent years revised their list of Roman bishops, called Popes. In the traditional list after Peter, came Linus, Cletus, Clement and Anacletus. It is now admitted by the Roman scholars that Cletus and Anacletus refer to the same man. There is also confusion of thought growing out of the tradition that Peter ordained these first three Roman bishops. With Peter's martyrdom in 68 it is difficult to understand how he could ordain Anacletus in 78 and Clement in 90. It is not difficult to understand that if Peter had been in Rome in 68 that he could have ordained (appointed) them all as elders as the same time.

By 190 Victor of Rome claimed to be "universal bishop" but he was ignored by the other churches. Cyprian (200-258) worked to give greater prestige to the bishops and after 250 the monarchal bishopric was almost universally established. After this date, (where there are no clarifying designations) the word bishop, in general usage, refers to the monarchal bishop. But before 250 and especially before 200 the student should question such usage in early literature, for, many times, the word bishop is used when the writer has in mind a bishop in the New Testament sense. It is also significant that the early writers, (Ignatius included) used the word "presbyter" in reference to these early church leaders; whereas, later writers refer to the same men as "bishops."

Irenaeus became bishop of Lyons in 177 and soon began to gather a list of the Roman bishops. He does not say that Peter was the first bishop, but that "when the blessed *Apostles* had found and built the church they gave the ministry of the *episcopate to Linus*" (italics J. M.).[2] In another place he states that Peter and Paul were preaching in Rome and founded the church there.[3] Such traditions gathered soon around the Roman church which had acquired a reputation for stability and soundness. It had been one of the most conservative of the churches and was noted for its great work of charity. Its leniency toward sinners enhanced its power. Both Ireneaus and Tertullian made agreement with the church in Rome the test of apostolicity. The church in Rome had earned this great reputa-

2. Against Heresies. 3:3:3
3. Ibid. 3:3:2

tion, but when it departed from the ways of the Apostles its good reputation made its example all the more dangerous. As Rome was looked to for its political leadership the churches began to look to the Roman church for spiritual leadership. Cyprian of Carthage (195-268) is said to have done more to establish the hierarchy than any other individual. He followed the thought set forth by Ignatius that apart from the bishop there is no church. These bishops were the successors of the Apostles, Christ overseeing their selection and giving them a special measure of the Holy Spirit. They constitute an episcopate and the unity of the church rests upon them. He accepted the tradition that the church at Rome had been founded by Peter and that Peter was the chief of the Apostles — the rock upon which the church was built. Cyprian believed all bishops to be of equal rank, but his views concerning Peter tended to encourage the exaltation of the Roman bishop. Cyprian also distinguished between clergy and laity and encouraged the acceptance of the clergy as actual priests with special powers.

By the close of the third century each congregation of any size had a bishop as its head with a group of elders under him. Each province looked to one bishop as greater than the rest with the authority to call councils. The bishops of Rome, Antioch and Alexandria received special recognition because of their apostolic origin.

II.   DEVELOPMENT OF A PRIESTHOOD

By 150 there is evidence of a distinction between those who served as ministers and the rest of the congregation. As this distinction grew the "clergy" patterned itself after the Jewish priesthood. The bishop took the position of High Priest, the presbytery priests, and the deacons Levites. Such a priesthood developed out of a prior separation of Christians into two levels, the spirituals and the carnals. The next step came quite naturally. Along with the development of an official priesthood came a changed attitude toward the services. Worship could be conducted only by authorized priests. This resulted in the ceremonialism and sacredotalism of later years.

III.   THE GROWTH OF SECTS

From the middle of the second century there was a rapid growth in the number of sects. Every generation produces a group of men with leadership ability who are not satisfied to leave the church as God created it. We have already seen the growth of Gnosticism and Montanism. The influence of Marcion has also been described, but there are certain other Gnostic leaders who need to be considered.

Basilides led a group of Gnostics in Egypt where he conducted a school and taught that there was one supreme God and three hundred and sixty-five angelic orders. He believed the one God produced seven beings who in turn produced the others. He believed this supreme being wanted to help mankind and sent Christ, but one of the lesser gods, the Jehovah of the Old Testament sent his servants, the Jews, to kill him. Rejection of the God of the Old Testament was a favorite Gnostic tenet.

Satornilus of Antioch is one of the earliest and most influential Gnostics. The basis of his system was dualism; matter is evil and the spirit good. He theorized that besides one great God there were seven lesser gods who ruled the seven planets. The Jehovah of the Old Testament was one of the lesser gods. The theory of creation was that these seven gods made the world and placed man upon it without the knowledge of the great God. Since these gods could not produce souls, man was just another animal. However, when the matter came to the attention of the great God, He was not pleased and gave each man a soul. Evil, nevertheless, was in the material world and soon the earth was corrupt. Christ came as an emissary of the great God to restore order. He appeared to have flesh, but actually did not have. He taught that man can reach salvation only by abstinence from all sensual gratification. Marriage was condemned and even nourishing meals were considered evil. With such influences prevalent, it is not hard to understand the development of asceticism within the church.

Gnosticism dealt with the problem of God and providence, the origin and destiny of the universe, Christ, intermediaries, redemption, and revelation. In general they held that matter is essentially evil, there is no resurrection of the dead, Christ did not come in actual flesh, God is far above and has no contact with this world. From 150 to 200 the Gnostics tried to remain in the church. Their influence as leaders, however, was thrown off and after 200 they formed their own societies. Through their influence the church was turned toward a type of mysticism that was to reappear in subsequent generations.

IV. NEOPLATONISM

About the year 240 Ammonius Saccas began to teach in Alexandria a new type of mysticism, attempting to harmonize pagan philosophy and Christianity. Some of his ideas are identical with other Gnostic conceptions. He taught the creation of man to be the result of eminations from the original "Absolute Being" and the purpose of man to be re-absorbed into this great force. The process by which this was to be accomplished involved mental contemplation of the higher things of art, nature, love and the spiritual things. When one reached, through this mental contemplation, an ecstasy that took him above the material world, he would be enjoying the highest state possible in this life. This attitude was conducive to a belief in the value of asceticism. Through Neoplatonism many Christians were influenced to think of Christianity as only another philosophy. Questions of such speculative nature were argued that practical Christianity was neglected.

Plotinus (205-270) studied under Saccas and then started a Neo-Platonic school in Rome. Porphyr (233-300) gathered up the ideas of Saccas and Plotinus, put them in logical order and attempted to substitute Neoplatonism for Christianity. In his *Life of Plotinus* Porphyr begins by telling us that Plotinus "was ashamed to be in the flesh." He would not allow his picture to be painted because of his theory that we must "retreat" from this material world and escape from the body. He wanted no remembrance of the mortal body and its evil. There is no doubt that this theory had some influence on the early ascetics.

V. MANICHAEISM

About the year 250, Mani (216-276) of Mesopotamia, formulated a philosophical system by mixing the teachings of Zoraster, the mystery religions and Christianity. Central to his theory was a conflict between light and darkness. The mother of light formed the soul of man from pure light, but the king of darkness enveloped this soul in an evil, material body, Salvation was a matter of releasing the soul from the burden of the body. This was to be accomplished by following the perfect light, Christ. Emphasis was placed upon asceticism. Marriage was permitted, but those entering it could not attain to the height of "perfection." This elite class spent their time in performing certain ceremonies designed to release more light. The carnal group could share in this light by supplying the material needs of the spirituals.

This development went far toward the general acceptance of a priestly class in the church. Mani was crucified for his faith, but his followers continued to flourish until about 450.

VI. THE EBIONITES

The Ebionites were a body of Judaizing Christians. They held that Moses was equal in authority to Christ. The "Gospel of the Hebrews" and various Apocryphal books became their guide. They held that Joseph was the natural father of Jesus and that all Christians were obligated to keep the law of Moses and the custom of circumcision. Since Paul taught differently, they held his writings in contempt. They considered Christ to be an ordinary man who was exalted because of his perfection in keeping the law. In view of this they reduced Christianity to a legalistic system and influenced later theologians who tended to regard Christianity similarly.

VII. MONARCHIANISM

The false doctrines which disturbed the church most of all were those that concerned the *nature* of Christ. The Ebionites in denying the divinity of Jesus by asserting that He was the son of Joseph and Mary, denied the virgin birth. They said that as Jesus kept the Law in such a perfect manner, God adopted Him to be the Messiah. Later, in the second and third centuries this view was known as Adoptionism or Dynamic Monarchianism. Those who belonged to this school of thought held that Jesus was just a man who so perfectly kept the Law that God adopted Him to be His son. Their emphasis on the humanity of Jesus laid the foundation for the Arianism of the fourth century.

During the third century the church at Antioch was led astray by Paul of Samosata who obtained the position of bishop. He was a man of great ability, but at the same time a demagogue, very unscrupulous, egotistical and self-centered. He denied the divinity of Christ in order to defend his idea of Monotheism. His view was that of modern Unitarianism.

There were others who emphasized the divinity of Jesus but

held that His human form was only an appearance. They were at first known as Docetists, then Modalistic Monarchians or just Modalists. Father and Son were two names for one person. Christ was just a temporary manifestation of one God. This view later came to be called Sabellianism after Sabellius, one of its leaders. It was also called Patriopassianism because one of its logical implications seemed to be that the Father suffered when Christ died.

Christians, attempting to find the truth fell into the use of philosophic language foreign to the Scriptures. They were trying to protect the divinity of Christ but in doing so used language not found in the Bible and thus opened the door to long centuries of conflict. The church had conquered the Roman empire, but in doing so had itself been conquered by creeds, ritualism and a kind of organization that destroyed the liberty and simplicity it was created to possess.

VIII. DONATISTS

During the severe persecution under Diocletian some Christians weakened under pressure and worshipped pagan gods. Others used schemes to obtain certificates that would be accepted by the police as evidence that they had worshipped the Roman gods. After the persecution was over and toleration was granted to Christians, many of these came back to the churches and confessed their weakness. Some had turned in copies of Scripture to be burned.

In 311 Donatus began to teach that these people had committed an unpardonable sin and could not be restored to the church, but Christians in general did not accept this view. A synod at Rome decided against the Donatist position and later councils confirmed the decision.

The first man to advocate the position taken by the Donatists was Novatian of Rome. After the persecution under Decius, Novatian would not restore the lapsed to the fellowship of the church and accepted no proof of repentance. He later went to Rome and reversed his position.

FURTHER DEPARTURE IN DOCTRINE

In tracing the development of the more popular sects we have seen certain doctrinal departures. There are others, however, that we will deal with independently from movements or individuals.

I. MILLENNIALISM

One of the doctrines that appeared in the church early in the second century and that has reappeared many times since, was a sort of millenarianism. It seems to have been a legacy from Judaism. Some of the Jews had expected a temporal Messiah and some early Christians had transferred the materialistic hopes of the Jews to the second coming of Jesus. Eusebius, on the authority of others, accused the heretic Cerinthus of being the first to bring this doctrine into the church. Cerinthus claimed to have special revelations from angels to the effect that after the resurrection, the Kingdom would be established on earth.

Early writers refer to the carnal nature of his descriptions of the coming age. Lust and pleasure would surround the marriage feast which would last a thousand years. Dionysius, commenting on the book of Revelation in opposition to this theory said:

> "Cerinthus too, who founded the Cerinthian heresy named after him, wished to attach a name worthy of credit to his own invention, for the doctrine of his teaching was this, that the kingdom of Christ would be on earth, and being fond of his body and very carnal, he dreamt of a future according to his own desires, given up to the indulgence of the flesh, that is, eating and drinking and marrying, and to those things which seem a euphemism for these things, feasts and sacrifices and the slaughter of victims."[4]

To emphasize that this doctrine was not held by John who wrote the book of Revelation, Polycarp tells that when John saw Cerinthus in a bath house he fled from the door saying, "Let us flee, lest the bath-house fall in, for Cerinthus the enemy of the truth is within."[5] Eusebius says that Papias taught the coming of the millennium in a material form on this earth. He describes Papias as a man of very little intelligence who failed to understand mystical and symbolic language. Irenaeus, who relied upon the antiquity of Papias was carried away by his teaching. He quotes Papias as saying:

> "The days will come, in which vines shall grow, each having ten thousand branches, and in each branch ten thousand

4. Eusebius. 3:28:4-5
5. Irenaeus, Against Heresies, 3:3:4

twigs, and each true twig ten thousand shoots and in each one of the shoots ten thousand clusters, and in every one of the clusters ten thousand grapes, and every grape when pressed will give five and twenty metretes (200 gallons) of wine."[6]

These millennial ideas are also found in the epistle of Barnabas, the Shepherd of Hermas, the Second Epistle of Clement, all of which are Apocryphal works bearing pseudonyms. Justin Martyr also held this theory but said he did not consider it a necessary part of Christian faith.[7]

II. ORIGINAL SIN AND BAPTISM

The doctrine of original sin teaches that children are born with the guilt of sin and through inheritance are depraved in nature. This idea is not found in any of the extant works of the Apostolic Fathers. In Irenaeus there is the first trend in this direction when he discusses the consequence of the fall of Adam. He taught that this brought man under the control of Satan and cost mankind the "divine likeness." There is, however, no indication that this cost man his freedom of will, which is an essential part of the doctrine. In the work of Clement of Alexandria there is no semblance of this doctrine. In Origen (185-254) we see a basis for it, but not the theory itself. Origen taught that all souls were created in the beginning of time. They all possessed freedom of will and some of them chose the pure and the good. These became angels. Others chose evil and these became the Devil and evil spirits. Other souls sinned, but to a lesser degree and whom God sent to earth as the souls of men. This theory holds that the sin is in the former state and is not the result of Adam's sin nor through natural birth. Origen did not teach original inherited sin.

Tertullian (160-220) is the first to formulate the doctrine of original sin. He taught that the soul shares in Adam's guilt and every man therefore is under condemnation and is punishable for his inherited guilt quite apart from any actual sin he may commit.

Cyprian, while bishop of Carthage (248-258) enlarged upon Tertullian's conception and declared that even though an infant had committed no actual sin it needed forgiveness for the sin inherited from Adam and this was received in baptism. He

6. Ibid. 5:33:3
7. **Dialogue with Trypho**, Chapter 80. "Ante-Nicene Fathers." I.

was the first to approve infant baptism, but he did not urge it. The doctrine of original sin, however, was not generally accepted at this time and accordingly infant baptism did not become common practice. It is logical for these two doctrines to rise and fall together. If children are innocent there is no need for baptism, but if they are in sin, baptism is the remedy.

There is a statement in Irenaeus before the year 200 that is quoted to prove that infant baptism is of early origin. The state- ment reads that Christ came to save all, "who through Him are born again to God — infants, and children, and boys, and youths, and old men."[8] As this reference is not conclusive, but a statement of emphasis that there is no salvation out of Christ, we do not believe it is proof that children were generally being baptized.

Origen stated that the church received the tradition from the Apostles to baptize the very young, but there is no record of its being done before the end of the second century.[9] Tertullian believed that baptism should not be performed before adolescence so the candidate would be old enough to fully understand its importance. Gregory of Nazianzus felt that infant baptism was of value, but that the child should be at least three years old. Infant baptism, however, did not become a general practice until the fifth century. It was the doctrine of original sin as taught by Augustine that brought about its general acceptance. He taught with persistence that because of inherited sin all infants needed baptism. The doctrine of original sin alone, however, would not have produced infant baptism. The doctrine of baptismal regeneration was also necessary. This view grew out of the Biblical teaching on baptism for the remission of sin, but went further and included the idea that baptism itself, apart from faith and repentance, removes sin. This view made baptism as valuable to the infant as to the adult.

While the doctrine of original sin and baptismal regeneration encouraged infant baptism, there was another teaching that worked against it. This was the idea that since baptism removed one's sins, there was no additional remedy for those sins committed after baptism and baptism could not be repeated.

8. Against Heresies, 2:22:4
9. There is no instance of an Apostle's having baptized anyone other than a believer in the New Testament.

Tertullian was an outspoken advocate of this idea and it was so commonly accepted that many people put off their baptism until old age. Constantine is the outstanding example of this. He delayed his baptism until shortly before his death so that it would cover all his sin.

Throughout all of this early period there is general agreement among Apostolic Fathers and Apologists that baptism is necessary to salvation and that the general practice was immersion. There were many false doctrines in the first three centuries of the church, but salvation apart from baptism was not one of them. This came later. During this period baptismal regeneration — the other extreme — was erroneously taught.

During the third century baptism was made a ritualistic ceremony performed by the bishop or one of his appointed assistants and conducted twice a year. The influence of the mystery religions is seen in this. The water took on magical power. The candidates went through a long period of trial and preparation, and just before baptism as he renounced the devil a group of people would gather around the candidate and with shouts and waving of arms drive the evil out of the one to be baptized. Following the immersion the new Christian was ceremoniously fed milk and honey, dressed in a white robe and given a crown to wear in a procession of victory back home. The desire to be like the nations round about has always been a curse to God's people.

The meetings of the church during this period varied in accordance with the circumstances. During persecution meetings were held after dark or early in the morning before daylight. At first the Jewish Christians continued to keep the Sabbath, or seventh day. They also observed the first day of the week in memory of the Lord's resurrection. Gradually the Sabbath observance was discontinued and the first day of the week was kept as the Lord's Day. In answer to the opinion that Constantine changed the day of worship from Saturday to Sunday, it should be observed that the writing of Justin, referred to earlier, shows clearly that the early Christians observed the first day of the week as the general practice one hundred and fifty years before Constantine. The Lord's Supper was a regular part of the Lord's Day worship. At times the congregation shared a meal together just before partaking of the bread and wine in memory of Christ. The wine often was mixed with water, not for ceremonial reasons, but to dilute its strength.

As the influence of pagan religions began to effect the church, the Lord's supper became a ceremony of pomp and ritualism. Gold and silver vessels came into use, and as in the cult mysteries all who were not members were excluded from the service. As time passed the elements took on a superstitious nature and became the "Medicine of Immorality."[10] As the elements took on magical powers they began to be administered just before death to remove sin. With the growing idea that ministers were priests, we see how the simple memorial service of the New Testament became the mass of medieval Catholicism.

Not all groups agreed in the changes that came about. The ascetics began to doubt that wine should be used. Tatian became so adverse to its use under any circumstances that he substituted water for it in the Lord's Supper.

DEPARTURE IN MANNER OF LIFE

I. ASCETICISM AND CELIBACY

As a result of the Gnostic emphasis that all matter is evil, some Christians were led to asceticism. The human body was considered evil. Normal human processes such as eating nourishing meals, marrying and child birth, to them, became evil. It was believed by some that any contact with normal society was contaminating. This gave rise to bodily abuse, self-starvation and residence in the wilderness. The celibate life began to be exalted above marriage, and ministers especially were considered unfit to serve if they were married. To combat this, Clement of Alexandria wrote a weighty treatise "On Marriage" in which he defends marriage as proper. He not only used Scripture as proof, but also referred to Peter's being married and having children and to the fact that his wife was with him until the time of his martyrdom. Clement also believed the Apostle Paul was married and referred to his wife as "true yoke-fellow" in Philippians 4:3.[11]

During the first three centuries there was no general rule

10. Ignatius, To the Ephesians, 20:2
11. Clement, On Marriage. 6:53. "Library of Christian Classics." I, p. 64.

against the right of marriage for ministers. It was the general practice. The pressure toward celibacy came from the common people who believed that demons could more easily control a married man.

As a result of the ascetic emphasis hermits emerged on the scene. Jerome tells of one Paul who fled under the persecution of Decius and lived for ninety years in the desert of Thebias. Others followed his example and soon began to form themselves into monastic communities.

II. EASTER CELEBRATION

Rather early some Christians tried to work out a yearly calendar and place in it all of the important events in the life of Christ. This would give the Christians special festivals and celebrations as were found among the Pagans and Jews. Where the large number of converts were Jews it was natural for them to transfer as far as possible the Jewish customs into Christian usage. The leaders of the churches were also desirous of making the church more attractive to Jews and Pagans. As these were accustomed to pompous ceremonies as a part of their systems, it was believed that they would hold the simplicity of Christian worship in contempt. To alleviate this prejudice, rites were made more elaborate and ceremonies expanded. The Jewish and Pagan priests had taunted the Christians, saying that they had no temples, altars, victims or priests, which to them constituted the essence of religion. Christians responded with special occasions and made a sacrifice out of the Lord's Supper.

Easter became one of the most elaborate of these celebrations. The time for its observance, however, caused serious differences. The church in Asia Minor wanted to keep Easter at the same time the Jews observed the Passover. They began a fast on the fourteenth day of the first Jewish month, the day of the crucifixion — and then celebrated the resurrection three days later. This made Easter fall on different days of the week. They claimed that the Apostle John and Philip had taught them this method of determining the day.

The Western church under the leadership of Rome said that Peter and Paul taught them to observe Easter day always on the first day of the week. About the close of the second century, Victor, bishop of Rome, excommunicated the church of Asia because they would not agree with Western custom in always celebrating Easter on Sunday. At this time it was generally believed that all bishops were of equal authority and Victor was considered out of place by such action. The churches of Asia would not change and Irenaeus got Victor to withdraw his rash declaration. Each continued its own practice until the first general council in 325 decided in favor of the Roman position. This was another step in exaltation of the Roman bishop.

III.   SUMMARY OF PART TWO

Through the writings of the Apostolic Fathers and the Apologists we have seen how the church became corrupt and how the predictions of the Apostles were fulfilled concerning the falling away. There were, throughout the first three centuries, strong, sincere Christians contending for the faith once for all delivered to the saints. Many of them were sacrificed during the persecutions helping to show the Roman officials the futility of fighting against the Eternal Kingdom that Christ died to establish.

The services of the church become more elaborate. The simple ordinances Jesus left became strangely interpreted and ceremoniously performed. The apostate organization produced a hierarchy unlike the original pattern. Yet in the midst of these changes there is evidence that many did not approve the departures. In every age "the Lord knows those who are his" and the Kingdom moved onward in spite of growing difficulties.

It is worthy of note that almost every controversy facing the church today was faced in the years immediately following the death of the Apostles. History teaches us how these false doctrines arose, and how each generation tried to deal with them. It should be kept in mind that inadequate solutions to these problems many times were the products of *expediency*. Scripture alone gives the true solution.

PART THREE

THE INCREASE OF ERROR
313 - 787 A.D.

Chapter Nine

The Influence of Constantine

Constantine the Great, as he later became known, grew up in the midst of the intrigue and jealousy of the ruling class of the Romans. In 292 he was taken to the court of Diocletian ostensibly "to be educated," but actually as a hostage. When Diocletian abdicated in 305, Constantine fled to join his father who had been governing Britain, Gaul and Spain. Constantius, his father, had been favorably impressed by the Christians and had protected them as far as possible. His mother, Helena, had espoused the Christian religion.

At this time the Empire had four Emperors. Diocletian and Maximian had the title of Augusti, while Constantius and Galerius were Caesars. When Diocletian and Maximian abdicated in 305, Constantius and Galerius became Augusti. In 306 Constantius died and his army proclaimed Constantine "Augustus." There followed a period of conflict out of which Constantine emerged sole Emperor in the West. He then decided to try to unify the empire under his authority. On his way to Rome to affect the overthrow of his opposition, he is said to have seen the sign of a cross in the sky with the statement under it, "By this conquer."

In 323 Constantine defeated Licinius who had been a claimant to the throne and a persecutor of Christians. Out of these conflicts he emerged sole emperor.

The part Christianity played in Constantine's thinking is difficult to determine. During his early reign it is doubtful that he accepted without reservation the idea of Christ as the Son of God and Jehovah as the only God. At least he outwardly supported the Christian religion and used it for his purposes. He no doubt recognized its value as a unifying force for he decided to stake his all on its support.

When Constantine marched on Rome, he overthrew with forty-thousand men an army of one hundred and seventy-thousand. Since his movements up to this time had been cautious, it requires some explanation to understand his rash decision to fight against such odds. The truth seems to be that he came under the conviction that the God of the Christians was the strongest supernatural force in the world. A series of circumstances led him to this decision.

Since 303 when Diocletian, at the instigation of Galerius, had issued his first decrees against Christians, authorizing the destruction of church buildings and the burning of all Scripture, the Christians had suffered greatly in the East, and the empire had been in turmoil. In the West, however, these decrees under Constantius had not been carried out, and peace and prosperity had been the result. This impressed Constantius. Also, the most ruthless persecutor, Galerius, had died a miserable death and had been compelled, almost with his dying breath to recognize defeat in his opposition to Christianity and to sign the edict of toleration. Then, according to the story, the sign of the cross appeared to Constantine. Eusebius says he heard the story of the sign of the cross from the Emperor's own lips, but for some reason he did not repeat it in his church history which was written during Constantine's life time. Whatever the truth may be in the matter, we do know that Constantine adopted a Christian monogram and inspired his soldiers with the belief that God would give them victory. After winning the victory, and becoming sole emperor, favor for the Christians was assured.

I. SUPPORT OF THE CHURCH

Constantine not only gave assurance that there would be no more persecution, he began to favor Christianity as though it were a state religion. He first decreed that all church buildings should be returned and the state would reimburse those who had obtained possession of them.[1] He then began to encourage the construction of additional elaborate buildings and authorized that state money be given to the Christians for this purpose. Eusebius preserves for us an imperial letter to the bishop of Carthage in which Constantine authorized three thousand 'folles' to be paid Caecilian, "the bishop," to be distributed to the ministers. The letter states that if this is not sufficient to take care of all of them that the commissioner of

1. Bettenson, pp. 22-23.

finance in Africa has Constantine's own instructions to supply out of his funds whatever additional the bishop would request.[2]

Besides building meeting houses and paying ministers, Constantine issued decrees that ministers should be excused from all public offices so they could give their time without interruption to the work of the church.[3] In this decree Constantine said it was the Divine Providence that was responsible for the welfare of mankind.

In order to preserve the unity of the church, Constantine took a hand in all internal affairs. A difference arose in Carthage in regard to the ordination of Caecilian by an accused traditor. Donatus, about 311, created a faction in opposition to Caecilian. When word of this reached Constantine, he ordered that Caecilian with ten bishops who favored his cause and ten bishops who opposed him proceed to Rome so that the matter could be tried by a synod under Constantine's authority and supervision.[4]

Constantine's favoritism to the church seems to be more a matter of expediency than of conviction. The church was to be used as a center of unity and culture to preserve the empire. Constantine had his son, Crispus, put to death in 326 upon charges of treason brought to him by his wife, Fausta. Soon after that he became displeased with Fausta, also, and ordered her executed. Perhaps more important to this consideration is the fact that he kept his position as chief priest of the Pagan state religion. None of these things can be said to be in harmony with Christian conduct. Constantine, however, continued to favor Christians. He issued an edict against soothsayers,[5] forbidding them recognition or favor from any man. One of his best known decrees related to working on Sunday. In this he states that "all judges, city people and craftsmen shall rest on the venerable day of the Sun."[6] He states, however, that farmers could work on Sunday if their crops required it. This decree has been considered by some to be the earliest authority for Christian worship on this day and constituting a change from Saturday to Sunday. This, however, is not the case. Chris-

---

2. Ecclesiastical History, 10:6:1.
3. Ibid., 10:7:2.
4. Ibid., 10:5:18-19.
5. Bettenson, p. 26
6. Ibid., p. 27.

tians had been worshipping on the first day of the week from the beginning.[7] This decree favored worship on Sunday by forbidding work on that day, thus making it possible for Christians to give themselves to worship without affecting their occupations unnecessarily.

II. Council of Nicaea

One of the outstanding examples of the relationship of Constantine to the church was his part in the first general council held in the city of Nicaea (325). This council grew out of a conflict over the nature of Christ. Constantine calling himself bishop of bishops, sat as the chairman of the council and paid the expenses of the delegates. His chief concern was not which side was right, but rather that a spirit of unity be achieved. If Christianity was to be a unifying force in the empire Constantine felt that he must keep unity within the church.

As long as the church had been under persecution the fine points of theology had not been a chief matter of concern. After the persecution ceased, the fine points of distinction came to the front and strong feelings developed over small differences. Not all of the problems facing the church were small, for opinions of the philosophers had crept in and the church needed to study the Scripture carefully to separate the truth from the opinions of men.

The problem concerning the relationship of Christ to God the Father is the question that brought out the differences of opinion. The earlier teachers had taken for granted the divinity of Christ without attempting to explain all that is involved in the doctrine of the Trinity. Justin had said that Christ was simply an attribute of God — the "Reason" or "Wisdom" that had proceeded from the Father by an act of His will. Tertullian had taught the unity of essence in the three personalities of the God-head.

Differences of opinion can exist in the church without disrupting fellowship. It is necessary that someone make an issue of a point for difficulties to arise. This is what happened in Alexandria. Alexander, "the bishop," had preached a sermon on the "Unity of the Trinity." Arius, one of the elders, who was

7. Acts 20:7; Barnabas 15:9, (about 100-130 A.D.), Didache 14:1 (About 100 A.D.), Ignatius to Magnesians 9:1, (About 108 A.D.); Justin Martyr, Apology I, (About 150 A.D.) Section 67.

a popular preacher, took issue with the sermon. He said Alexander did not make enough distinction between God the Father and Jesus and that his views made three Gods instead of one. In order to defend the idea of the oneness of God Arius believed that Christ was above man but beneath God.

The position Arius took was immediately challenged. He was accused of denying that Christ was divine. Alexander called a synod to consider the matter. In the discussion the nature of Christ and the length of His existence were debated. Arius said that He was in existence long before the world began, but that He had not existed eternally as had the Father. He also contended that Christ was of different essence than the Father. The synod condemned Arius as a false teacher, and he had to leave Alexandria. Eusebius of Nicomedia, (not the church historian) had taken the part of Arius and welcomed him to his city.

Theodoret, bishop of Cyrus, gathered up information concerning this controversy and presented it in a History of the Church which was designed to continue where the history of Eusebius left off. It covers the years 322 to 427. Theodoret quotes a letter from Alexander which gives the view of Arius. In it Alexander said that Arius denied the divinity of Christ and declared Him to be on the level with other men, assuming there was a time when Christ had no existence and thus placing Him among other created beings.

In a letter to Eusebius of Nicomedia, Arius states his own position by saying we teach, "that the Son is not begotten, nor in any way unbegotten, even in part; and that he does not derive his subsistence from any matter; but that by his own will and counsel he has subsisted before time, and before ages, as perfect God, only begotten and unchangeable, and that he existed not before he was begotten, or created, or purposed, or established. For he was not unbegotten. We are persecuted because we say that the Son had a beginning."[8] Arius states that Alexander held "that the Son has always been; that as the Father so is the Son; that the Son is unbegotten, without having been begotten; that neither by thought nor by any interval does

8. Theodoret. Church History. 1:5

God precede the Son, God and the Son having always been; and that the Son proceeds from God."[9]

These differences of opinion caused so much dissension that Constantine wrote letters requiring the two parties to come to an understanding. When the letters did not bring unity, Constantine called the first general council. Theodoret says, "He commanded that the bishops, and those connected with the councils, should be mounted on asses, mules and horses belonging to the public in order to repair" to Nicaea. Three-hundred and eighteen bishops assembled. All their wants were supplied by Constantine who sat as chairman of the meeting to direct it toward the preservation of unity. He made the keynote address and exhorted them to unanimity and concord. In this speech Constantine said, "the gospel, the Apostolic writings, and the ancient prophecies clearly teach us what we are to believe concerning the divine nature. Let then all contentious disputation be set aside; and let us seek in the divinely inspired word, the solution of all doubtful topics."[10]

It is interesting that although Constantine had not been baptized and held no church office, he yet took a very active part in discussing this difficult theological problem. His arguments and his authority carried the meeting and when the entire group was called upon to subscribe to the creed which was drawn up, all but six agreed. The council then took action. Arius was excommunicated and only two bishops continued with him. The council adopted a final form of the creed with unanimous consent. Alexander and Athanasius had been the outstanding spokesmen against Arius. Eusebius, the church historian, had sat next to Constantine and had taken down the proceedings. At heart he favored the view of Arius, but he drew up a statement of faith to present to the council that affirmed a middle of the road position. After Constantine changed some of the wording it became the adopted creed. It reads as follows:

" 'The Articles of Faith maintained by the Council.'

"We believe in one God, the Father Almighty, the Maker of all things visible and invisible. And in one Lord Jesus Christ, the Son of God, the only begotten of the Father; he is begotten, that is to say, he is of the substance of God, God of God, light of light, very God of very God, begotten and not

9. Ibid.
10. Ibid., 1:7

made, being of one substance with the Father; by whom all things both in heaven and on earth were made. Who for us men, and for our salvation, came down from heaven, and took our nature, and became man; suffered, and rose again the third day; he ascended into heaven, and will come to judge the living and the dead. And we believe in the Holy Ghost. . . . The holy catholic and apostolical church condemns all that who say that there was a period in which the Son of God did not exist; that before he was begotten he had no existence; that he was called out of nothing into being; that he is of a different nature and of a different substance from the Father; and that he is susceptible of variation or change."[11]

Another decision of the council was that Easter should be celebrated on the same day in all churches. Constantine sent a letter to all of the churches saying that it was not right that differences of customs prevail and called upon them to "obey this decree." In this letter Constantine gave the council the position of speaking for God. He said "all that is transacted in the holy councils of the bishops, is sanctioned by the Divine will."

Throughout the council Constantine dealt very kindly with the bishops. He presented them with gifts, and served them elaborate banquets. He then wrote letters that widows and orphans (presumably whose husbands and fathers had been killed in persecutions) be cared for from the public treasury and that bishops and ministers be given a liberal annual allowance from state funds. He then wrote an open letter to all his subjects exhorting them to renounce their superstition and accept Christianity. He exhorted bishops in every city to build churches and furnish them with money. He also called upon Eusebius to have made for him fifty copies of the Scripture "on fine parchment" to be placed in the churches in Constantinople.

Constantine specified that the bishops of Jerusalem were to build elaborate buildings.

"My most intense desire," he said, "is to erect beautiful edifices upon that consecrated spot. . . . Take every care and precaution that these edifices may not only be magnificient, but that they may be incomparably superior to all the most beautiful structures in the world. . . . The governors will provide all that you may deem requisite. . . . Let us know what

11. Ibid., 1:12. Bettenson, p. 36

columns or marbles you may consider would be ornamental
and we will have them conveyed to you. Whatever wants you
mention will be supplied."[12]

In order to encourage the construction of these elaborate
buildings in Jerusalem, Helena, the mother of Constantine,
carried the above letter to the bishop. She engaged actively in
the work of securing the best workmen and materials. To make
the services more impressive, Constantine gave the bishop a
robe of golden cloth to wear when he administered the ordinance of baptism.

This active interest in behalf of the church led Christians to
exalt Constantine and rely on his decisions. He soon took the
affairs of the church into his own hands and became dictatorial.
The followers of Arius continued to defend their views and
won over a large number of people to their way of thinking.
This caused a disturbance that was brought to the attention of
the emperor. To settle it he ordered a meeting of the bishops at
Tyre. He wrote:

"If any one should dare to disobey our command, and refuse
to come to the council, which however, I do not think possible, we must send him into immediate banishment, that he
may learn not to oppose the decrees enacted by the emperor
for the support of the truth."[13]

After the council of Nicaea the Arian bishops succeeded
in gaining the Emperor's ear, and in the closing years of Constantine's reign, they were in the ascendancy. The council of
Tyre was to examine charges against Athanasius, bishop of
Alexandria. Although the charges were false the council found
him guilty and sentenced him to death. Constantine changed
the sentence to exile. The Arians next held a council in Jerusalem and readmitted Arius to fellowship. He died, however,
the day before he was to be received in triumph and receive the
communion. The opponents saw in this sudden death the hand
of God against a heretic. Constantine did not accept it thus and
received baptism and communion on his death bed at the hands
of an Arian bishop, Eusebius of Nicodemia.

The controversy over Arianism was long and bitter. The

12. Theodoret, 1:17.
13. Ibid., 1:29.

most violent period was from 325 to 381, which will be treated more fully in the discussion of the councils.

This is sufficient, however, to show the influence of Constantine upon the church. Out of respect to Constantine for the favors he showed, the church gave up her independence and began to rely upon the head of the state for its organization and authority. The leaders seemed too concerned with present problems to see the danger in these developments.

Constantine selected the city of Byzantium (later called Constantinople) in 324 to be rebuilt as his capital. In 330 he removed to this new city and dedicated it. There is a story that the city was dedicated to the Virgin Mary, but this is a later tradition and is doubted by many writers. Constantine had planned for the new city to be the center of government for the church as well as for the empire. All heathen worship was excluded from the city, elaborate churches were built and the bishop exalted to a place of prominence.

Chapter Ten

The Growth of Episcopacy

I. Chronological Development

When Constantine called the bishops together for the first general council, they all came to Nicaea as equals. We have previously noted how these monarchal bishops came into existence. The chairmanship of the elders became a permanent position and the word bishop was applied to the holder of this office. Soon this bishop was elevated in authority over the elders. Each congregation had its own bishop, and gradually the city bishops grew in prestige over the country bishops, absorbing their functions. This was the stage of development at the time of the council of Nicaea.

We have already noticed the Synod in Rome called to decide the matter of ordination by a traditor. This was held by Constantine's order. In the letter to Militades, bishop of Rome, concerning this, Constantine gives him high respect, calling him "Your Firmness" and "Your Carefulness." This however, is characteristic of Constantine and does not indicate any special recognition. In a letter to Chrestus, bishop of Syracuse, Eusebius preserves for us a copy of the form letter sent to the bishops, calling the second Synod over this problem. In it Constantine said, "I have given orders" that the bishops meet to discuss this problem. He continues, "In as much, therefore, as we have commanded that very many bishops from various and numberless places should assemble . . . do thou be present."[1] He then refers to him as "Thy Firmness" and states that by unanimous consent a decision is to be reached.

Throughout all of the work of Constantine in his efforts to unify and organize the church there is no idea of any centralized church organization. The bishop of Rome had no position above other bishops. Constantius, the son of Constantine, continued his father's policy of calling the bishops together to settle disturbances. In 359 he assembled the bishops of the West at

1. Eusebius, 10:5; 21-24.

(134)

Rimina to discuss further the doctrine of Arius. However, the bishop of Rome was not pleased with these developments, which were attempts to reinstitute Arianism. He accordingly called together ninety bishops in Rome and took a stand against Arianism. The facts show that the Bishop of Rome had nothing to do with this first general council. He himself did not attend, and less than ten of the 318 were from the West. If the bishop of Rome had "selected" the delegates the Western bishops would have been more numerous. It was rather the emperor who convened the council. Constantine said, "God it was, on whose suggestion I acted in summoning the bishops to meet in such numbers." The council also declared at its close, "it was by the grace of God and the piety of the emperor in assembling us that the great and holy synod came together."

It is clear that at the beginning of the fourth century the organization of the church had not developed into any centralized control. By 359, as we have seen, the bishop of Rome was claiming authority outside his diocese. In the same letter quoted above, he condemns the synod at Rimini because "they assembled without the sanction of the bishop of Rome, whose opinion ought to have been consulted before that of any other bishop."[2] In spite of these claims the bishop of Rome had no authority outside his diocese. The bishops of Alexandria, Constantinople, Antioch or Jerusalem had as much authority in their respective dioceses as the bishop of Rome had in his, and no one of them had authority outside of his own territory.

Eusebius gives us lists of bishops in a number of cities, but in all his effort to exalt the bishops he does not go beyond the rule just stated. When he wrote his church history, the growth of episcopacy had not developed above the monarchal bishop. Theodoret in 450 wrote the history of the church for the next 105 years, from 324 to 429. It was intended to be a continuation of the history of Eusebius and in it there is no indication that the bishop of Rome received any recognition above the bishops of Antioch, Constantinople or Alexandria. At the conclusion of his history Theodoret gave a list of the bishops in Rome, Antioch, Alexandria, Jerusalem and Constantinople from the year 300. If the bishop of Rome had any special recognition at this time he would have referred to it. He tells

2. Theodoret. 1:22.

of the work of many bishops, but refers to them all as though they were equals, yet the highest authority in the church in their respective territories. In terminology he uses the word pope, but applies it to Alexander, bishop of Alexandria. Thus we see that the churches in the East gave the Roman bishop no more honor than they did the Eastern bishops.

The churches in the West, however, began to exalt the bishop of Rome. They eventually gave him the title pope (papa) and considered him the universal head of the church. The process by which exaltation developed may be clearly traced.

325. The Council of Nicaea exalted the bishops of Rome, Antioch, and Alexandria to the position of patriarchs (or Metropolitans) and gave them charge over the church in their respective provinces, placing all bishops under the authority of their Metropolitan. The bishop of Rome had authority over the bishops of Italy only, as the bishop of Alexandria had over Egypt, Libya and the Pentapolis.

341. Julius, bishop of Rome, wrote a council at Antioch that questioned that dispute should be settled at Rome as that is "the tradition handed down from the blessed Apostle Peter."[3]

343. The Council of Sardica agreed that the retrial of bishops should be held in Rome to "honor the memory of the Apostle Peter." The Bishop of Rome was to preside or appoint arbitrators.[4]

376. Damascus, bishop of Rome, hired Jerome to translate the Bible into Latin and Jerome appeals to him for a decision saying, "I think it my duty to consult the chair of Peter . . . for this I know, is the Rock on which the church is built."[5]

380. Theodosius I recognized the bishop of Rome as 'Pontif.'[6]

381. One hundred and fifty bishops of the council of Constantinople gave the bishop of Constantinople the first place of honor in the church next after the bishop of Rome. This gave him control of the church in the East and exalted him over the bishops of Antioch, Alexandria and Jerusalem.

382. Valentinian the Emperor agrees to back up with imperial force the decisions of the bishop of Rome affecting the trial of church officials. Metropolitans had to come to Rome for trial before the Roman bishop.[7]

3. Bettenson, p. 111.
4. Ibid., 112
5. Ibid., 113.
6. Ibid., 31
7. Ibid., 30

417. The Bishop of Rome tells African bishops, "Nothing should be taken as finally settled unless it came to the notice of this See, that any just pronouncement might be confirmed by all the authority of this See, and that the other churches might from thence gather what they should teach."[8] Notice that decrees from Rome are to take the place of Scripture in determining the truth.

424. The African bishops in the Synod at Carthage rejected the interference of the bishop of Rome and reminded him that at Nicaea the Metropolitan had authority in his own district.[9]

445. Valentinian III decreed in favor of the Roman bishop's having universal authority. He said, "Inasmuch as the pre-eminence of the Apostolic See is assured by the merit of St. Peter, the first of the bishops, by the leading position of the city of Rome and also by the authority of the holy Synod, let not presumption strive to attempt anything contrary to the authority of that See. . . . We decree . . . that nothing shall be attempted by the . . . bishops . . . without the authority of the venerable pope of the Eternal City."[10]

541. The Council of Chalcedon reaffirmed the decision of council of Constantinople (381) exalting the bishop of Constantinople. They did not accept the idea of the "chair of Peter" but said, "For to the throne of Old Rome, the Fathers gave privileges with good reason, because it was the imperial city. And the 150 bishops, with the same consideration in view gave equal privileges to the most holy throne of New Rome." (Constantinople). They then gave the bishop of Constantinople the right to ordain the Metropolitans in the East, who had the responsibility of ordaining bishops under them.[11]

Until this time there were five Metropolitans: Rome, Alexandria, Antioch, Constantinople and Jerusalem. Rome in the West and Constantinople in the East, however, had risen to greater prominence because of the position of these cities, and there now arises a conflict as to which of these should become dominant. The council of Chalcedon had decreed the two were equal.

II. THE BATTLE OF THE BISHOPS

From the first distinction between elder and bishop there may be seen a steady development in organization in the direction of one universal head of the church. At the council of

8. Ibid., 113
9. Ibid., 114.
10. Ibid., 32.
11. Ibid., 116.

Nicaea (325) there was effected an organization in the church parallel to Constantine's organization of the Roman government. The Patriarchs authorized at Nicaea were given territory identical to that of the provincial governors. Very early there was developed in the church positions equaling the lower offices in the imperial administration. With this development it was natural for the organization to move upward also and some one be selected to stand on an equality with the emperior as universal head of the church. Rome and Constantinople were the logical opponents in this struggle, and although the world council decreed that they were equal in authority there were forces at work which favored Rome.

In the first place the prestige of Rome was tremendous in the Empire at this time. Valentinian referred to the "leading position of the city of Rome" in his Edict of 445 A.D. She was the capital city of the world. Her reputation, in the second place, was well known in the areas of benevolence and sound doctrine. Much of this is reflected in the correspondence of Clement to Corinth. Further, the tradition was quite strong that Peter and Paul had founded the church there sealing their faith with martyrdom. Much of this was based on the spurious "Acts of Peter," an evident pseudepigraphical work of the late second century or earlier. Nevertheless, the idea that Peter was the first bishop of Rome was early accepted as incontrovertible. To strengthen this position, various passages of the New Testament were explained in such a way as to insist upon Peter's identity as the foundation of the church. For example, Matthew 16:18 is used frequently in this regard from the time of Cyprian (250 A.D.) onward.

In addition to these there were other reasons for the rise in prestige of the Roman bishop. Rome had been the mother church for much missionary activity in Western Europe and it was only natural that these churches newly founded should turn to her for their needs. It should not be surprising either that support should come to the church in the capitol city from the Emperors who resided there. Leo I considered the bishop of Rome a successor of Peter, possessing the same powers Christ had given Peter — and some indeed that were not delegated him. Finally, it might be mentioned that the breach between the Eastern and Western churches eventually widened to the extent that many supported the Roman bishop out of resentment to the undue exaltation of the Eastern bishop.

It looked as though this favorable position concerning Rome would be all that was needed to give the Roman bishop recognition as head of the church. Conditions developed in Constantinople, however, that delayed such recognition and for a time it looked as though the bishop of Constantinople would receive this honor instead of the Roman bishop. In 527 the Emperor Justinian gave the bishop of Constantinople the title of "Ecumenical Patriarch," and the succeeding bishops tried to hold on to this title. John the Faster, as late as 588, claimed he was world bishop and that this honor belonged only to Constantinople. The bishops of Rome denied all these assertions, and circumstances soon favored their position.

The claims of Apostolic Succession themselves soon favored the prominence of the Roman bishop. As early as the third century the bishops everywhere were looked upon as successors of the Apostles. As Rome was the only church in the West whose origin was ascribed to Peter, the Roman bishop considered himself a successor of Peter and viceregent of God.

Further, in time of danger the churches sought a closer fellowship with Rome taking the lead against heresy. The Roman bishop wrote letters attempting to promote unity among the churches with the unfortunate result that his "advice" became "authoritative decree." As the barbarian invasions began and the imperial administration broke down, the Roman bishop took over. The churches of Africa, oppressed by the Vandals, began to look to Rome for guidance. Eastern churches sought her approval also, but denied her presumed authority.

It is clear, also, that prominent personalities in Rome contributed to the elevation of the bishop. Leo I, later called "the Great," became bishop of Rome in 440 and served twenty years. He stressed the theory of Roman supremacy on the basis of Apostolic succession. He taught that the Lord held the Roman bishop responsible for the care of all the churches and that other bishops were assistants to the Roman bishop in administration, but could not share his authority. To the bishop of Constantinople, he said:

> "Constantinople has its own glory and by the mercy of God
> has become the seat of the empire. But secular matters are

based on one thing, and ecclesiastical matters on another.
Nothing will stand which is not built on the Rock which the
Lord laid in the foundation. . . . Your city is royal but you
cannot make it Apostolic."

Leo thus became the first pope. His claims did not stand
unchallenged but remained steadfast nevertheless. Weaker men
who succeeded him were not able to defend these claims successfully, and after a period of ascendency for the bishops of
Constantinople, another strong personality became bishop of
Rome. Gregory I, who was also given the title "the Great,"
ruled from 590 to 604. At the close of his reign the theory of
the the primacy of Peter and the Roman bishop as his successor and universal head of the church was definitely established.
The episcopal order of government secured the submission of
worshippers to a system of priesthood. The pattern set by
paganism that priests were representatives of the gods and the
emperor high priest had become customary in the church, and
the New Testament teaching that man may approach God
directly was destroyed. The New Testament arrangement consisting of a plurality of bishops in each congregation was forsaken, and while there were here and there sincere Christians
trying to do the will of God as revealed in His word, the Eternal Kingdom largely disappeared from the pages of history.

That the development of a pope was a gradual process is
clearly seen. None of the Apostolic Fathers evidence such a
situation. The Apologists and the bishops of the early councils
never had to reckon with papal authority. Christians today who
respect the authority of the New Testament are forced to recognize the entire hierarchy as a human development which is to
be rejected in favor of the simple organization found in the
New Testament — the last Will and Testament of Jesus Christ.

Chapter Eleven

The Ecumenical Councils

The term ecumenical means universal or world wide in extent. As applied to church councils it refers to the first seven councils to which all of the bishops were invited. They were held at: Nicaea, 325; Constantinople, 381; Ephesus, 431; Chalcedon, 451; Constantinople, 553; Constantinople, 680; and Nicaea, 787. There was an eighth council conducted at Constantinople in 869 that some count ecumenical but it is not generally considered to be so. Some protestant scholars do not count as ecumenical any council after Chalcedon in 451 as by this time the pope began to influence the decisions. On the other hand the Roman Catholics claim that the Pope-in-Council guarantees their ecumenical character and on this basis claim twelve additional councils as ecumenical.

The Christian who accepts the Bible as an inspired revelation from God can place no importance upon such councils, because they are subject to error being human. Since the Apostles, no man or group of men have been given the right to speak for God. Contrary to this, the Roman theologians maintain that the church as an organization does have the right to speak for God and that the bishops in council cannot err. The decision as to where final authority resides constitutes a vital difference between Romanism and undenominational Christianity.

After the rise of the pope as universal head of the church there was a conflict over who had the final authority, the pope or the council. During the time we are considering, the council claimed that it had the final authority but later the pope gained ascendancy over the councils. After this development councils were seldom called, and when they were, their decisions would be accepted only if pleasing to the pope.

I. COUNCIL OF NICAEA, 325

Since this council was discussed in connection with Constantine, we will deal with it here only briefly.

Constantine called this first general council to meet in Nicaea in Asia Minor, June 19, 325. Its purpose was to settle the controversy over the nature of Christ. Arius, a popular preacher of Alexandria, contended that Christ was not eternal and that His substance was not the same as that of God the Father. Athanasius opposed Arius saying that the substance of Christ was the same as the Father. Constantine thought the differences were unimportant, too subtle for the average man and confusing to the people of the Empire.

During the council popular feeling supported Alexander, bishop of Alexandria and Athanasius who was the chief spokesman against Arius. The council excommunicated Arius and drew up the first creed. It also settled a difference between the East and West over the time to observe Easter, decreeing that it must always be observed on Sunday. The council also created the office of Metropolitan, or Patriarch, by exalting the bishops of Rome, Alexandria and Antioch.

The council and its creed did not remove Arianism. Although only two bishops stood with Arius in this condemnation, many of the bishops had signed the creed without agreeing to it. These bishops began to work for a reversal of the decision. Soon they gained the ear of Constantine, changed his thinking and through false charges had Athanasius sent into exile. After the death of Constantine the Empire fell into the hands of his three sons and during their lives the Arians were able to keep imperial support. In 359 the council of Ariminum accepted an Arian creed, and even the bishop of Rome, Liberius (352-366), after defending Athanasius, at last gave way to the Arian views and the entire church seemed to be in the hands of the Arians. For a time the decisions of the first council were reversed.

This Arian ascendancy, however, was not to last. Strong men arose to oppose this doctrine because it tended to lessen the divinity of Christ. Many synods were held and the Arians seemed to lose all sense of integrity. In their efforts to bring discredit upon Athanasius, many false charges were brought against his moral character. From 325 to 381 contention over which party would control the church was characterized by extreme bitterness. The doctrine of Arius was rejected in later councils, but it has continued in the world until today and can be found in part in Unitarianism, which says there is true diety only in God the Father and Jesus was purely human.

II. COUNCIL OF CONSTANTINOPLE, 381

The Emperor Theodosius convoked the second general council in Constantinople in May, 381. One hundred fifty bishops attended. Their first decision was that the position taken by the three hundred and eighteen bishops of Nicaea was the truth and that this doctrine "shall not be set aside but shall remain dominant."

A second important decision had to do with the nature of the Holy Spirit. Macdonius, a bishop of Constantinople from 341-360 had taught that the Holy Spirit was subordinate to both the Father and the Son and was on the level of the angels. This was a denial of the place the Scripture gives the Holy Spirit as the third member of the Godhead and is as harmful to the true conception of the Holy Spirit as Arianism is to the deity of Christ. The council condemned this teaching and stated its faith in the "Holy Spirit, the Lord and the Life-giver, that proceedeth from the Father, who with Father and Son is worshipped together and glorified together . . ."[1]

The council also decreed that Christ was human as well as divine. This was necessary to counteract those who opposed Arianism to such an extent that they emphasized the divinity of Christ to the extent that it constituted a denial of His humanity. Apollinaris, bishop of Laodicea, had strongly opposed Arianism, but he began to philosophize as to how Jesus could be both human and divine, concluding that He was born with a natural body and soul, but that instead of having a human spirit He had the divine logos. The logos dominated the body and the soul and made Him divine. This view was condemned by the council because it minimized the manhood of Christ.

III. THE COUNCIL OF EPHESUS

The doctrine that Christ had two natures which were distinct continued in the church. In order to emphasize that Jesus was truly divine at the time of birth the theologians began to call Mary the mother of God (Theotokos). This was not done to exalt Mary, but to emphasize the divinity of her child.

Nestorius denied that the divine nature was truly united

1. Bettenson. 37.

with the body of Jesus. He taught that Mary gave birth to the human body only, and therefore she should not be called the "mother of God."

This doctrine caused so much confusion that Theodosius, the emperor, called a third council in 431 to meet in Ephesus. The council decreed that Christ had perfect unity in His being and personality and that He was not of two different parts joined together in some mechanical way as Nestorius had taught.

From this time on the statement "Mary, the mother of God," is commonly used. It was not used to exalt Mary, but rather to exalt Jesus, her son, as God. The statement, however, was soon removed from the controversy that called it forth. The divinity of Christ became generally accepted. Then the emphasis in the statement was changed and Mary began to be exalted as though she were the source of Christ's divine nature.

IV. Council of Chalcedon, 451

The controversy over the nature of Christ continued in the church. As Nestorius had given Christ two natures, Eutyches said that after the incarnation the two natures were fused into one—the divine. This again minimized the humanity of Christ, and to try again for a settlement of this question Marsian, who became emperor upon the death of Theodosius in 450, called the council of Chalcedon.

To this council, Leo, the bishop of Rome, presented a document condemning the teaching of Eutyches. The council said that "Peter has spoken through Leo" and drew up its decision on the basis of his arguments. The decree says that Christ is:

> At once complete in Godhead and complete in manhood, truly God and truly man, consisting also of a reasonable soul and body; as of one substance with the Father as regards his Godhead, and at the same time of one substance with us as regards his manhood . . . begotten . . . of Mary the Virgin, the God-bearer; one and the same Christ, Son, Lord, Only-begotten, recognized in two natures, without confusion, without change, without division, without seperation. . . .[2]

In the council's effort to make everyone conform to this creed, Theodoret, bishop of Cyrus, was required to say, "An-

2. Bettenson. op. cit., p. 72.

athema to all who do not confess that the Virgin Mary is the mother of God."[3]

This council also decreed that the bishop of Constantinople was due all of the rights and powers bestowed upon the bishop of Rome. That as Rome ruled the West, Constantinople would rule the East. Leo, bishop of Rome, strongly opposed this but without success. This placed the bishop of Constantinople in position to become a strong contender for the honor of world bishop and shows clearly that there was no one man at this time who was recognized by the bishops of the churches as universal head of the church.

V. COUNCIL OF CONSTANTINOPLE, 553

The doctrine of Eutychus, that after the incarnation Christ had only one nature, continued after its official condemnation. This is true of all of the decisions of councils. It is impossible to change ideas through legislation. The councils accomplished nothing except to draw up a statement that might help in clarifying thinking.

The doctrine of Eutychus was called Monophysitism. (Mono, one; Physis, nature). This theory so disturbed the churches in the East and persisted to such a degree that the Emperor Justinian called a council to meet in Constantinople in 553. At this time the bishops strongly condemned this theory. Before the decision was finally reached, however, the bishop of Rome as well as the Emperor and other influential leaders had changed opinions several times.

VI. COUNCIL OF CONSTANTINOPLE, 680

As Monophysitism had declared that the divine nature of Christ made inactive His human nature, there arose a companion theory that Christ had only a divine will. This is known as Monotheletism (Mono, one; Thelma, will). Those holding this view taught that although Christ had two natures, He had only one personality and only one will. If He had two wills He would have been two persons.

The ideas expressed by the orthodox party failed to explain the real unity of the two natures in Christ. Monotheletism was an effort to explain this by subjecting the human will to the divine. This could hardly be accepted, for if Christ had only a

3. Theodoret, 9.

divine will His human nature would be repudiated and His overcoming human weaknesses would be ascribed to a lack of real temptation. The strife grew bitter. The Emperor took a position in favor of the Monothelites and sent the leading opponents into exile.

Finally in 678 the new emperor Constantine Poganatus entered into negotiations with Domnus, bishop of Rome, and they agreed that a settlement should be reached by a general council. The Emperor called the council to meet in Constantinople in 680. The Emperor presided as chairman of the council. The idea that Christ had two wills was sustained by the council, and those who said Christ had only one will were condemned.

VII. COUNCIL OF NICAEA, 787

The chief reason for the Nicaean council of 787 was to settle a disturbance over the use of images in the church. This is known as the "iconoclastic controversy." An "icon" was a representation of a true historical person. It is believed that this type of Christian art began in Syria. One of the favorite subjects was the crucified Christ. Constantia, the sister of Constantine, wrote Eusebius and asked that he send her an "image of Christ." Eusebius was shocked at this and wrote back that images were forbidden by the Law, that they were unknown in the churches and that to have such would be to follow pagan idolatry. He went on to say that Christians have the living Christ and do not need artificial images of Him.[4] From the fourth century, images and pictures came into use as teaching aids. As the study of the Bible itself declined, icons were relied upon to a greater extent. Pictures or images were arranged to portray the life of Christ from His birth to the ascension. The crucifix came into use as an aid to worship and as superstition developed these icons took on a special significance for the ignorant. People began to fondle and kiss them and bow down before them in the same way that pagans were dong before their idols.

The emperors were alarmed at this situation, but the bishops of the West, especially the pope, favored the use of the

4. See the article by George Florovsky, "Origen, Eusebius, and the Iconoclastic Controversy," in the journal, **Church History**, XIX, No. 2, page 77, June, 1950.

icons. They became an important part of the Roman Catholic religion eventually.

In the East, Mohammedanism became a threat to the Empire and to the Romanized church. The Mohammedians reproached the Christians as idolaters. Images were a stumbling block to efforts to convert these non-Christian peoples. In 730 the emperor, Leo the Isaurian, issued a decree that all images and pictures must be removed from the churches. This decree was opposed by the Patriarch of Constantinople so the emperor had him removed from office.

John, bishop of Damascus, defended the use of images and said that God was in the images in the same way that Christ was in the Lord's Supper and that the image is an actual representation of the Invisible. He believed that the common people could not visualize Christ apart from a material representation.

The emperor, however, by imperial edict cleared the churches in the East of their images. This was no sooner done than word of it reached Pope Gregory III in Rome. The pope took immediate action, and in 731 excommunicated the emperor and all church officials who would not restore the images. As many believed, the council in 754 condemned the use of images, but the pope rejected this council. To end the confusion, the emperor Constantine VI called a world council to settle the question. The council restored the images to the churches, but said worship should be given to God alone and the images could receive no more than veneration. As veneration is the first step to worship it was not long before worship was again being offered to the images as well as through them.

As was to be expected, this council did not solve the problem, and it was another one hundred years before the pope and his assistants could persuade the emperors to cease opposing the use of images. Finally in 860 a Council of Constantinople decreed that the images should be "worshipped with the same honor as the books of the holy gospels."

The ecumenical councils, it should be remembered, were called by the Roman Emperors, not the popes. They were chiefly interested in the unity of the empire, but they also looked upon themselves as theologians and wanted to have a part in directing the course of the church.

These councils reflect the confusion which arose when men

tried to harmonize human philosophy and Christianity. The councils settled no problems and each controversy had to wear itself out in time. The writing of creeds, which was meant to bring unity, forced open division and crystalized the differences. No decisions were made without lengthy discussion. At times the decision was adopted by a very small majority and that obtained by the power of eloquence in one individual. With the same eloquence on the opposite side of the question the decision, condemned as heresy, might have been praised as orthodoxy. If the controversy over images had come to the front while emperors dominated the councils rather than later after the pope had gained power, one wonders how much difference it would have made in the development of Romanism.

Chapter Twelve

Life, Worship and Doctrine
Under Romanism

In order to present in brief form a variety of developments that took place during the period of the general councils, this chapter will consist of such developments as have not previously been discussed.

I. THE ESTABLISHMENT OF CATHOLICITY

The increase of heresy led the bishops to desire more centralization of authority and a set pattern of doctrine. The New Testament was recognized as authoritative, but they believed it needed an authoritarian interpretation. After the development of the episcopacy the church had an organization which could demand conformity. The bishops became the spokesmen of orthodoxy and officially representives of the organism. They developed and enlarged the rule of faith. Their interpretations began to crystalize, and from the beginning of the sixth century, there was a pattern of doctrine designated as "Catholic."

The word Catholic began to be used in the second century. Its primary meaning is "universal." The church from the beginning was the universal church of Christ. In this sense it may still correctly be called Catholic. The term, however, was soon applied to doctrine and organization that received the approval of the majority of the bishops. Some modern scholars refer to the church before the first church council, as the old Catholic church, to distinguish the early church with its simple organization and worship from the development of Roman Catholicism.

II. SACREDOTALISM

From the scriptural position of the priesthood of all believers there grew up a distinct priestly class. The New Testament teaches that Christ is the only mediator between God and man. The early leaders warned against falling from this idea, but soon a priestly class was developed and the priests began to

(149)

do things for the common Christians that, they were told, they could not do for themselves. This was not only a retrogression to Jewish days, but was also a compromise with paganism. If the ministers were to be priests they had to interpret the items of worship in such a way as to give themselves special functions and to justify their position. The priestly idea grew up with the episcopacy. The administration of the Lord's Supper and baptism became the sole privilege of the bishop. As the bishop enlarged his responsibilities he authorized elders to perform these services. The services then became official in nature and could be performed only by a specially ordained individual. From this point on the full priesthood required only a little time to develop. Along with these devolepments was a general increase of ceremonialism. Simple services became ritualistic.

III. BAPTISM

In the Apostolic period baptism was a simple act of initiation into Christ. Faith in Jesus as the Son of God and desire to be baptized were the only things necessary. Later baptism became a ceremony that could be performed only by an approved official. It was performed only on Easter and on Pentecost. The candidates were required to go through a period of training before baptism was permitted. The act itself became an elaborate ceremony where the candidate renounced the Devil, had salt sprinkled on his head and after his immersion received milk and honey as a token of entering the spiritual promised land. The baptized were then dressed in white robes and paraded home wearing crowns of victory.

In some places the baptisms were performed by three immersions. Once for each member of the Godhead, but the general practice was one immersion into the Father, Son and Holy Spirit.

Infant baptism was occasionally practiced before 325, but it was not until after Augustine, about 450 that it became common practice.

Sprinkling for baptism was accepted during this period only on an emergency basis. It developed through baptisms of the sick. Baptism throughout this period was recognized as necessary for the remission of sins and for salvation. Since many unbaptized would become seriously ill and immersion seemed unwise, the priests poured small amounts of water on the subject's head and called it baptism. The first known case of this was Novatian in 251. What was introduced as an exception later became the rule. Sprinkling was not commonly practiced in this era.

IV. THE LORD'S SUPPER

In the period of the Apostolic Fathers and the Apologists the Lord's Supper was a memorial service conducted in a simple way in harmony with the universal priesthood of all believers. However, the seed for the Roman doctrine of the Eucharist were planted early.[1] Justin and Irenaeus both speak of the Lord's Supper as an offering, somewhat as the Jews offered incense unto God. Members of the church began to bring bread and wine and give it to the bishop who in turn presented it to God and a portion was used in the communion service. This took the form of an oblation or offering. It was a small step from this to the idea that the gift was a sacrifice as well as an offering. At first it was considered a sacrifice of man unto God, but since it represented the sacrifice of Christ, the service became an offering of Christ unto God. Cyprian added the idea that the service reinacts the offering of Christ, as a high priest, made when He presented His blood to God. In this the priest takes the place of Christ, the emblems stand for the body of Christ and the priest offers the body and the blood for the sins of men. This is the idea of sacrifice. Tertullian believed that the bread and wine were only symbols, but that the Lord's Supper could also be applied to the dead. This idea, however, was not clearly stated, and we do not know to what extent or in what way this was practiced. Cyril of Jerusalem (315-386) was the first to clearly advocate that the Eucharist had power to help the dead. Chrysostom (347-407), bishop of Constantinople, separated the idea of sacrifice from communion and believed the priest offered the sacrifice to God, and the people took communion. Augustine supported the idea that the Supper is a sacrifice, and by the time of Gregory the Great (540-604) the sacrifice of the mass was fully established.

1. "Eucharist" is a word transliterated from the Greek **Eucharistao** "to give thanks" — a word used by Jesus in instituting the Lord's Supper (Matt. 26:27). It is now used synonymously with "Lord's Supper."

The church was slow in accepting the idea of the actual body and blood of Christ in the elements. Eusebius and Athanasius strongly repudiated the idea of partaking of real flesh and blood. Origen had taught that the elements were only symbols. Cyrpian calls the emblems the "body and blood of Christ" but means that they are symbolic. Augustine refers to the elements in this same way, using realistic language but in symbolism also.

Cyril of Jerusalem spoke of the elements' being transformed into the body and blood of Christ, but to him this was a spiritual change and not literal. Chrysostom uses such language but explains he does not mean literal flesh and blood.

John of Damascus (700-750) seems to be the first to clearly defend a literal change from elements into actual flesh and blood. This idea was first accepted by the church in the East and then gradually accepted by the West and read into the statements of Ambrose and Augustine. It is interesting that the bishop of Rome, Gelasius (496), who later was claimed to be in the line of Popes, definitely stood against the idea of transubstantiation.

V. INCREASE OF SACRAMENTS

In the idea of sacrament there is suggested the relationship of an outward sign to the spiritual purposes of God. Man is in a two-fold world of matter and spirit. He is capable of understanding and appropriating physical-spiritual relationships. God has given certain ordinances by means of which man is to be drawn spiritually to God. Christ set forth only two such ordinances that might come under the definition of a sacrament. These are baptism and the Lord's Supper.

As the priesthood developed the bishop authorized his subordinates to perform the act of baptism, and he later confirmed the baptism as valid. Also, as infant baptism came into common practice, after the middle of the fifth century, it was believed necessary to have a confirmation service for such children after they became old enough to realize the nature of worship. This ceremony consisted of the laying on of hands by the bishop. Soon the bishop began also to annoint the child with oil in this ceremony. This was considered necessary before the child could partake of communion. With this development confirmation was given the status of a sacrament.

In dealing with Christians who fell into sin there developed the idea that simple repentance and confession of wrong were not sufficient. Here the priesthood inserted itself. It became the duty of the priest to determine whether the contrition was genuine and whether or not the church should require some proof of good intentions before it would grant readmittance to its membership. The priest might require the penitent to make some satisfaction for the sin he had committed, and then after all requirements were fulfilled he would pronounce the sinner absolved from his sin and readmitted to his place in the church. This was a big step in increasing the power of the priests. It gave them a fourth sacrament with which to subject the common Christians to their dictates. Gregory the Great was the first to clearly set forth penance as a sacrament.

Since the priesthood was becoming so important, it was natural that elaborate rites should be developed to initiate one into such an exclusive order. As it developed the priesthood was looked upon with an unusual respect, and the mysterious event that bestowed a common man with such privileges and powers became looked upon as the sacrament of ordination.

In keeping with the growing power of the priesthood it was believed that through special ceremony the sick could be anointed with oil and receive special grace. Also, by anointing a baptized person just before death all sin would be removed. This became the sacrament of unction. The ceremony and services of a priest were believed to convey special grace that could not be obtained through the earnest prayer of an individual.

Tertullian was the first to apply the term sacrament to significant Christian rites. In all ages baptism and the Lord's Supper have been looked upon as such. Augustine used the word sacrament in a very loose way and applied it to all spiritual things. He gave some definitions and said the word sacrament indicated a visible sign of an invisible grace. By the time of Gregory the Great the original two had grown into the seven sacraments of the medieval Catholic church and are still held by both the Greek and Roman Catholic churches.

VI.   INSTRUMENTAL MUSIC INTRODUCED

Throughout the early literature of the Apostolic fathers

and Apologists there are abundant references to singing in the church, but no indications of the use of instrumental music. The Jews used instrumental music, and the Greeks in their idol worship sang to the accompaniment of instruments. It is thus obvious that the early Christians were familiar with its use. Justin, Tertullian and Origen all speak of singing in the early church, and Eusebius quotes Irenaeus and Meliton concerning the songs sung in praise to God, but not one of them mentions the use of instrumental music in the worship. Among later writers Ambrose, Basil and Chrysostom all admonish Christians to praise God in song. Only Basil mentions instrumental music and he condemns it as ministering to the depraved nature of man. It must be generally admitted that the early church used no instrumental music. Chrysostom states,

> "It was the ancient custom, as it is still with us, for all to come together, and unitedly to join in singing. The young and the old, rich and poor, male and female, bond and free, all join in one song. . . . All worldly distinctions here cease, and the whole congregation form one general chorus."

Along with other changes in the fourth century as the service was becoming formal, special singers were appointed as a distinct class of officers in the church. This encouraged singing by a choir and by the fifth century some mechanical music began to be introduced. Organs were not used until the eighth century.

VII. MONASTICISM

Many early Christians, in attempting to overcome the temptations of life, were influenced by the Gnostic philosophy that everything connected with the flesh was evil. In order to crucify the flesh asceticism began to be practiced. Some went out into the deserts to escape the temptation and contamination of society. It was believed that the Apostle Paul taught that marriage was a hindrance to spirituality. Origen, Cyprian, Tertullian and Jerome all taught that celibacy was necessary to obtain the highest spirituality. As society was becoming increasingly corrupt the most devout sought closer contact with God in isolation.

In the East conditions were favorable to life in the caves along rivers and streams and soon every cave was occupied.

One of the best known hermits was Anthony (250-356). When only twenty years old he gave away his possessions and went to live in a cave. He was soon the leader of a group of hermits who had taken up their abode near him. Later on he became known as the "star of the desert" and "the father of monks." He did not organize his followers into a group, but each lived to himself in his own cave.

In the fourth century these hermits began to organize monastic groups. The moral and political decay of the Roman Empire made life insecure. The churches were taking on pagan customs and becoming filled with ritualism and ceremony. The monastery offered an opportunity to escape these influences and in solitude purify the soul by simple worship.

It is believed that Pachomius (292-346) was the first to organize the hermits around him and form a monastery. This was done in 340 when he took a group of hermits to an island in the Nile River. From this beginning he organized other groups, and soon several thousand monks in Egypt and Syria were under his supervision. He worked out a system for division of their time in prayer, study and work. He made obedience a requirement and set the pattern for monastic life.

Most of these early ascetics were reasonable in their activities, but there were also fanatics called anchorites. These extremists exposed themselves to all manner of hardship. Some refused to wear necessary clothing; others devised coarse, uncomfortable clothing and still others weighted themselves down with chains. One group refused to eat anything but grass and would graze as a herd of cattle. Gregory Nazianzus tells of monks in Syria who wore iron fetters, slept on the ground, fasted for twenty days at a time and stood immovable in prayer in the rain, wind and snow.[2] Theodoret tells of a Jacob of Nisibis who lived on the top of the highest mountain. In the summer he stayed in a thicket in the woods and in winter he lived in a cave. He used no clothing or fire and ate only herbs and roots.[3]

Ephraem of Edessa tells of monks who lived with the animals, ate grass and perched on the rocks like birds. They en-

---

2. See the article by Arthur Voobus, "The Origin of Monasticism In Mesopotamia" in Church History, XX, No. 4, Page 27, December, 1951.
3. Ibid.

dured severe fasting, spent their time in prayer and took no precaution against snakes or savage animals.[4]

The aim of such monks was to destroy themselves through suffering. They believed every torment was endured for the sake of Christ and that they would be blessed if they killed themselves through torture and starvation. Some of them burned their bodies and others purposefully endangered themselves before snakes and carnivorous animals.

Such extreme asceticism came into the Christian communities by untaught monks who came under the influence of Mani. Mani had been influenced by the monastic practices of the monks of Buddhism and Jainism of India. The Manichaean monks thought that all physical existence was the work of the Devil. The so called "pillar saints," in efforts to get away from the world, lived on top of stone columns left in the ruins of the temples. The most famous of these was Simeon (386-459) who lived on top of a column sixty feet high for thirty-six years. He gained quite a reputation by preaching to any who would listen. He also sat as judge in cases of dispute.

The bishops discouraged the radical type of asceticism and urged the monastic development. Basil of Caesarea (330-379) urged all monks under his rule in Cappadocia to render useful service, study, pray and help their fellow man through good deeds.

As the weather was colder in the West the ascetic life there did not follow the pattern of life in caves as it had in the East. Monasteries, however, provided an outlet for ascetic tendencies and soon covered Europe. The writings of Jerome, Augustine and Ambrose encouraged this development.

Benedict (480-543) became the organizer of Western monasticism. While still a boy he dedicated himself to asceticism. Because of the sin in the church at Rome he withdrew from society and lived apart for three years in a cave. As he became known for his piety disciples gathered around him. He first formed them into group of twelve under a "father" to represent Christ and His Apostles. Later in 529 he established his monastery at Monte Cassino which was to become world famous and the example to be followed. Not far away Bene-

4. Ibid.

dict's twin sister, Scholastica, founded a convent which set the pattern for organized societies of female ascetics.

The rule of Benedict was not new. It consisted of the three "virtues," poverty, chastity and obedience. After a person chose the monastic life he was supposed to remain a monk until death. The monasteries were to be self supporting by each member working at some productive occupation six hours a day. Four hours were given for prayer and worship, eight hours for sleep and the rest for writing, teaching, or study. Each monk was expected to discipline himself, keep his body in subjection, talk only when necessary and remain in the monastery's walls. Food was largely vegetable as meat was forbidden except for the sick or invalid.

Benedict went far toward eliminating the radical element in Monasticism. To an ascetic who chained a rock to his foot, Benedict said, "If thou art truly a servant of God, confine thyself not with a chain of iron, but with the chain of Christ." By the year 550 it is estimated that there were one hundred monasteries in Europe after the pattern of Monte Cassino.

The monastery was ready to receive all who wanted to take the sure way to heaven. This idea took from the church the most devout, whose leadership was badly needed. The monasteries, however, during the "dark ages" kept learning alive and preserved manuscripts that have been priceless as sources of information.

VIII. CONTROVERSY ON THE HUMAN WILL

Throughout the Apostolic Fathers there is no teaching that man is depraved by original sin or that he does not possess freedom of will. After the doctrine of original sin entered the church, there arose a violent controversy over the relation of the human will to divine grace and regeneration. One group emphasized that man of his own will could turn from sin and accept saving grace. The other group reasoned that man's sin so removed him from God that it required grace to bring man into a position to accept salvation. This controversy centered in the opposition of two men — Pelagius and Augustine.

Pelagius was a devout monk supposedly born in Briton. About the year 400 he visited Rome and was astonished by the state of morality he found among professed Christians. In

stressing the moral responsibility of the individual he emphasized that man had it in his power to overcome sin. After some
opposition to his views he formulated a system of theology
based upon the freedom of the human will. Leaving Rome and
visiting Palestine and North Africa in 411, he was opposed
strongly by Augustine and then condemned by two North African Synods. He believed that each human is born with no tendency toward either good or bad and with complete freedom to
choose his course. It is possible for a human to live without
committing sin and some probably have. Sin is an act of the
will and not transmitted through heredity. Each soul is created
at the time of birth and being made by God has no sin. Each
infant is born in the same condition as was Adam before his
fall. Children dying in infancy are saved and in no need of baptism. Baptism of infants cannot remove sin and could do no
more than consecrate them. Baptism for believers does remove
sin and is necessary for salvation. Death is not a result of
Adam's sin, and sin is not inherited but is the result of temptation. By good works a person can be saved apart from the death
of Christ. Grace is available to the sinner after he proves himself worth of it.

There are many worthy ideas in this view, but by nullifying
the need for atonement and over exalting man's ability to merit
goodness, the effect of sin and the need for the death of Christ
was misunderstood.

Augustine was born in Tagaste, North Africa in 354. His
mother, Monica, was a Christian and taught him the Christian
religion as a child. His father, however, was a pagan and
Augustine grew to manhood unconverted. He gives his own
life story in his confessions and tells how his evil desire came
on him early and how he became guilty of all the immorality of
his day. When nineteen years of age he became an auditor in
the sect of the Manichaeans and remained with this group for
nine years. He was interested in truth but thought Christianity
was for people who could not understand true philosophy.
Hearing Ambrose, bishop of Milan, he became more interested
in Christianity, but he had a strong desire to be married. He
thought that to be a real Christian one had to remain unmarried. His desire to both marry and become a Christian pro-

duced a strong mental conflict. Finally through violent emotional experience he overcame his desire to satisfy the flesh and gave himself to spiritual life. His experience with sin led him to believe that the individual was not responsible for his sinful nature and that became basic to his theological system. Augustine opposed Pelagius and taught that Adam had the choice of following God or sin. When he sinned, however, his soul became depraved and perverted. He not only was cast out of the garden, but he also could no longer have fellowship with God. This deprived him of any connection with good, and his nature was such that he could no longer choose the good. All of this depravity was transferred through heredity to his posterity. In this way every child shares the reality of original sin and is under the curse of the penalty imposed upon guilt. He makes birth itself the result of sinful concupiscence. This makes salvation the result of God's grace. It requires grace to start man in the direction of salvation; then grace is further given when through baptism past sins are forgiven. The Christian life is lived by grace, and it is not in man's power apart from this grace to move toward holiness.

Augustine does not deny man's freedom, but his explanation that "no one believes unless he wills" must be understood in the light of his belief that God makes it possible for man to will. This excludes any real freedom for man. His system maintains that those elected by God are predestined to eternal life and cannot resist His grace, but will persevere unto salvation. No one, however, can be sure that he is one of these elect.

It was not difficult to see that the view of Pelagius was unscriptural, for if man could save himself without the death of Christ, that death was in vain. The views of Augustine were accepted by many as the truth, but some were not satisfied. Pelagius held some truth and Augustine some error. Soon there appeared a compromise theory.

Chapter Thirteen

Theory and Organization of Roman Catholicism

THE THEORY OF ROMANISM

The theory that produced Medieval Romanism is centered in the idea that Christ left with the church officials all of the powers and privileges that He had exercised while on earth. These responsibilities were not only left with the church under the Apostles, but also were to continue in all ages to come. As this was contemplated it appeared that Christ had a three-fold ministry, and in Him resided the work of the prophet, the priest and the king of the Jewish era. These three functions were taken over by the hierarchy. In the prophet was seen the teaching functions of the church; in the priest was found the authority to mediate God's grace to man; and in the king the right to demand obedience and punish nonconformists.

I. THE TEACHING MINISTRY OF THE CHURCH

Because Jesus taught with infallible authority while on earth it was assumed that the church officials had the same authority. This did not mean that these officials taught the principles of the Bible as authoritative, but that these officials had the same right as Jesus in deciding what was true teaching. This supplied the hierarchy with authority to introduce traditions not found in the Scripture and give them an equal place of prominence with the Scripture itself.

As the hierarchy, through synods and councils, reached conclusions on points of differences the priests were held responsible in conveying the doctrines to the common people. If the priesthood enjoyed the same prerogative that Jesus had in teaching with authority, whatever the hierarchy handed down all Christians were under obligation to accept. This gave the priest a position of tremendous power. Since Christianity had been made the state religion, every citizen was considered a member of the church, and any who rejected the authorized doctrine was dealt with as a heretic. It was this theory and these assumed powers that brought the population of Western Europe under the domination of the papacy. In the enforcement of conformity to this theory there were sincere Christians who, continuing to follow the New Testament pattern, were eliminated for their opposition.

This theory made it unnecessary for the church membership at large to study the Bible as it was the priesthood's responsibility to tell them what to do. It also became unnecessary for the priest to study, because his instruction came from his superiors, and, accordingly, the services consisted of ceremonialism apart from instruction.

II.   THE PRIESTLY FUNCTION OF THE CHURCH

In the work Christ came to do there is nothing more vital than His work as High Priest. After atoning for man's sin on the cross He offered His blood to God as our priest and obtained eternal redemption for those who believe. The New Testament teaches this was done once and is valid for all time to come (Heb. 7:27; 9:12; 10:10-14). Through the high priesthood of Christ all Christians are priests.

The Medieval Roman church, however, functioned on the theory that when Christ left the earth, church officials were given the power to perform the services of the Priesthood, which were formulated into seven sacraments. The priesthood through these sacraments was to mediate God's grace to man.

All men are sinners through their own thought and act. To this was added the idea that children inherit sin and are born in a state of guilt before God. Salvation can be only by grace which was placed in the hands of the priesthood. Baptism took on magical powers — the act itself regenerating and removing sin. A baby's guilt of original sin was accordingly removed by baptism. This was supposed to be performed by a priest, but it was so important that the church made provision for others to perform it in cases of emergency. Through confirmation by the hands of a bishop a child from seven to twelve years of age was made capable of partaking of the communion and of receiving full church membership. The communion was given special significance. A properly ordained priest could do what no ordinary Christian, under any conditions, could do. He could by miracle turn the bread and wine into the actual body and blood of Jesus. This was done by going through a stipulated ceremony and uttering the proper "magical" words. After the ceremony the priest took the goblet of "blood" and held it up to God as an offering of the sacrifice of Christ. This is why it began to be called the "Sacrifice of the Mass." Christ was sacrificed every time communion was administered. No one seemed to recognize that this contradicted the Bible statement that the offering Christ made of His blood to God was "once for all" and that by "one offering he hath perfected for ever them that are sanctified," (Heb. 10:14). The Bible was not generally available among the membership of the churches of this period. This must account for much of the prevalent ignorance.

The sacrament of penance also gave the priesthood control over their subjects. When a person sinned he could not take communion until he had confessed to a priest. After the sinner had confessed his sin from a contrite heart the priest would make some requirement to impress the sinner with his guilt and to turn him to righteousness. It was believed the sin increased the amount of evil in the world, and to offset this the sinner must be required to do something to increase the amount of good. Whatever the priest required the person to do was called "satisfaction." Then after this "satisfaction" was performed the sinner went back to the priest to hear his sin pronounced forgiven. This step is called "absolution." Penance then consists of contrition, confession, satisfaction and absolution.

The fact that the pope represented God and through the priests could bestow or withhold God's grace made salvation impossible without submission to the terms of the priesthood. Marriage also came under the church's power with the result that no marriage was considered valid unless performed by a priest. In these ways the church officials were supposed to be able to bring men to God. It was made clear that apart from the services of the priesthood no man could reach God.

III.   The Kingly Function of the Church

As a king is supposed to make laws, judge conduct and punish the disobedient, the medieval Roman church assumed these kingly powers. Upon the basis that Christ left all of His powers with the church, officials began to act upon their assumed royal prerogative. Laws were created, and the disobedient were punished. These laws were taken from Roman civil law, from Scripture, from decrees of councils, decrees of popes and from Germanic law. All together these laws are known as "canon law." They deal with the organization, administration, worship and conduct of the church, morality, family life, vital statistics, education, business practice and every other phase of life.

Out of this theory grew an entire legal system that paralleled the civil courts and took over many of their cases. Offenders who were found guilty were punished and heretics, at times, were put to death. The medieval church officials had no question in their minds about having approval of God when they executed those who rejected their authoritative interpretation of religious matters. They overlooked that the sword of Christ is His word.

ORGANIZATION OF THE ROMAN CHURCH

Roman Catholicism is organized on the basis of a sharp line of cleavage between clergy and laity. It is a system of hierarchy and priestly rule. The clergy is carefully classified according to several divisions and standards.

I. The Regular Priests

After the development of monastic orders those priests who took up the monastic life were termed "regular" clergy, and the priests who lived and worked with the people were called "secular" clergy. The word regular comes from the Latin word "regula" and means under rule. These clergymen, then, who are under the rule of some order must be separated from those who serve in the parishes. The regular clergy may be sent as missionaries, or special teachers, or they may be assigned to care for the sick or to minister to the poor. They are ordinarily recognized by special robes or insignia representing their order.

II. The Secular Clergy

The secular clergy worked directly with the people in every day religious matters. They baptized babies, performed the ceremony of the mass, heard confessions, performed marriages and buried the dead. These priests were limited in their services by what is called "powers of orders" and "powers of jurisdiction."

III. POWERS OF ORDERS

Powers of orders had to do with stratification within the priesthood. There are two divisions—minor clerical orders and major orders. A young man desiring to become a priest must begin at the bottom and work up through the minor orders before he can become a priest and enter the major orders. Janitor is the first step. This is the responsiblity to keep the church roll and know the members. The next is the level of Reader, and as the name implies, such a one can read the Scripture in the service. The third step is called Exorcist and this gives the prospective priest the right to hold the water while a priest sprinkles babies. The next advancement makes one an Acolyte and brings him closer to sacred things and allows him to handle the vessels and assist in the mass. The last level of the minor orders is called Sub-Deacon which is the stage immediately prior to ordination.

After ordination the young priest enters the major orders and is called a Deacon. He works in connection with another experienced Priest for a time and then advances to the level called Priest. As a Priest he can administer five sacraments. Upon the death of a bishop, the priest might be selected to this high position and then be empowered to administer all seven sacraments. Archbishops and Cardinals are selected from among the Bishops, and the Pope is selected from among the Cardinals.

IV. POWERS OF JURISDICTION

Powers of jurisdiction refers to the size of geographical territory over which a priest is authorized to serve. A man may be a fully ordained priest, but until he is assigned a territory he is not allowed to use his abilities. The arrangement of territory is as follows:

1. Parish Priest

The smallest territory alloted to a priest is called a parish. The actual size depends upon the density of population and the number of church members. In this territory the priest teaches the people, administers five sacraments, mediates grace and imposes punishments upon the disobedient.

2. *Rural Dean.*

As the Roman system took form every priest was to be checked on by one in higher authority. The Rural Dean is a parish priest who has been given the added responsibility of checking on seven to twelve parish priests. He is supposed to see that they do their work properly and keep their financial records in good order.

3. *Vicar General*

To assist in the administration of dioceses, special migratory agents are used to check on the Rural Deans or Parish Priests. These officials, called Vicar General, are personal representatives of the bishop and with his authority can hold court and judge church officials, audit accounts and remove incompetent personnel. The Vicar General is selected or dismissed by the Bishop.

4. *Bishop.*

The Bishop is the highest ranking official in a diocese. He is supposed to visit each parish once a year and confirm the young people who have been prepared by the local priest. Confirmation and ordination are two sacraments that only the bishop administers. The Bishop holds court for cases that have been appealed from the decision of a Vicar General. He is also superintendent of education in his diocese and is supposed to maintain an institution for training priests.

5. *Archbishop.*

The Archbishop is a bishop with full responsibilities in his own diocese but is given added responsibility to check on twelve other bishops. He has a large staff of assistants to make this possible. The Pope selects the Archbishops and gives them a special pendant to hang around their neck as a symbol of special authority. This pendant is made of wool taken from the Pope's own sheep that graze in the Papal gardens. The Archbishop may have a territory as large as an entire nation.

6. *Papal Legate.*

The Roman system was thorough in seeing that no offiicial was left without a supervisor. To check on Archbishops or any official under them, the Pope selected Papal Legates to serve as his personal representative. They had power over all others and represented the Pope on special occasions. In this way there was erected a closely knit system in which responsibilty was carefully delegated and inefficiency easily located.

7. *The Pope.*

In the Roman organization the Pope is an elective monarch who rules by divine right and is an autocrat. This development was possible only after the episcopacy had prepared the way for it.

Leo I (440-461) was the first to set forth Papal claims on the basis of Scripture as proof. Matthew 16:16-19 was used as proof that the church was built upon Peter. Luke 22:32 was used to prove that Peter was given responsibility for the other brethren as an overseer, and Leo said John 21:15-19 gave Peter the responsibility to feed the sheep, which meant clergy, and feed the lambs, which meant the laity.

This sermon did much to change the course of history. The tradition that Peter was bishop of Rome gave great significance to the claim of his primacy. That Peter was martyred in Rome is in the realm of possibility, but the stories of his Roman bishopric are without foundation. Regardless of their accuracy, the stories — in apocryphal writings — were circulated as matters of fact and had almost as much influence.

The Pope relied upon the advice and support of the other bishops in the vicinity of Rome. These he formed into an advisory cabinet. They were looked upon as "hinge" men and given the name Cardinals from the Latin word "cardo" which means hinge, like the hinge on a door. At first there were seven men selected who served as an active cabinet. Later the number was increased and the position became somewhat honorary. In theory there are to be seventy cardinals. They are ranked in three levels. Fifty are Cardinal Priests, fourteen are Cardinal Deacons and six are Cardinal Bishops. All are either Bishops or Archbishops in the powers of orders, but in the college of cardinals they hold these additional ranks. The chief function of the college of cardinals is the election of the new Pope. When a Pope dies the cardinals meet in Rome and elect one of their own number to be the new Pope. The voting is done by secret ballot. This takes place behind closed doors (in "conclave" which means "under the key") and continues until a majority is reached.

In addition to the council of Cardinals there is an extensive bureaucratic organization with which the Pope must deal. This is called the "curia" and includes all of the administrative and business offices necessary to take care of such an extensive operation. Here is found directors of missions, of education or publications, etc. Such officers with their bookkeepers and secretaries require thousands of persons to keep up with the book work.

V. Undenominationalism Contrasted With Romanism

New Testament Church Based Upon Bible Authority

Apostolic Authority — Bible Authority — Departure

- Heresy
- Bible Neglected — Greek Catholicism
- The New Testament Church — Roman Catholicism
- Greek Catholicism — Protestantism
- Roman Catholicism — Modernism — Bible Authority

The Undenominational Church Remains Constant

1. Apostolic authority was left in the written Word, the New Testament, 1 Cor. 14:37; 2 Tim. 3:6; 2 Tim. 2:15.
2. Authority of Scripture remains constant in all ages and available to all generations.
3. Individuals coming to Christ through the inspired Scripture constitute the true church.
4. Faith centers in God through the inspired Word.

Roman Catholicism Based Upon Human Tradition

Apostles	100	150	325	440	600	1545	1875	1955
	Elders	Monarchal bishops	Patriarch, Monarchal bishops	Papal Claims	Pope	Tradition made equal to the Bible	Papal Infallibility proclaimed	Authority of hierarchy Papal Decrees
	Deacons	Elders		Patriarchs	Cardinals			
	Bible	Deacons	Priestly orders	Dioceson bishops	Curia			
		Synods	Council	Priests	Hierarchy			
		Bible	Tradition	Councils	Tradition			
			Bible	Tradition	Bible			
				Bible				

The Roman Church is the Result of Growing Tradition

1. Apostolic authority was left with church officials who were uninspired men.
2. Church officials kept oral traditions of men as commandments of God.
3. Tradition was enlarged.
4. The hope of salvation depends now upon submission to the hierarchy.
5. Faith centers in a blind hope that the traditions of the hierarchy are acceptable to God.

Chapter Fourteen

The Rise of Mohammedanism

Mohammed, the founder of Mohammedanism, was born in April 570 A.D. in the city of Mecca, Arabia. His father, Abdallah, died two months before his birth, and his mother, Amina, died when he was six years of age. When his mother died she gave him to his grandfather at whose death two years later he was given to an uncle.

One story is told that when he was born he opened his mouth and said, "God is great! There is no God but God, and I am his prophet." Another story has it that he was born with a symbol between his shoulders which indicated that he was going to be a prophet.

Mohammed's uncle, a merchant, took a great interest in him, and by taking him on caravans, taught him his trade. These journeys became the source of a story that, at the age of twelve, while Mohammed was on his first journey with the caravan to Syria, while traveling through the burning sands, that an angel hovered over him and protected him from the heat with his wings. At another time he was protected from noontide heat by a cloud over his head. At the age of twenty-five he became the chief merchant and camel driver for a rich widow named Khadija who wanted to carry on the business her husband had left. She offered Mohammed double wages to conduct a caravan to Syria, and he accepted the offer. On his return home she was so pleased with him she gave him double the amount they had agreed upon.

Mohammed was very handsome and Khadija fell in love with him. One day as Mohammed returned with a caravan she sent her slave, Maisara, out to him to propose marriage for her. He accepted the offer, and after the marriage Mohammed spent a great deal of time in meditation in a cave near Mecca. There he claimed to have received visions from the Almighty. He told how that God through the angel, Gabriel, had given him revelations concerning doctrines and precepts that heaven was designed for his countrymen. His wife did not believe him at first, but he finally converted her as well as his servant.

At the age of thirty-eight he went to the cave and stayed for two years. Then at forty he assumed the title, Apostle of God, with only his wife, his freed slave and his nephew, Ali, as converts.

It was not until four years later that he began to tell the people the things he had experienced at the cave and how he had received the Koran from God.

The leading ideas of all his discourses were that God is one, and that he himself was the prophet of God sent to declare His will to men. His opposition to idolatry turned the people against him. They tried to kill him and cast him out of the city, but his uncle protected him. During the first year of his public efforts he won only eight converts. After three years he announced his plan to overthrow the three hundred and sixty idols of Mecca. This created such opposition that he, with about eighty men and seven women, fled to Medina. This flight, known as the Hejira, took place on July 16, 622[1], which became the beginning date of the Moslem calendar of events.

At Medina, by eloquent preaching, he converted the whole city, except the Jews, and became dictator of the city. He set forth a six-fold program: (1) We will not worship any but the one God; (2) We will not steal; (3) We will not commit adultery; (4) We will not kill our children; (5) We will not slander; (6) We will not disobey the prophet in anything that is right.

At Medina by eloquent preaching he converted the whole vans. Those who would not become Moslems were killed. He said that anyone who died fighting would have a place in paradise. Hence the men fought with great courage because the point of the sword was their passport to heaven.

In 630 when he set out against his native city, Mecca, he traveled with ten thousand men, because he wanted to take the city by surprise. As they approached the city one of the leading men of the town was captured and brought to Mohammed. He proclaimed the faith and asked Mohammed not to destroy the city. Mohammed told him he would spare the people if they

1. Latourette calls the date "erroneous." Kenneth Scott Latourette, **History of Christianity**. (New York: Harper and Bros., 1953), p. 286.

would accept the faith. Accordingly, Mecca was taken with very little bloodshed.

Mohammed destroyed all the images in the Caaba and proclaimed the ground between Medina and Mecca holy ground. No non-believer should put foot on it. Upon becoming a conquering ruler Mohammed persecuted the Jews and reduced the Christians to dependency. He was sixty years old at the subjection of Mecca, but immediately planned further conquests. He unified Arabia and set the pattern followed by his successors who conquered three continents before his fanatical zeal was lost. A part of his power came from his dynamic personality, but part of it also came from the certainty with which he described his visions as actual events.

Among the many visions that Mohammed had one of the most outstanding was his night flight from Mecca to Jerusalem and from there to heaven on Alborah, his horse. Gabriel came one night and woke him up and told him he was sent to conduct him to the divine presence of God. They went out to get on Alborah, and he began to kick and buck. Gabriel told him to be still and let the prophet of God mount. After Mohammed told Alborah that he would have a place in heaven, he let him mount and they sailed through the air to Jerusalem where they briefly stopped and then went on to the first heaven. There they tied Alborah to a stone and began to climb the stairs to the gate where they found Adam. He embraced the prophet with great tenderness and thanked God that He had given him so great a son. He also saw the stars hanging from the roof on golden chains. This first heaven was pure silver. They then went on to the second heaven. At the rate of travel on earth it would have taken five hundred years, yet they reached it in an instant. It was pure gold. Here he met Noah. The third heaven was of precious stones and Abraham stayed here. He was a very large man. The distance between his eyes was seventy thousand days' journey, and his height was five million, forty thousand or four times as high as all his heavens put together. Joseph dwelt in the fourth heaven which was made of emerald. The fifth was the residence of Moses, and in the sixth was John the Baptist. In the seventh he found Jesus Christ and a very remarkable angel who had seventy thousand heads. In each head were seventy thousand tongues, and each tongue spoke seventy thousand distinct voices at once. Mohammed then came within two bow-shots of the throne of God and had his face covered with seventy thousand veils. Here he received things that were not lawful to utter, and he was told that he was the greatest man on earth. He returned to the rock where Alborah was tied and presently found himself at home. The next morning he related this to his followers, affirming that it was not just a vision, but that it was real. His followers accepted it and believe it until this day.

The sacred book of Mohammedanism, the Koran, means the "thing read." It is made up of speeches, statements and prayers of Mohammed. Some were dictated and some were written from memory. After his death they were gathered up and arranged according to length — the longest being placed first. The book contains many contradictions, but there is no way of separating the early teaching from the latter.

The Koran recognizes Adam, Abraham, Moses, Christ and John the Baptist all as prophets, but considers Mohammed the last and greatest. Many ideas are taken completely from the Old Testament such as the idea of God, the Devil and the Creation. The concept of heaven is that of a continuation of earth with all its sensual pleasures and the absence of evil. Marrying and childbirth will continue in heaven with each faithful man possessing a harem of beautiful ladies.

There are five obligations that each Moslem must assume. (1) Recite the Creed, "There is no God but Allah and Mohammed is the prophet of God; (2) Pray five times a day facing Mecca; (3) Partake of no food from sun-up till sun-down during the month of Ramadan; (4) Give alms to the poor, and (5) Make a pilgrimage to Mecca, if at all possible, during one's lifetime.

Friday is the day for public worship with every Moslem acting as his own priest. There is a strict moral code that allows no gambling or the use of wine. Pork is not to be used as food. Mohammed would allow no images. Children were to reverence their parents. Protection was to be given to widows and orphans and charity extended to the poor. Kindness was to be shown to slaves and animals. Wives were treated as property, and the husband was allowed "only" four at a time but there was no objection to making changes.

There are several reasons why the Arabs accepted the leadership of Mohammed. His plan offered an outlet for their energy. The excitement of conquest and the desire for plunder appealed to the desert peoples. As the movement gained momentum it became more economic and political than religious. The "heathen" who did not accept the new religion were allowed to worship as they pleased so long as they paid the required taxes. This within itself became a motive for conversion, for only the unbeliever had to pay taxes. In less than twenty-five years from the Hejira the followers of Mohammed had taken control of Egypt, Palestine, Persia and Syria. Within another one hundred and fifty years North Africa and Spain were included.

PART FOUR

THE GROWTH OF PAPAL POWER
787 - 1294 A.D.

Chapter Fifteen

Sources of Support for the Papacy

I. PAPAL RECOGNITION BY SECULAR RULERS

Shortly after Christianity received recognition by the Roman rulers, there was great impetus on missionary activity. Christians began to take the gospel to the heathen tribes outside the Roman empire. In the empire, heathen worship with its priesthood and temples began to fall into discredit. Soon Theodosius the Great (in 392) declared all heathen sacrifice treason, and Christianity was declared the state religion.

In the year 300 Constantine had moved his seat of government to a town called Byzantium. It was completely rebuilt and later named Constantinople. This move left a lesser official in Rome and gave opportunity for the Roman bishop to gain greater power. One reason for the move from Rome was to get further away from the pressure of the Northern Barbaric tribes.

These Northern tribes were soon successful in their push to the south, coming in hordes, overrunning Western Europe. In 476 the last of the Western Empires was dethroned.

A number of barbaric kingdoms were then set up; Visigoths (415-711) controlled Spain and Southern France; Ostrogoths (493-544) controlled Italy; Burgandians (443-534), South-Eastern France; Vandals (429-533), North Africa; and the Lombards (586-774), Northern Italy.

All of these Teutonic tribes accepted some form of Christianity either before or just after coming into the Roman Empire. Clovis, king of the Franks (481-511), decided to be baptized and then commanded that his whole army be baptized. In this manner the pagans were "Christianized" and the church paganized. It should be stated that although the barbarians "accepted" Christianity that fact did not keep them from capturing the city of Rome, plundering it of its treasures, burning its library and stabling their horses in the church buildings.

These Germanic tribes had accepted the Arian type of

(177)

Christianity and upon conquering the Empire found themselves in conflict with the theology of the Roman church. For a time there were two types of churches, the Arian and the Catholic. The pagans, however, felt inferior to the Romans because of their lack of culture and learning, which gradually brought them under the influence of the Roman church. The Franks accepted the Roman ideas, and as they became more powerful and influenced the other tribes they, too, soon came under Roman dominance.

It should be kept in mind that these invaders were illiterate and through their destruction of culture illiteracy soon swept the western world. Learning was kept alive in some monasteries, but the average person could not read or write. This was true of the average priest as well as layman.

In the midst of political turmoil and chaos the people longed for a strong centralized authority which could restrain lawlessness and restore order. The rulers remembered the power and glory of the Roman Emperors and desired such distinction, but centralized political power was not to be again seen for many years.

Throughout this period the Roman Bishop was a stabilizing influence in society. The chain of universal authority over all religious activities gave encouragement to would-be emperors and provided a means of unification for one king.

The invasion of Western Europe by the Moslems necessitated a unification of forces if their advance was to be stopped. Charles Martel (714-741) with the aid of the pope arose to the occasion and repulsed the Moslems. The people of Europe had been duly frightened, and in this way it was Islam which indirectly consolidated the political power and increased papal power. The pope used his position to achieve political unity, and in return the ruler was glad to acknowledge and increase his spiritual power.

When Charles died in 741 and his son Pepin took the throne, the pope gave him his official blessing with Pepin's returning the favor by protecting the pope and giving to him the temporal rule of territory which he took from the Lombards. This, in 756, was the first time a pope was given temporal rule. This, however, laid the foundation for the church-state and for the pope's being called the Duke of Rome.

When Pepin died in 768, the kingdom was divided between Charlemagne and his brother Carloman. When Carloman died in 771 Charlemagne took control of the entire kingdom, attempting to strengthen and enlarge it. He desired the blessing of the pope, hoping it would strengthen his position and remove any claim of Carloman's children to part of the Empire. His opportunity came when the Lombard king invaded the pope's territory. Charlemagne entered Italy with a great army, defeated the Lombards and went to Rome to enlarge the pope's temporal kingdom. He was received with a great celebration, and on Christmas day, 800, Pope Leo III placed a crown upon his head and proclaimed him crowned by God, Augustus. In return Charlemagne increased the pope's territory and assured his continuation as a secular ruler.

Charlemagne looked upon himself as a king in the same position as David, telling the pope:

"It is my bound duty, by the help of the divine compassion everywhere to defend outwardly by arms the whole church of Christ against every attack of the heathen, and every devastation caused by unbelievers; and, inwardly, to defend it by the recognition of the general faith. But, it is your duty, holy father, to raise your hands to God, as Moses did, and to support my military service by your prayer."

From this time the Western Emperors worked to strengthen the papacy. Although Charlemagne submitted to coronation by the Roman pope, he neither looked upon the church as his superior, nor did he recognize the pope as having supremacy over the crown. On the other hand, Charlemagne assumed active leadership in the work of the church. He directed missions, sponsored ecclesiastical legislation, strengthened church government and supervised the election of bishops and was quite active in the establishment of schools and monasteries and in the formulation of educational standards. He was very energetic in the selection of missionaries and in sending them to all parts of the world. However, he boldly opposed the pope on the question of the worship of images. As the result of his activity image worship was not practiced in the churches north of the Alps until the beginning of the eleventh century. Charlemagne further organized the church by adopting a system of metropolitans. As he divided his empire into twenty-one chief districts he set up an archbishop in each one of these districts and increased the number of bishoprics as well. He bestowed large grants upon monasteries and provided property for the support of the parish priests. He made church property tax-free and decreed that church matters should be settled in ecclesiastical courts instead of being brought into the regular secular courts.

After the death of Charlemagne his empire was divided between his three grandsons, but in 962 Otto the Great re-unified the empire and was crowned Emperor of the Romans. With him what is known as the Holy Roman empire of the German nation had its beginning.

At this time the secular empire with the Emperor on one hand and the spiritual empire with the pope at its head on the other, were theoretically counterparts of one another. However, in actual historical development, they were in mortal combat. Three theories developed in regard to the relationship of pope and Emperor. (1) The pope and the Emperor were each independently commissioned by God to rule in a separate sphere. (2) The Emperor was superior to the pope in secular affairs. Advocates of this theory worked upon the basis that Pepin the Second and Charlemagne, by granting gifts to the pope, had made the popes vassals to the Emperor. (3) The temporal power was subordinate to the spiritual even in worldly affairs. During the latter medieval period there is evidence of the struggle between the pope and the Emperor as to who would emerge with the greatest power. During the eleventh, twelfth and thirteenth centuries feudalism was the dominant social, political and economic order and no effective central government could be maintained. Under a form of feudalism, the land was held in trust by a vassal to a lord, and there existed a very close personal bond between the vassal and his landlord. The vassal was to give service to his lord in return for protection. The lords were considered vassals to the kings and the kings in turn considered vassals to the Emperor. The Emperor was considered God's vassal. The pope, however, claimed that he was God's vassal on earth and, accordingly, the kings should receive their authority from the pope. To strengthen his own position, Otto the Great (936-973) donated large estates of land to the church and elevated certain bishops to feudal lordship. He attempted to restore the Holy Roman Empire by relying upon the power of the church. The result of this policy was to strengthen the secular power of the church. Since the church was dependent upon the Emperor for the increase of its temporal authority and territory, the bishops of the church were willing to receive their appointment from the Emperor. The appointing of an official to a church position is referred to as investiture. Beginning with Otto the Great, it became traditional for the king or Emperor to invest the bishops with their offiice by giving them his staff and episcopal ring. These symbols bestowed not only temporal jurisdiction, but also the right to serve as officials in the church. The Emperor granting investiture in this way brought the displeasure of the pope upon himself, for by doing so the Emperor rather than the pope was claiming to be God's representative on earth. With the growth of nationalism and the power of investiture in secular hands, it looked for a time like the Roman Catholic Church would be divided into national churches. However, the Emperor kept only a semblance of authority over the entire Empire, and the church was held together with the theory that as the Emperor was the head of the Empire, he was also nominal head of the church. During this period the Emperors appointed the popes. In 1046 Henry III deposed three rival popes and appointed a German bishop head of the church. The German Emperor following this procedure also appointed the next three succeeding popes. During this period there is no question but that the Emperor was the head of the church and was so recognized by all in Western Europe. The popes would not acknowledge that they were subservient to the Emperor as head of the church, however, and the time was to come when the popes would gain complete authority not only over the church but also over Emperors as well.

The Emperors had exalted the popes by granting them secular power and made them second in authority only to themselves. The story of the conflict between the Emperors and the strong popes that were to come will be discussed in a later chapter.

II. PAPAL SUPPORT FROM FALSE DOCUMENTS

From the time of Leo I (440-461) there were elements in

the Latin church which tended to exalt the Roman Bishop. In every period of religious ferment there is an inclination to strengthen the opinions of the present by an appeal to the past. The desire to elevate the papacy above the emperor continued throughout the entire medieval period. In a contest such as took place between the pope and the Emperor, it is not surprising that evil forces would come to the front with skilled forgeries and shrewd manipulation of historical events in order to place the pope in supreme authority.

During the seventh century a Spanish Archbishop by the name of Isidore began to make the church in Germany acquainted with a number of important classical and patristic writings. Isidore died in 636 and left behind a great reputation for mental and moral accomplishment. His reputation was used as authority for forgery which favored the authority of the Roman bishop above that of the political rulers. The age was uncritical, and for a while the entire church was deceived. It seemed the church officials welcomed the deception, and the true nature of the false documents was concealed long enough to strengthen every branch of the ecclesiastical authority and to place the pope in a position of supreme authority.

These false documents are known as the Pseudo-Isidorian Decretals. Isidore, during his life time had written a collection of important works which were used legitimately to contribute to the centralization of ecclesiastical authority in Rome. The idea came to someone that additional works could be set forth under his name that would add great prestige to the Roman bishop. Such writings were designed and set forth as the decrees of former councils. It was pretended that these decrees had recently been discovered and were authentic. It was not long before they were scattered over the entire Empire and used extensively to build the prestige of the Roman Bishop. The forger boldly set forth alleged decrees of unknown councils and quoted letters that claimed to have been written by Clement of Rome and Anacletus who were Bishops at Rome contemporary with the Apostles. The forger continued by quoting about thirty of the Apostolic Fathers themselves, producing statements that they never made. The document was divided into three parts. The first contained additions to the authentic Apostolical canons by adding fifty-nine spurious writings of Roman bishops from Clement I to Melchiades and extending from the end of the first century to the beginning of the fourth. It was claimed that Constantine made a donation of territory to the papacy and recognized the spiritual superiority of the Roman bishop over all other bishops. The second part of the work consisted of authentic canons of various synods. The third section presented some true decrees but in addition added thirty-five spurious ones, which were purportedly written at various times from Sylvester I who died in 335 to Gregory II who died in 731.

Before discussing the relationship of the pope to the bishops as set forth in these false decrees, let us notice first the section referred to as the "Donation of Constantine." This document tells how Constantine was afflicted with leprosy and states that Peter and Paul appeared to him in a vision, telling him to have Pope Sylvester come and baptize him three times for the cleansing of his leprosy and removal of his sin. According to the document, Constantine did this and was healed of his leprosy. He then exalted Sylvester and states that:

> "Since he (Sylvester) is seen to have been set up as the vicar of God's Son on earth, the pontiffs who act on behalf of that prince of the apostles should receive from us and our empire a greater power of government that the earthly clemency of our imperial serenity is seen to have conceded to them; for we choose the same prince of the apostles as his vicars to be our constant witness before God. And inasmuch as our imperial power is earthly, we have decreed that it shall venerate and honor his most holy Roman Church and that the sacred seed of the blessed Peter shall be gloriously exalted above our empire and earthly throne."[1]

The document exalts the pope above all religious officials in the world, sets forth the Roman Bishop as a successor of Peter and Paul and then grants to him temporal authority. The palace and jurisdiction over Rome and all Italy as well as the regions of the west were also among the "donations."

This part of the document played a very important part in subsequent controversies over the authority of the pope. Its authority was unquestioned until the fifteenth century when its authenticity was questioned by many eminent scholars and its falsity finally proved by Lorenzo Valla. It is now completely

1. Bettenson, 140.

discredited by scholars of the Roman church as well as all other students of church history. Although the document is entirely discredited, it exercised very great influence upon the development of the Roman papacy. On the basis of it later Emperors donated territorial privileges and sovereignty to the bishops of Rome.

It is believed that Nicholas I (858-867) was the first pope to make use of the Decretals to increase the spiritual authority of the papacy in the world. The rest of the document, dealing with the relationship of the pope and the bishops, was used to strengthen the papacy within the church. This section of the document sets forth the bishops in the same relationship as the Apostles to Peter. This emphasis seems to have been made especially to curtail the development of power by the archbishops and to bring them into greater subjection to the pope. It is apparent that certain archbishops were keeping the bishops of their territory in subjection to themselves rather than the bishop of Rome. This is further indicated in the fact that the document declares that provincial synods cannot be held without being summoned by the pope. This seems to indicate rather definitely that the author of the document was working to bring the archbishops into submission to the papacy. The document further distinguishes between clergy and laity, designating the clergy a divine family or "spirituals" and the lay people "carnals." This indicates that the priests were setting forth a distinction between clergy and laity. Another reason for this conclusion is that the document declares that none of the clergy were to be summoned before a secular court, that a layman could not accuse a priest, and that if a charge was brought against a bishop it could not be received in the ecclesiastical court unless there were seventy-two trustworthy witnesses to substantiate the charge.

On the basis of this false document Nicholas I exalted the papacy in every conceivable manner. He not only claimed supremacy, but also carried out the claim by deposing and excommunicating Photius, the patriarch of Constantinople, and by humbling John, the archbishop of Ravenna, to complete submission. He likewise humbled Archbishop Hinkmar of Reims, whom he forced to reinstate a deposed bishop. Nicholas was also successful in demanding that King Lothair II take back his divorced queen. Such action distinguished Nicholas as the strongest pope that had ever occupied the position. In exercising such assumed authority he set a pattern for still stronger popes that were yet to come.

The Pseudo-Isidorean Decretals were questioned as early as the fifteenth century, but it was the seventeenth century reformed theologian Blondel that proved them to be false. After his evidence was presented, scholars of the Roman church acknowledged that they were false documents, but by this time they had accomplished their purpose. These false documents gave the papacy a strength that it would not otherwise have been able to achieve. After having gained the power which it did, the Catholic Church refused to surrender it even though the basis on which it was attained was proven to be false.

III. PAPAL SUPPORT FROM HIERARCHY

In tracing the rise of papal power one is impressed with the many forces which were used to strengthen papal claims. We have seen how the pope strengthened the Emperor and how the Emperor in turn strengthened the pope. In a similar way the hierarchy supported the pope and the pope provided for the hierarchy.

There can be no doubt that the establishment of the papacy was the result of a gradual development toward centralization of authority. From congregational autonomy — each church ruled by a plurality of elders — there developed in order the monarchal bishop, diocesan bishop, patriarch and finally the pope.

This organization was supported by the theory of apostolic succession with the pope as the successor of Peter, head of the church and God's representative on earth. After recognition of the pope on this basis the hierarchy became the army of obedient followers supporting his claims and carrying out his orders. We have seen the type of line and staff organization which developed. Each priest was made to feel a dependency upon his superiors. Obedience without question was required. This system gave the pope loyal, obedient, servants in every community who could effectively influence the life of Western Europe.

In order to enforce the pope's will two weapons were

ready at hand. One was excommunication and the other the interdict. By excommunication the priest could cut off any individual from receiving divine grace. As the pope was God's representative he could use the keys and bind or loose man's sin. Since this power came from the pope down through the hierarchy, each parish priest could prevent the disobedient from reaching God. During the medieval period there was no question in the mind of the average person but that this was according to God's will. Because of this the priest was a man to be feared and obeyed. Excommunication, however, not only severed one's connection with the church, it also made one a social outcast and during this period removed all privileges of citizenship. This weapon was sufficient to keep the average person in a state of submission to the pope.

In conflict with temporal rulers the pope used a more powerful weapon, the interdict. This required the priests to refuse to serve in their priestly capacities. If a king or prince was displeasing to the pope, the pope could retaliate by requiring all priests in his territorly to refuse to serve mass, perform marriages or bury the dead until the ruler repented. In this way pressure from the people would force the ruler to submit.

As administrators of the sacraments the hierarchy further strengthened the papacy. For the people were taught that the sacrament had no value unless performed by a properly ordained administrator. Since ordination found meaning only through the pope, the sacraments in turn received their validity through papal authority.

With this understanding of the sacraments and the hierarchy, one can readily think of the common people constituting the base of a pyramid. Above them were the parish priests, the bishops, archbishops and the pope at the top reaching with one hand into heaven to receive his authority from God and exercising his authority downward through the hierarchy to the common people. This is a clear picture of the medieval Catholic church. Church officials mentioned that man could reach God only by going through the hierarchy and the pope. Outside of this arrangement there was no hope of obtaining God's grace. This demonstrates how the secular clergy strengthened the papacy.

The regular clergy in the monastic orders also was used

to increase papal power. The orders themselves were chartered by the pope, and each monk was made to feel his dependence upon papal authority.

In all of the monastic orders obedience to superiors was strongly emphasized. Gregory the Great, who was the first strong pope, had served as a Benedictine monk, and after having been made pope he did much to strengthen the Benedictine order. Through his efforts the monasteries were unified and brought together under his will. Throughout the history of the church the monastic orders have been one of the strongest sources of support for the papacy.

The college of cardinals, a special advisory council to the pope which began as a small committee of priests in the churches of Rome, was gradually expanded into an international organization. By the year 1059 the Lateran council approved this expansion program, and from that date on Cardinals have been found in all countries where the Roman Catholic church had any strength and have become an important agency for expanding papal power toward world supremacy. The papacy has lost no opportunity to strengthen its position wherever possible. Through the use of papal legates formal alliances have been made with kings and feudal lords expanding the power of the pope in this manner to every part of the world.

In addition to the pope's being supported through the hierarchy in these matters of practical application of his authority, the hierarchy has also rendered great service toward papal supremacy by setting forth a literary defense of the papal claims. This reached its height during the work of a group of men known as the Scholastics. The word Scholasticism goes back to the schools as founded in the monasteries. Especially is this true after the time that Charlemagne re-established Christian learning and gave emphasis to the ecclesiastical schools. Scholasticism is a system of philosophy which emanated from these schools and became the expression of Catholic faith for several centuries. The purpose of the Scholastics was to defend the truth of Catholic Christianity by the process of cold logic. The Scholastics did not question Catholic dogma but accepted all of the conclusions of traditionally developed Catholicism and set out by the use of logic to prove that this doctrine and organization was correct. Beginning in the ninth century it continued its influence until it reached its height in the early part of the thirteenth century. Most of the Scholastics were monks from the various monasteries who spent their time in systematizing and organizing the faith and doctrine of the church on the basis of the Scripture interpreted in the light of tradition. They made an analysis of grace as it is manifest through the sacraments and worked out a system of legalistic emphasis. They maintained strongly that the service of a priest was essential to the efficacy of the sacrament. This secured the place of the Roman hierarchy as serving in a mediatory position between God and man. As a result of the work of these Scholastics the Lateran Council in 1215 gave official sanction to the doctrine of transubstantiation and the requirement that every individual must make confession to the priest at least once a year. The Scholastics also reorganized and systematized cannon law to give absolute power to the pope. The result of their work was to bring the common people into strict adherence to the laws of the church, obedience to the clergy and regular use of the sacraments. Thus they established a rational explanation for the Roman system of religion.

The system of sacraments and a hierarchy found its greatest support in the theory of papal power. The stronger the pope the more dependent the people became and the more important grew the priesthood. Theory, system and operation all worked together to strengthen papal power. Before the papal system could be overthrown the fallacy of its foundation claims had to be pointed out. This was the work of the Reformers.

Chapter Sixteen

The Strong Popes

Leo I (440-461) attempted to establish the historic papacy. He was a man of strong intellect and did much to bring power and prestige to the Roman bishop. It cannot be accurately said, however, that Leo ever became head of the church on a world-wide basis.

By the time of Gregory I (590-604) conditions had so changed that it was possible for him to put the papacy on a stronger foundation. Gregory was born in an ancient Patrician family at Rome in the year 540. His family had great hopes that he would give himself to the service of the government. The family had all the advantages which wealth could bring and accordingly received an excellent education. He very early became interested in the affairs of the church and became a deacon under Pelagius who was at that time bishop. Working with Pelagius, he was sent as a representative of the court of the Emperor to Constantinople. Upon the death of Pelagius he returned to Rome and was selected bishop. Gregory was very active in literary work as well as administrative. He wrote a commentary on the book of Job and being himself a brilliant preacher wrote a handbook entitled *Pastoral Rule*. After becoming a bishop he devoted himself without reservation to strengthening the position of the Roman bishop. He began to enforce strict monastic discipline and took great interest in missionary activity. He seemed to have the greatest interest in evangelizing England and was especially solicitous in sending detailed instructions for this work. Gregory became active in reorganizing church finances and was so successful that he was able to raise an army and pay the expenses of war. On the basis of his own successes he made peace with the Lombard king and enjoyed a greater position of honor in secular administration. One of his chief conflicts was with the patriarch of Constantinople, John the Faster, who had assumed the title "universal bishop." Gregory was successful in causing a revocation of this title, but instead of adopting the same title for himself he said that he was a servant of the servants of God. As an administrator he established the Archbishopric of Canterbury and brought the churches of France, England, Spain and Africa substantially under his control. In doctrinal matters he established the doctrine of purgatory, the merit of good works and placed greater emphasis on the mass and the eucharist. After Gregory the Great no pope following him until Nicholas I (858) was able to maintain the same authority. Between Gregory and Nicholas there are listed in the Catholic Abstract of Title the names of forty-one popes. Many of these tried to maintain papal supremacy but were unsuccessful. The bishops of Constantinople consistently refused to recognize the supremacy of the Roman bishop. With the ascension of Nicholas I in 858, however, the situation changed. Nicholas was an able administrator and in practice demanded obedience to the pope as the supreme head of the church who was responsible for the spiritual welfare of all people. He insisted both in actual practice and through weighty written documents that the pope was not only head over the church but was also head over temporal rulers in matters of morals and religion. Nicholas made extensive use of the Pseudo-Isidorian Decretals for proof that the claims he made were recognized from the beginning as the will of God. Acting upon the support of these false documents, he forced bishops to become submissive to his will and created such pressure upon Lother II of Loraine that he set aside a second wife that he had married and reinstated his first wife to her rightful place. Nicholas decreed that a bishop could appeal directly to the pope without going through his archbishop. On occasions he reversed the decisions of archbishops and brought them into submission. In a conflict with the patriarch of Constantinople Nicholas supported Ignatius a former patriarch whom the Emperor Michael had removed from office, replacing him with Photius. Nicholas declared Photius deposed, but a synod under the leadership of Photius accused Nicholas and the Western church of heresy. The Eastern bishops refused to acknowledge the "pope" in the West.

After the death of Nicholas there came to papal power forty-three popes of lesser ability. Benedict IX, who became pope in 1033, created such a scandal that he was driven from

Rome and replaced by Sylvester III. Benedict, however, managed to return to the city and maintain his claim that he was the rightful pope. On the basis of his claim he sold the papacy to Gregory VI. Gregory began to claim papal power, but Benedict decided that he would continue in office, and so for a period of time there were three men claiming the title of pope. Henry III, who at this time was Emperor of the Holy Roman Empire, called a council to meet in the city of Sutri in the year 1046. This council deposed both Benedict and Sylvester and then required Gregory to resign. Clement II replaced him. Clement soon died, however, and Henry the Emperor exalted his cousin Bruno to the papal throne as Leo IX. The official Abstract of Popes of the Catholic Church lists Benedict IX (1033-1044), Gregory VI (1044), then skips to Clement II (1046) which indicates that during this two year period the Catholic officials have not come to a decision as to who was the rightful pope. Leo IX, a strong man in his own right, had a very able assistant in the person of Hildebrand, who became an advisor of popes and later pope himself (Gregory VII). Leo IX, however, had a very serious problem on his hands. His army was defeated by the Normans in Italy in 1053, and Cerularius Patriarch of Constantinople, began to bring discredit upon the authority of the Roman bishop. Cerularius was able to close all of the monasteries and the churches of Constantinople which were loyal to the Roman pope. He also influenced the Patriarch of Achrida of Bulgaria to write to the bishops of southern Italy and refer to all of the errors propagated by the Roman church. This instigated a very bitter struggle between Rome and Constantinople. Leo sent delegates to Constantinople in an attempt to bring about unity and restore his authority over certain churches and monasteries. But rather than producing unity the conferences led to a permanent division of the Eastern and Western churches. This final break took place July 16, 1054, and shall be discussed in detail later.

During the reign of Victor II (1055-57) and Stephen X (1057-58) Hildebrand continued to be the power behind the throne. In 1059 Nicholas II was made pope and served for two years under the supervision of Hildebrand. In order to strengthen the position of the pope Hildebrand was able to have the election of the pope taken out of the hands of the Roman people and put under the control of the college of Cardinals. This took place in 1059, and the law creating this machinery has remained in effect until today and is considered the oldest election law in existence. Hildebrand worked diligently to reform the church and increase the papal power according to the ideals set forth in the Pseudo-Isidorian Decretals. He made great effort to eliminate abuses from the conduct of the clergy and to suppress both simony and marriage. Hildebrand was especially eager to take the power of ordaining church officials out of the hands of secular rulers and establish it firmly in the hands of the pope. Nicholas began to use papal legates in a very effective manner, and soon the international aspect of the Roman church began to be felt. Under the guidance of Hildebrand an alliance was made with the Normans of Southern Italy which provided the pope with a strong army. When Nicholas II died in 1066, Hildebrand was able to influence the college of Cardinals to select the candidate he desired, Alexander II (1061-1073). Hildebrand was becoming very successful in bringing the papacy to its great height as a real power in world affairs. With Alexander II sitting in the papal chair Hildebrand was able to form an alliance with the king of France and subdue feudal lords who were successful in bringing the entire Spanish church under the control of Rome. With the aid of the Army of Normandy. William the Conqueror invaded England at Hildebrand's suggestion and brought the church of England under Roman control. The church in Germany was the next stronghold to be completely subjected to the Roman pope. Up to this point Hildebrand felt that he could accomplish more for the papacy by not serving as pope than he could by holding the position. But after strengthening the papacy to this extent he was willing in 1073 to accept the position himself. Upon acquiring the office he immediately set forth his theory of papal power. He believed that the entire world should be in subjection to the pope as God's representative on earth. He claimed absolute world supremacy and acted in harmony with his conception. He stated:

"The Roman Church was founded by God alone; the Roman pope alone can with right be called universal; he alone may use the imperial insignia; his feet alone shall be kissed by all princes; he may depose the Emperor; he himself may be judged by no one; the Roman church has never erred, nor will it err in all eternity."[1]

Hildebrand as Pope Gregory VII caused the Lateran Council of 1074 to decree that celibacy of the clergy must be enforced. Although it had been talked about for years, up until this time nearly all of the priests had maintained wives or concubines. In many places the priestly office had been transferred from father to son. This decree would eliminate the hereditary principle in holding church offices and strengthen the authority of the pope over the clergy by requiring papal appointment. In conflict with the German rulers who had assumed power to appoint church officers, Gregory VII through the Lateran Council of 1075 issued a decree forbidding any priest or bishop to receive his bishopric or any abbot to receive his abbey from the hands of a secular prince. This included the king and the emperor. Gregory insisted that investiture should be from the pope only as God's supreme representative in the world. Due to the system of feudalism the kings of Germany had placed bishops in their Sees over church lands, making them feudal lords who felt a responsibility and loyalty to the secular authority. Gregory determined to change this loyalty from secular rulers to the pope. This is referred to as the "investiture controversy." Henry IV, king of Germany, immediately declared Gregory VII deposed as pope. Gregory replied by excommunicating Henry IV and placing Germany under the interdict. This was in 1076. Gregory then made a trip to Germany for the purpose of bringing the German official under his control. The excommunication weighed so heavily upon Henry that he saw the futility of trying to continue under it. So hearing that Gregory was coming into Germany, he made a trip to Canossa to request that the excommunication be removed. Gregory refused to admit Henry to his presence and required that in penitence he wait three days in the court yard outside the castle where Gregory was staying. Finally at the conclusion of the period of penance Gregory allowed Henry to kneel at his feet and receive forgiveness.

Henry had bowed before Gregory but it was an unwilling submission. This did not at all end the investiture controversy

1. B. J. Kidd. Documents, illustrative of the History of the church. (London Society for promoting knowledge, 3 volumes, 1920-1941), Vol. 3. pp. 129-130.

for Henry continued to work against the power of the papacy. Gregory later excommunicated Henry a second time, but by this time Henry had the support of Germany behind him and he invaded Italy and drove Gregory into exile where he died in 1085. Henry then selected Wilbert as pope and had him crown himself before he left Italy. The controversy over investiture, however, was not settled until a later time. And after all Gregory's efforts to raise the power of the papacy it looked at this time that it might all be in vain as the pope was again appointed by the emperor. But Gregory had established the ban on clerical marriage and to some extent reduced the practice of simony. In 1211 at the Concordat of Worms the pope and the emperor finally agreed that all elections of bishops and abbots should be done according to the laws of the church but under the supervision of the emperor and that the right of spiritual investiture by ring and staff belonged to the pope. The emperor should exercise the right of investiture by a touch of the scepter as an emblem of secular authority. Thus the investiture controversy was finally settled by a compromise. The church would supervise spiritual matters with the state giving legal and secular sanction.

During the next one hundred years eighteen popes attempted to maintain the papacy on the level set by Gregory VII. But it was Innocent III who occupied the papal throne from 1198 to 1216 who brought the papacy to the zenith of its power. He was born into a family of Roman nobility and given an excellent education in law and theology. He was characterized by sincerity, humility, piety. But at the same time he was a man of great vigor and intelligence. He accepted as an established fact the theory that the pope was the supreme authority on earth and believed that kings and princes derived their authority from the pope. On this basis he thought that he had power to excommunicate or depose any emperor on earth. He used the illustration of the sun and the moon to illustrate that as the moon is inferior to the sun in radiance so the secular authorities are inferior to the spiritual; that as the moon gives the reflected light of the sun so the secular authorities reflect the glory of the pope, who in turn receives his radiance directly from God. The first contest between the pope and civil rulers came when Philip Augustus of France forced the French bishops to annul his marriage to Ingeborg, his first wife, in 1193. Philip then married Agnes De Meran. Ingeborg appealed to the pope, and Innocent ordered Philip to put away Agnes and take her back as his lawful wife. When Philip refused to obey this command, Innocent placed the entire nation of France under the interdict. By this move the priests of France went on a sit down strike and were not permitted to open the church buildings to perform the mass or render any of the customary services of the priesthood. This created such resentment on the part of the people of France against Philip that he was forced to put away Agnes and bring back Ingeborg as his lawful wife. Likewise Innocent used the interdict in England to force King John into placing the archbishop that Innocent had selected in a position of authority. In 1213 John was forced to acknowledge that he held the kingdom of England as a feudal vassal of the pope and agreed to pay the pope an annual sum of one thousand marks. Innocent then took a hand in the selection of the emperor of the Holy Roman Empire and was successful in having his candidate elected. In order to accomplish this Innocent had strengthened the king of France and used him against the Holy Roman Empire. Later this powerful French state was to turn against the pope. By skillful manipulation Innocent III stood as the leading figure of Europe in his day. He took a hand in the crusades against the Moslems and also led a bloody crusade against the Albigenses who were a protestant type religious group opposing papal supremacy. While the pope was increasing this power over secular rulers the spirituality of the clergy was not maintained.

It is said that Boniface VIII (1294-1303) "came in like a fox, ruled like a lion and died like a dog." The story is told that he inserted a reed between cracks in the masonery next to where the former pope slept and each night whispered, "It is God's will that thou shouldest resign." The old pope decided that it was God talking to him and on his resignation Boniface VIII succeeded in obtaining his position. He began to rule with all of the authority of Innocent III. It was not long, however, before he came in conflict with Philip the Fair of France. In order to support his army Philip taxed the land held by the clergy. The church held one third of the land of Western Europe and had been paying no taxes on the property. In 1296

Boniface issued a decree that forbade the priests' paying taxes to temporal rulers under threat of excommunication. Edward of England had also been levying taxes upon the clergy and he replied to the pope's decree by having Parliament pass an act forbiding the clergy to regard the pope's demands. Philip responded to the decree of Boniface by forbidding the exportation of any money out of France into Italy, thus depriving the pope of all of French revenue. In the conflict that followed Philip called the French Estates General, the legislative body, into session and asked for their support in opposition to the pope. Since at this time a new nationalism had arisen in France, the people supported the king against the Roman Pontiff. Boniface replied by setting forth the papal claims in the bull Unam Sanctum (1302). In this he stated that outside the Catholic church "there is neither salvation nor remission of sins." Peter was the successor of the Lord and had been given responsibility over all the peoples of the earth. The church, through Peter, wields two swords, the spiritual and the temporal, both of which are in the control of the church. He goes on to state that if the earthly power err it can be judged by the pope. If the pope err he can be judged by God alone. He concludes by saying, "Furthermore, we declare, state, define and pronounce that it is altogether necessary to salvation for every human creature to be subject to the Roman Pontiff."[2]

Boniface had no army to support his claims, so Philip with the backing of the French people invaded Italy and temporarily imprisoned Boniface. Such humiliation resulted in the loss of his sanity and he soon died. Philip then had Clement V proclaimed pope, and under his control Clement annuled all the papal acts that were contrary to the desires of Philip. The papal court was then transferred from Rome to Avignon where it remained for seventy years. This period is referred to as the Babylonian Captivity of the church during which time the papacy became a toy in the hands of French kings. It never again regained the prominent position that it had held under Innocent III.

2. Ibid., 163.

Chapter Seventeen

The Crusades

The twelfth and thirteenth centuries are characterized by mass migrations of people from Western Europe into the near East for the purpose of recovering the Holy Lands from the Turks. These are referred to as the Crusades.

From the time that Helena, the mother of Constantine, surveyed Palestine for the purpose of establishing the location of important events in the life of Christ, devout Christians have desired to revisit the land where Jesus spent His earthly existence. After the development of the sacrament of penance, pilgrimages were looked upon as a peculiar means of acquiring merit in heaven. When the Mohammedan Arabs took possession of Palestine in the seventh century, it became difficult for Christians to visit the places where Jesus lived and died for their sins. The Seljuk Turks captured the Holy Land in 1073 and it became even more difficult to safely visit these sacred places. The Turks were also threatening the borders of the Empire, and the Emperor Alexius was greatly disturbed at their increasing power. In 1092, upon the death of Malik Shah, the Turkish Empire was thrown into civil war, and Alexius saw an opportunity to gain a victory over the Turks if he could obtain support from the West. Accordingly, he appealed to the pope of Rome, Urban II, to assist him in driving the Turks out of the Holy Land.

Urban convened a synod at Clermont, France, in 1095. On this occasion he urged that the people of France with the support of western Europe lead a crusade to drive the Turks from Palestine. It is difficult to know all of the motivating influences that caused the people to respond to this call. A number of influences, however, can be determined. Among these is the consideration that famine in Western Europe had created economic distress, and many men were eager to go on a crusade hoping to re-establish themselves financially. It is also known that the Normans were interested in plunder and in setting

(197)

themselves up as feudal lords in territories that they would take from the Moslems. The Venetians were interested in developing easier trade with the near East. No doubt, many were willing to go out of love for military adventure or to escape the boredom of domestic life. Soldiers of fortune were not unknown. Some perhaps went to escape punishment from crime. The direct cause, however, was the appeal that the pope made to rescue the holy places from the infidel Turks. Urban set forth the crusade as a holy war having as its objective the liberation of the Holy Land. The first crusade was called, organized and conducted under the auspices of the pope, and he emphasized that those who lost their lives while participating would be absolved of their sins. Urban further promised to care for the lands of those who went on the crusade holding out before them the prospect of plunder. His desire to make the pilgrimage to Jerusalem safe was the direct appeal for the war. He, however, wanted to establish fraternal relations with the Christians of the East. Some have suggested that he was interested in establishing a feudal state in Palestine under his own authority. There seems to be little doubt but that he was interested in increasing the power and prestige of the papacy. In consideration of the fact that he immediately established cordial relations with the Byzantine Emperor, it seems certain that he had some hope of ending the schism and ultimately unifying all Christendom under the Roman See. For over fifty years there had been no communication between the churches of Constantinople and Rome. And although the re-establishment of communion lay behind many obstacles, the pope believed that if he could get full support from the Emperor, the Emperor could in turn force the Greek church to do his bidding. There were a number of political considerations that made this favorable to Alexius. Urban removed the excommunication which had been imposed on the Byzantine Emperor by Gregory VII and in return the Latin churches in Constantinople were reopened. The pope had hoped that this beginning would produce unity among the churches, and the Emperor saw in it an opportunity to raise troops in the West to fight his wars against his enemies. It is very apparent that Alexius used the papacy at Clermont for the recruiting of troops to carry out his purposes although the ambassadors from Alexius to the pope placed their emphasis upon the necessity of liberating the Holy Lands. One of the chroniclers who reported these events said:

"Having considered therefore that it was impossible for him alone to undertake the battle on which everything depended he recognized that he would have to call on the Italians as allies and he affected this with considerable cunning adroitness and deeply laid planning. For finding pretext in the fact that this nation considered unbearable the domination of Jerusalem and the life giving sepulchre of our Saviour Jesus Christ by the Persians and seeing therein a Heaven sent opportunity he managed by dispatching ambassadors to the bishop of Old Rome and to those whom they would call Kings and Rulers of those parts and by the use of appropriate arguments to prevail over not a few of them to leave their country and succeeded in directing them in every way to the task. That is the reason why many of them numbering thousands and tens of thousands having crossed the Ionian Sea, reached Constantinople with all speed. And having exchanged assurance and oaths with them he advanced toward the East. With the aid of God and their alliance and by his own efforts he speedily expelled the Persians from Roman territories, liberated the cities and restored his sway in the East to its former glory. Such was this emperor, great in the conception of plans and the doing of deeds."[1]

From these considerations it seems that Urban was moved by three dominant motives: the desire to make the Holy Land available to Christian Pilgrims, the desire to bring succor to the Eastern Christians, and the hope that he might bring an end to the schism in the church.

After Urban had made his speech to the council of Clermont, the entire assembly replied with a shout that God willed it. The enthusiasm that followed sent multitudes of peasants who were poorly armed and without discipline to Palestine. In Asia Minor they were either massacred or taken prisoner and sold as slaves by the Turks. The organized portion of the first crusade, however, was led by noblemen from France, Belgium and northern Italy. These leaders with their armies arrived in Constantinople in the spring of 1094. Beginning their attack they took the town of Nicaea and marched on to Antioch. During the battle of Antioch, which was fought during the winter of 1097-98, the crusaders having just entered the city were con-

1. Church History, June, 1952. p. 127.

fronted with a new Turk army. When their spirits were about crushed by the sight of reinforcements, someone claimed to have found the spear the Roman soldier had used to pierce the side of Christ. When the word went through the ranks they were rejuvinated and threw themselves against the Turks with such force that they were forced to withdraw. They then marched on to Jerusalem, captured the holy city and worshipped with rejoicing upon the completion of their objective. It has been estimated that thirty to fifty thousands soldiers went on the first crusade and that one fourth to one tenth remained to reach Jerusalem. Godfrey of Bouillon who had been the moral leader of the crusade set his brother Baldwin up as king over the kingdom of Jerusalem with the title, Defender of the Holy Sepulchre. The kingdom, however, was very weak. The territory was divided among over-lords who were eager to establish themselves as feudal lords and scattered themselves out along the coast. The conquerors composed only a minority of the total population. During this time two new orders of knights were established on a religious basis — both being military orders. The Hospitaliers and Templars were organized for the purpose of helping maintain control of the Holy Land. The crusaders controlled the territory they had conquered until 1144 not because of their own strength but because of the weakness of the Moslems. In 1144, however, the Moslems became somewhat unified and retook the city of Edessa, which brought on the second crusade.

In 1147 Bernard of Clairvaux was successful in stirring up the King of France and the Emperor of the Holy Roman Empire to lead a crusade to recover the land taken by the Moslems. Under the leadership of Louis VII of France and Conrad III of Germany the crusade began very favorably. It ended, however, in miserable failure with thousands killed in Asia Minor. The Crusaders reached Damascus and after a seige of a few days became discouraged and returned home. Upon this failure Saladin unified the Moslems and retook Jerusalem in 1187. When news of this reached Europe the third Crusade — the Kings Crusade — was organized under the leadership of Philip Augustus of France, Richard of England and the Emperor Frederick Barbarosa of Germany. Frederick was nearly seventy years of age at the time he started for the Holy Land

and was accidently drowned soon after reaching Asia Minor. Upon the loss of his leadership many of his soldiers were discouraged and returned home. Philip and Richard reached Palestine by sea and successfully captured the town of Acre. However, they soon quarreled over the control of the captured territory and Philip, discouraged, returned home. Richard stayed on for fourteen months making very little headway. Finally he formulated a treaty with the Moslem leader Saladin, which permitted Christians to visit Jerusalem on pilgrimages. This being the most he could accomplish, he returned to England having gained the title "Lion-Hearted" for his tenacious efforts.

Innocent III, eager to restore the prestige of the crusaders, encouraged a fourth crusade. Being a shrewd manipulator, Innocent was successful in bringing the Greek church and the Eastern Empire again under the papacy for a brief period of time. The lasting result, however, was to deepen the hatred that the Greek church held for the papacy. No king assisted Innocent in the fourth crusade, but many knights followed his leadership. There were no lasting results of the effort.

The fifth crusade under the leadership of Frederick II was successful in negotiating a treaty in 1229 that brought Jerusalem and a small section of Palestine under the control of Christians. The Moslems, however, were permitted to keep the Mosque of Omar in Jerusalem. Several later attempts were made to bring the Holy Land under the permanent control of Christianity but without success. The Saracens overpowered the Seljuk Turks, and Palestine again was in the hands of a unified Moslem group.

During the period of crusades there were many tragedies. One of the saddest was the Children's Crusade of 1212. Two boys named Stephen and Nicholas succeeded in assembling the children of France and Germany and marched across southern Europe to Italy. Stephen led children ill clothed and poorly fed on a trek toward Palestine thinking that the purity and innocence of childhood would be able to accomplish what the strength of adulthood, because of its sin, could not. The children who finally reached the seacoast fell under the dominion of conspiring men who put them into boats by pretending to be their friends and sold them into Egyptian slavery. Although the crusades failed to make Jerusalem available to pilgrims from Western Europe, it is believed by some that certain advantages arose from these efforts. Feudalism was weakened in favor of a growing nationalism, and although the papacy was temporarily strengthened through its part in the crusades, the growing nationalism was a factor which was to take from the papacy its assumed powers. There were apparently economic results since trade with the Near East began to flourish.

It is especially noteworthy that the crusades Urban instigated at Clermont became an institution which was used for centuries to promote the interests of the papacy. It is significant that as the crusades developed they could only be authorized by the papacy. True, the original plan was to use the crusades to support Christianity against the infidel, but the result was that the interests of Christianity came to be looked upon synonymously with the interests of the pope. In the centuries that followed, the crusade was not only used against infidels but also against any group that arose to question papal authority, not only against those considered heretics — such as the Albigenses — but also against secular rulers whose policies were at variance with those of the pope. As long as there were followers who were eager to receive absolution from the pope it was not difficult for him to use such persons for the accomplishment of his purposes. It is to be seriously doubted that any real benefits were derived from the crusades. It is certain that the crusades did much to harm both in the East and in the West and that the so-called benefits were actually logical developments which would have materialized anyway without the crusades.

Chapter Eighteen

Opposition to Papacy

When the mother of the sons of Zebedee asked that they might receive special consideration in the kingdom, the other disciples were moved with indignation. Jesus took advantage of this opportunity to say unto them, "Ye know that the rulers of the Gentiles lord it over them and their great ones exercise authority over them. Not so shall it be among you." (Matt. 20: 25-26). Jesus thus stated that in His kingdom there would be no one with authority such as the Gentiles exercised in civil government. It is no wonder then that as the papacy began to develop into a position of world power opposition increased with papal claims.

Opposition to the Roman bishop began very early. Hippolytus (160-235) opposed very strongly the arrogancy of the Roman bishop of his day. He started a congregation in Rome which opposed three men that were later called popes. It is interesting that the Catholic church, in spite of this, later canonized Hippolytus as a saint. From this beginning there continued strong opposition to the claims of the Roman bishops. Tertullian, one of the most prolific writers among the Christian Apologists, who lived in the latter part of the second century and early third, was a very strong opponent of the growing hierarchy. These are only two outstanding men who opposed the growing power of the Roman bishop.

In spite of opposition the Roman bishop continued to gain influence in the West. With the change of the seat of the Imperial Government from Rome to Constantinople, the bishop of Constantinople came into prominence and became the leader of the church in the Eastern part of the Empire. With this development there was continued rivalry between the Patriarch of Constantinople and the Bishop of Rome. As a result of this rivalry the church in the East never did fully submit itself to the Roman supremacy. The church in the East began to enjoy full support of the Emperors in their oposition to the Roman pope. The second Trullian council held in 692 set forth principles that finally led to a complete break in fellowship between the Eastern and the Western churches. This council approved the marriage of the clergy, with the exception of the bishop, archbishop and patriarch, and reaffirmed the decree of the Council of Chalcedon (451) that the patriarch of Constantinople was of equal rank with the pope in Rome. It also passed decrees in regard to minor points of worship and ceremony that were opposed to the Roman church. Among these was a rule making it illegal to require fasting on Saturdays during lent. The council also prohibited the eating of animals that had been strangled or suffocated. This was done in opposition to the Roman church which permitted this practice. The council also forbade any pictorial representation of Christ as a lamb, a practice quite popular in the West. These decisions indicate something of the difference in temperament of the people of the West and the East. The Greek mind was more speculative, fanciful and excitable, yet through their emphasis on allegorical interpretation the Greeks had remained more interested in doctrinal matters than the Western church. On the other hand the Western church was more interested in practical matters which would increase the authority of the hierarchy.

One of the chief differences between the two groups arose in regard to the "procession of the Holy Spirit." Photius, who became Patriarch of Constantinople in 858, made powerful attacks on the claims of the Roman Pope. He pointed out that the pope had approached idolatry in his attitude toward the use of images and claimed that he was a heretic by his changing the doctrine set forth in the first ecumenical council at Nicaea. The Nicaean creed in its original form said that the Holy Spirit "proceedeth from the Father." This doctrine had been unchanged in the church for a period of three hundred years until the Roman church began to add the phrase "and the Son." This interpretation affirmed that the Holy Spirit had a "double procession" — from both the Father and the Son. When the Western theologians with the approval of the pope added the word "Filioque" which means "and the son" to the Nicaean wording, Photius declared that this changed the decision of Nicaea and that, accordingly, the Roman pope held the council of Nicaea to have erred in doctrine. Because of this Photius and Pope Nicholas I excommunicated each other.

In 869 at a council in Constantinople the division was temporarily healed and for the next one hundred years there was no open break. During this time the church in the East enjoyed remarkable growth while the church in the West was suffering decline. The occasion for the final break came in 1054. The Emperor at Constantinople, Constantine IX, in conflict with the Normans appealed to the pope at Rome for help. In order to obtain this support he was ready to recognize Leo IX as universal bishop of the church. The Patriarch of Constantinople, however, who at this time was Cerularius, had planned to make himself head of the Eastern church and separate the Eastern church from the West. To carry out his plan he closed the Latin churches and monasteries in Constantinople and influenced the Bulgarian patriarch Leo to write a letter to the bishops of Southern Italy in which he set forth all of the errors of the Roman church. This stirred Pope Leo IX to action, and a bitter controversy arose between Rome and Constantinople. In attempting to bring about unity the Roman pope sent papal legates to Constantinople. These legates and the officials of the Eastern churches discussed all of the differences between them. Cerularius, the patriarch of Constantinople, being dissatisfied with proposed solutions, burned a dialogue drawn up by the Roman legates. The lack of respect caused the legates to write out an excommunication of the Patriarch of Constantinople and the Eastern church. On July 16, 1054, the three papal legates placed this decree of excommunication on the altar of the church of Sophia. They then left the church and shook the dust off their feet against it. Cerularius immediately replied by excommunicating the pope and the Western church. This crystalized the schism between the East and the West and it has remained so until the present time. The Eastern church is known as the "Holy Orthodox church" and the church at Rome the "Catholic church." There are several major differences between the two bodies. In the West the pope is head of the church but the Eastern church recognizes four patriarchs of equal authority. The Eastern church declares the Holy Spirit proceeds from the Father only while the Western church affirms that the Holy Spirit proceeds from the Father and the

Son. The Eastern church uses leavened bread in the Lord's Supper while the Western churches use only unleavened bread. The Greek church has practiced triune immersion since the fourth century and has never accepted sprinkling for baptism. This is because they understand the meaning of the Greek word used by the Apostles to mean "immerse." The Western church on the other hand changed its method of baptism from immersion to sprinkling. The Eastern church permits the clergy, with the exception of the bishops, archbishop and patriarch, to marry while the Western church holds to clerical celibacy. The Eastern churches permit no images in their worship, allowing only pictures with flat surfaces to be used, while the church in the West has employed statuary since the iconoclastic controversy was settled. The Eastern church did not accept the use of mechanical instruments of music in later centuries as did the church of Rome.

I. OPPOSITION GROUPS

From the beginning of the development of the Roman hierarchy there was opposition both to organization and to the changes which came about in doctrine. Information concerning these groups in opposition to the developing hierarchy is very brief due to the fact that these groups were considered heretical by the hierarchy, and, accordingly, records concerning them were not preserved. What information we do have comes almost entirely from the Catholics who preserved their history and refers to these groups only in discussing their efforts to keep the church free from "heresy."

II. CHURCH SUCCESSION THROUGH OPPOSITION GROUPS

From the days of the Reformation there have been groups who were interested in trying to trace their own history back to the days of the Apostles. One of the recent efforts in this direction was made by Ben M. Bogard for the Missionary Baptist church. His book is called "The Baptist Way Book." It was set forth as a manual designed to be used in Baptist churches and was published by the Baptist Sunday School Committee. In this work Bogard attempts to establish the claim that the Baptist church can be traced through ten links back to the days of the Apostles.

Bogard states that following the Apostles, the second link

in the Baptist line is found in the Montanists of the second century. The Montanists rejected the authority of the Roman bishop but cannot be considered identical with the Baptist church of today. The Montanists believed in progressive spiritual revelation. The church was not complete in the days of the Apostles, but was brought to completion in the person of Montanus.

According to Bogard the third link is found in the Novatians of the third and fourth centuries. This group taught that if a person fell away from the faith it would be impossible to receive him back into fellowship. They also emphasized that baptism itself removed sin. They had no objection to the growing hierarchy and assumption of priestly duties. There is really very little similarity between them and present day Baptists.

Concerning the fourth link he says "the Baptists were called Donatists in the latter part of the fourth and fifth and sixth centuries." The Donatists also believed in baptismal regeneration. In this they even went beyond the Catholics themselves by maintaining that the human nature of Christ needed to be cleansed by baptism. They practiced infant baptism and were very intolerant of any one opposed to their views.

Bogard finds a fifth link in the Paulicans of the eighth and ninth centuries. This group did not baptize infants and finally would admit to baptizing only the adults who had gone through a period of testing. Those who were proven worthy were sprinkled three times.

The sixth link, Bogard finds in the Albigenses of the tenth, eleventh, twelfth and thirteenth centuries. The term Albigenses applied to a large number of sects in Southern France who opposed Catholicism. Although these sects differed greatly among themselves, most of them agreed in rejecting marriage as fornication and an ordinance of the devil. They denied that Christ and His Apostles actually healed the bodies of men. Most of them agreed with the view that the Old Testament was written by the Devil. And according to all sources these groups rejected water baptism altogether, practicing rather the laying on of hands.

The Petro-Brusians of the thirteenth and fourteenth centuries furnish the seventh link in the chain. Information in regard to the doctrine of Peter of Bruys is very scant, consisting only of what the persecutors said concerning him. It is stated that he opposed infant baptism and the papacy. In his objection to the doctrine of transubstantiation he rejected the ordinance of the Lord's Supper altogether.

The next association is made between the Baptists and the Waldensians, prominent from the fourteenth century to the Reformation. From the information we have concerning them they were hesitant to break from the doctrine of the Catholic church and continued to hold to the practice of infant baptism and the doctrine of transubstantiation. They gradually moved toward Protestantism, and their successors, who have remained until today in the Alps, are substantially Presbyterian in their doctrine and organization.

The attempt of Bogard to establish a "chain" connecting the Baptist church with that of the first century is as skillfully done as possible from the information we have. Yet it must be acknowledged that the attempt is unsuccessful. Conditions being what they were during the period generally referred to as the dark ages in Western Europe, the Catholic church was in supreme control. All opposition groups were annihilated, and no adequate record remained of their work and teaching. We have sufficient evidence, however, to know that there were groups which opposed the papacy in every generation. We believe that the true undenominational church of Christ — the Eternal Kingdom — continued throughout this entire period. The gates of Hades did not prevail against it. It is not necessary to maintain apostolic succession in order to know that we are members of that church today. Christ is the foundation and other foundation can no man lay. The Gospel is the seed of the kingdom, and when individuals yield themselves to Christ and follow the teaching set forth in the New Testament there is every assurance that such individuals constitute the church of Christ in that generation.

III. THE CATHARISTS

From the ninth century on there are glimpses of thousands of persons who opposed the Roman hierarchy and were persecuted as heretics. These were found especially in Greece, Italy, Germany, France and Holland. They were known by various local names, but Catharists or Paulicans seem to be the general designations given them by the hierarchy. In local and more restricted areas they were known by such names as Arnoldians, Paulicans, Petrobusians, Albigenses and Waldenses. All of these groups were similar in that they opposed the Roman hierarchy, accepted the Scripture as their only authority, claimed to be the only true Christians in their generation and lived puritanical lives. It is impossible to ascertain their beginning, but thousands were persecuted as early as the ninth century. In their services they read the Scripture aloud and had the Lord's Supper at every service. They refused infant baptism, baptizing only believers. They rejected all human authority, had no formal creed or confession, denounced the ignorance and vice of the clergy. Their chief mistake was in accepting some of the ideas of the early Gnostics and the later Manicheans. Many of them accepted the basic principle of dualism which emphasized that nature is evil. This led them into an extreme asceticism and in some instances to the rejection of the Old Testament. Many believed that marriage was from the Devil. One wonders, however, from the emphasis they placed upon the study of the Scripture, that if among these widely scattered groups who differed greatly from each other there were not true saints of God, following the New Testament pattern and constituting the Eternal Kingdom. One cannot put his finger on evidence of such, but we believe it to be the case.

IV. ARNOLD OF BRESCIA

Arnold was born about the year 1100 and was educated in Paris under Abelard. Becoming intensely interested in the study of the Scripture, he began to oppose the corruption he found in the clergy. Although his knowledge of the truth was incomplete, his views of baptism and the Lord's Supper were far more Scriptural than those held by the Roman church. With the emphasis he placed on a return to Scripture, he was strongly opposed by the clergy, and Innocent II pronounced a decree against him which forced him to flee from Italy. He went to France and then to Switzerland, locating at Zurich. Becoming prominent as an opposition leader at one time it looked as though his reformation would change the entire papal order. Having influenced the new pope in the direction of reform, he appeared at Rome and preached publicly against the hierarchy.

Here the tide was soon turned against him and under strong opposition he was deserted by his supporters. Soon a new pope, Hadrian IV, who came to power in 1155, started a persecution that brought Arnold to trial. He was hanged as a heretic, his body burned and the ashes thrown in the Tiber River.

V.   PETER OF BRUYS

While various opposition movements were developing over Western Europe, there came into prominence about the year 1110 a priest by the name of Peter. Peter began to denounce Catholicism, taking the New Testament as his guide. He set out to correct all of the abuses in the church but was too radical for his movement to succeed. He was permitted to preach over a period of twenty years before the church took action against him. He had gained great crowds of followers who under his leadership tore down altars and images in various church buildings. Out of contempt for the Catholic ceremonialism his followers gathered up wooden crucifixes, on a Good Friday built a fire of the crucifixes and cooked meat to show their contempt for the regulations that Christians should not eat meat on that day. Peter insisted that the priests should marry and that the Catholic worship should be returned to a simple service. As opposition developed against him he was seized in 1130 and executed.

While Peter was preaching in France a zealous Christian in Switzerland named Henry, through a careful study of the Scripture, had reached similar conclusions. He set out to restore primitive Christianity and in 1116 began preaching his convictions. Henry was also radical in his techniques, going about in a coarse robe with wooden sandals denouncing the clergy. He succeeded in stirring up the people against the clergy while Hildebart, bishop of the city, was visiting in Rome. When Hildebart returned, however, Henry was forced to leave. He then went to Southern France where he met Peter and upon the death of Peter, assumed the leadership of his movement. Henry was later caught and brought before a council at Rheims in 1148 and sentenced to life imprisonment. He died very soon after being committed to the prison.

VI.   PETER WALDO AND THE WALDENSES

The opposition to Romanism in Southern France through

the work of Peter of Bruys, Henry and Arnold had created a movement that could be turned against the hierarchy with effectiveness. Peter Waldo was a wealthy merchant of Lyons who about the year 1160 began to study the Bible. He persuaded certain monks to translate the New Testament and certain teachings of the early church fathers into his own language. Peter then gave away his possessions and organized a small group of men to study the Scripture with him and to go about preaching what they learned. In order to oppose more effectively the rich and corrupt clergy these men decided to abandon all property and go about preaching the Gospel as the early disciples did without purse and without possessions. Because of this they were called the "poor men of Lyons." At first they had no intention of leaving the Catholic church but merely desired to reform the abuses of the clergy. As a result of their study, however, they decided that priestly ordination was unnecessary and that the doctrine of purgatory was not taught in the Scripture. They advocated a return to the pure teaching of Scripture and stood firmly against the worship of saints and the idea that the priest could absolve one of his sin. They opposed strongly the idea that salvation was dependent upon Catholic clergy. They believed that the real church of Christ embraced many more believers than the papal church. The Archbishop of Lyons began a persecution and Peter fled from the city. He then traveled about strengthening various groups of Catharists that he found and organizing new groups in opposition to the Catholic church. He spent his last days in the mountains of Bohemia where he died in 1179. By this time opponents of the pope had become so numerous that Pope Alexander III issued a decree forbidding all men to receive these heretics in their houses. In 1181 another edict was published by Lucius III which states:

> "More particularly we declare all Catharists, Peterines, and those who call themselves 'the poor of Lyons,' the Passagines, the Josephists, the Arnoldians, to lie under a perpetual anathema. . . . but without any further hearing they be forthwith delivered to the secular power, and their goods confiscated to the use of the church."

These decrees brought on very severe persecution against the opponents of the pope. The secular authorities were expected to execute the "criminals." We have a record of one group of thirty men and women who under persecution in Germany fled into England and there continued to teach against the doctrine of purgatory, believing that prayer for the dead was useless. They also opposed the reverence of the saints, and for teaching these doctrines they were branded with a red hot iron on the forehead and whipped through the streets of Oxford. The inhabitants were prohibited from giving them either shelter, or food, or any other type of relief. After severe punishment they gave their lives for their faith.

VII. THE ALBIGENSES

In spite of persecution that followed the Catharists they continued to increase in number. By the year 1200 Southern France was covered with people of this persuasion. They became so numerous around the town of Albi that they were called Albigenses. One reason for their rapid increase in this region was that a number of princes of the territory gave them protection. This was especially true of Count Raymond VII of Toulouse. Some of the Southern French noblemen supported these teachers by lending them the use of their castles and using their authority to curb any punishment that the Monks were trying to inflict upon them. This so filled the pope with alarm that papal legates were sent to investigate the situation and curb their activities. These emissaries, however, proved to be of little service and were dismissed, their efforts being replaced with force. Innocent III, the strongest of the popes, in the year 1206 began a serious effort to exterminate all of the Albigenses. His attitude may be seen in one of his letters:

> "We exhort you wholly to destroy this wicked heresy of the Albigenses and do it with more vigor than you would use towards the Saracens themselves. Persecute them with a strong hand; deprive them of their lands and possessions; utterly banish them, and put Roman Catholics in their room."

A strong crusade emerged against the Albigenses. In order to stir up hatred special rewards as well as indulgences were promised by the pope to everyone who would leave his occupation for forty days to join the war against the Albigenses. Multitudes accepted this opportunity to trade their services for remission of sins. Others joined the papal army out of the desire for the loot that they would be permitted to take. In this manner over fifty thousand soldiers were mounted and equipped for battle. The unhappy Albigenses were unarmed and unprepared to defend themselves, so the papal force with fire and sword easily ravaged the entire country around Toulouse. They then took the city of Beziers. This city was a stronghold of the Albigensian party. Thus, to prevent any heretic's escaping, the city was surrounded and its surrender demanded. There were many devout Catholics who were loyal to the pope in the city and they pled for an opportunity to prove their loyalty to him, but the reply was, that unless all in the city submitted they would all be put to the sword. According to the reports, twenty-three thousand persons were massacred indiscriminately there. The city was reduced to ashes. When some of the soldiers hesitated to kill people who were declaring their loyalty to the pope, they turned to a papal legate for instruction, who commanded, "Kill them all, the Lord knoweth them that are his." After this, the only hope that the Catholics in Southern France had of saving their own lives was to join the pope's army and sew the symbol of the cross on their clothing. As the destruction continued the army grew until it numbered three-hundred thousand.

A chronicler for the occasion said:

> "Hundreds of villages had seen all their inhabitants massacred with a blind fury, without the crusaders giving themselves the trouble to examine whether they contained a single heretic; the harvest of the country people and the provisions and merchandise of the citizens were divided at discretion among the maurading assailants. There was scarcely a peasant who did not reckon in his family some, unhappy one whose life had been cut off by the sword of Montfort's soldiers, and whose property had not been repeatedly ravaged. More than three quarters of the knights and lorded proprietors of the district had been dispoiled of their castles and Feifs."

Conservative estimates state that two-thirds of the people of Southern France were killed in this effort to wipe out the heresy of Albigensianism. The effort apparently was successful from the pope's viewpoint, for we read no more of opposition to the Roman church under the Albigensian name. Large numbers, however, had escaped to the valleys of the mountains where their descendants continue until today as Protestant groups.

VIII. The Inquisition

The papacy learned through its experience with the Albigensians that some organization must be developed which could deal with individual heretics before they developed large numbers of followers. The answer to individual heresy was found in the inquisition. The legal foundation for this institution is found in the decrees of the Latern Council of 1215. The theory promulgated was that religious authorities would pass on each individual's orthodoxy, and those found to be heretics would be turned over to state officials for execution. As the institution grew it became an organization of terror. Any individual could accuse any other person for heresy, and when the accused was called for trial he was not allowed to know who his accuser was or to defend himself. The inquisition was organized in every diocese throughout Italy. The laws governing it were incorporated into later additions of Corpus Juris as a part of the canon law and are in force to the present day. The inquisition was placed in the hands of the Dominican monks who were very zealous in the extermination of heresy. These monks were subject to no authority, civil or ecclesiastical, other than the pope. When the accused was to be brought before the inquisitor he was generally arrested suddenly and at night. Wives, children or servants were not permitted to give evidence in favor of the accused, but if their testimony was adverse it was welcomed and consider particularly strong. The suspected heretic was prejudiced. The effort of the inquisitor was not to determine guilt but to force the admission of guilt. The only means of release was confession of the charges made and acceptance of whatever punishment might be imposed. To those who would not confess guilt, torture was applied. The degree of torture was left to the discretion of the inquisitor. For those who confessed that they had been heretics but had denounced their heresy there was a terrible period of penance imposed that consisted of the penitent's presenting himself every Sunday to the priest with a rod in his hand so the priest could soundly scourge him in the presence of the congregation. Many were required to make pilgrimages wearing yellow crosses on their garments which were never to be laid aside indoors or out. The inquisition was introduced into France in 1233, Aragon

1238 and Italy in 1254. Perhaps the most terrifying forms of the inquisition were found in Spain.

Attempts have been made to justify it on the theory that it was not intended to be used on non-Catholics but only by the church as punishment upon her own children. Since all were declared to be subject to the pope this argument has no validity. It has also been emphasized that torture was never applied more than once to the same individual. These claims are entirely contrary to the facts involved for cases of torture were dragged out over several weeks. There was no time limit involved. Each successive period of torture to the same individual was counted a "new" torture.

It is of little satisfaction to state that Calvin and some of the American colonists also used torture and decreed the death penalty to human beings. The Catholic officials would like to place the responsibility for these excesses on the secular arm, claiming to have no responsibility in regard to their excesses during this time. The inquisitors, however, were members of the Franciscan and the Dominican orders, and the "secular" officials were loyal Catholics who killed religious heretics — not criminals against the state. Catholic officials have consistently held the opinion that the Catholic church alone is the true church, and all who were out of harmony with its doctrine were correctly designated heretics.

In view of the historical development we are forced to conclude that religious toleration did not develop by Catholic consent. Such necessitated the forfeiting of countless lives during the religious wars. Catholicism had to be overpowered. When the Catholic church could no longer take the lives of dissenters it reluctantly "permitted" others to live and hold a faith at variance with its doctrine.

IX. THE TRUE CHURCH

During this period the church as a Scripturally organized body worshipping according to the New Testament pattern, is entirely lost to view. It should be remembered, however, that the Eternal Kingdom could have lived on hidden from the pages of history — overshadowed by the power and grandeur of an apostate Romanism. God had spoken of an everlasting kingdom of the prophet Daniel, and although we cannot discern a body of Christians functioning throughout this period according to the New Testament pattern, we can believe that such existence with every assurance that there has never been a time when the gates of death prevailed against God's kingdom.

PART FIVE

REFORMATION BEGINNINGS

Chapter Nineteen

The Need for Reformation

Having traced the gradual apostasy from New Testament purity and the consequent corruption of the dark ages, it remains to note the specific abuses that precipitated the Reformation of the sixteenth century. These abuses had their origin in the teaching of the church itself and worked as an aggravated malignancy to destroy the unity of the body.

I. CELIBACY

The effect of asceticism was to be seen in the current conception that the conjugate life was inferior to the celibate. Since the priests were considered superior in living to the average layman, it was a simple step in the evolution of thought for the two ideas to amalgamate and produce the notion that priests should be unmarried. This was easier thought than practiced, however, resulting in widespread immorality among the clergy. It is obviously against nature and a mark of apostasy (1 Tim. 4:3), but was nevertheless enforced by Gregory VII. Prior to his reign the doctrine of compulsory celibacy had been discussed but not universally accepted. It was one of the points under consideration at the first ecumenical council of Nicaea in 325. Since Gregory this unnatural prohibition has only produced immorality. In the years preceding the Reformation movement it was a matter of considerable resentment among the religious minded of Europe.

II. SIMONY

In these crucial years it has been estimated that one-third of the wealth of Europe in terms of real estate lay in the hands of the church.[1] In addition to revenue from its land the church also taxed its members. The clergy paid dues to the papacy for the right of holding offices. The priests reimbursed themselves by charging exhorbitant fees for their services. The process became a lucrative business known as "simony" reminiscent of

1. Although Smith feels that this is an exaggeration. Preserved Smith, The Age of the Reformation (Henry Holt & Co., 1920), p. 21.

Simon the Sorcerer's attempt to purchase spiritual things with material possessions (Acts 8:9-23). Leo X made more than one million dollars annually from the sale of over two-thousand offices. At a time when monastic preaching and Christian idealism centered in "apostolic poverty" the riches of the clergy constituted a scandal to the pious. The offices of the churches were held often by men who neither lived in the city nor cared for the church situated there. The office was frequently purchased by some wealthy nobleman for his son as a scholarship to guarantee his education. The income from one or more of these positions would provide a young man with the means necessary to complete his schooling. The value of such an arrangement can be seen in the estimate that only one person in every ten thousand in Western Europe during the latter medieval period (about 1000 to 1300 A.D.) could read or write. The clergy was characterized by widespread ignorance and found no stimulus to reform in the disgusting business of simony.

III. INDULGENCES

One of the richest sources of ecclesiastical revenue was the indulgence, closely related to the sacrament of penance. When one sinned satisfaction had to be made both in heaven and on earth. Penance was sufficient for the former, but temporal guilt had to be alleviated by temporal satisfaction. So the purchasing of an indulgence for a specified sum of money by one who had sinned enabled the pope to draw on the "treasury of merits" in heaven and apply the goodness of departed saints stored in this treasury to the sins of the penitent individual. One might even shorten the time of a departed friend in purgatory by the purchasing of an indulgence in his name. The practice arose in connection with the crusades as enticement to enlistment. The pope granted full indulgences guaranteeing the remission of sins to anyone who would go on a crusade. During Martin Luther's day the practice was revived and greatly exaggerated in an attempt to finance the construction of St. Peter's Cathedral in Rome. It was commonly stated by indulgence salesmen that "as soon as a coin in the coffer rings, another soul from purgatory springs."

The indulgence trade worked on a percentage basis, each salesman receiving ten percent of the sale. However, it is doubtful that more than 30 to 45 percent of it ever got to Rome. The result of the practice was that it drained the money out of the lands involved and produced financial as well as religious repercussions. Overly enthusiastic salesmen finally offered the forgiveness of sins not yet committed to those who would purchase an indulgence. This was an open license to immorality and crime as people soon realized. It was at this point in the picture that Martin Luther raised his voice in protest and offered to debate anyone in Germany about the matter. His *Ninety-Five Theses* were debate topics in their inception but became the spark that inflamed the whole of European Catholicism. However, long before Luther issued his challenge Duke George of Saxony had remarked of the clergy that "they cheated the simple layman of his soul," and Ulrich von Mutten had said of Pope Julius II that he sold to others the heaven he could not win for himself. Perhaps the indulgence traffic more than anything else served to ignite the Reformation.

IV. HAGIOLATRY

Hagiolatry, the worship of departed saints, had begun in the early centuries of the church's history but was not made official until 788. By the time of the Reformation this practice that had once been considered a stepping-stone had become a stumbling-block. It was more polytheism. Erasmus, a noted scholar of the age, said fugitive nuns prayed to saints for help in hiding their sins — rather than praying to God for forgiveness. Merchants, he said, prayed for a rich haul, gamblers for luck and prostitutes for generous patrons. Not only were saints worshipped but relics as well. Erasmus said there appeared to be enough wood from the true cross of Christ to make a ship. There were exhibited at various times five shin-bones of the ass on which Christ rode into Jerusalem during His triumphant entry. Simple faith in the efficacy of the blood of Christ as a propitiation for the sins of man was no longer the essence of religion. It had been replaced by ceremonialism, legalism, hagiolatry and sacredotalism.

Throughout professed Christendom the corruption of the Roman church was felt. Reformation was the only answer. The power of the papacy over the minds of men had to be broken. From the reigns of Gregory VII, Innocent III and Boniface

VII, it had become the greatest force on earth producing the greatest corruption on earth — the defilement of things sacred. The need of reform was everywhere apparent.

Chapter Twenty

Early Reform Movements

Since the papacy had reached the zenith of its power and was using this power to promote its selfish interests the entire church could be characterized as being morally bankrupt. It is to be expected that under these conditions sincere reformers would arise to work for a moral and spiritual regeneration. There were a number of forces which arose to check the glaring immorality of the church and a number of theories of reform presented. One theory was that a general council should be called which would have greater authority than the pope. Thus, by placing the pope in submission to the council he would be made to assume a greater degree of responsibilty.

As there was a growing nationalism it was felt by some that the pope's power should be limited to Italy and that each national state should govern its own religious affairs. There was also growing interest in mysticism which emphasized personal communion with God and tended to break down the authority of the established church. The mystic concept did not depend upon institutionalism or sacramentalism and was strongly opposed to the authority of the Roman church.

Another force strongly felt was individualism. Men were becoming conscious of their own worth as individuals. In the period of feudalism an individual had very little recognition as such. Each was a member of a rigidly organized social system in which the individual had little status. Along with the rising individualism was a secularization of thought that caused religion to be considered of secondary importance in the thought and interest of the citizen.

Many of these ideas were set forth in 1324 by Marsilius of Padua and John of Jandun. They taught that the church should become more democratic and limit itself to the spiritual welfare of mankind. They set forth a democratic type of state government in which the sovereignty rested with the common people controlled by a legislature elected by popular vote. They also believed that the executive power should be in the hands of an elected king who would rule according to an adopted constitution. These democratic thinkers also believed that the authority of the church should rest upon the common people and that the people themselves should elect their own priests and officials who would constitute the general council — the highest spiritual power on earth. Such a council would replace the papacy. The priest should preach the gospel, administer sacraments and have no responsibilities in secular matters. The Bible itself should be the only source of faith. These ideas soon began to influence the thinking of the world.

I. WILLIAM OF OCCAM (c. 1300-1349)

One of the most influential thinkers of his time, William of Occam began to build upon the ideas stated above. He taught that the pope is not infallible and that a general council was higher authority than the papacy. He also advocated that the Bible is the only infallible source of authority in the church and that in secular matters, the church and the pope should be subordinate to the state.

II. JOHN WYCLIFFE (1320-1384)

The need for reformation was being felt in every part of the world. In England there arose a man of great intellectual ability who saw clearly the need for a return to New Testament simplicity and authority. John Wycliffe was educated at Oxford University where as a student he opposed the Mendicant orders. He opposed the pope, also, declaring that in the Scripture there are only two orders of officers in the church, elders and deacons. In his effort he defended the English king's refusal to send money from England to Rome. He was soon granted a doctor's degree and appointed professor of theology in Oxford. In 1374 as a member of an embassy to Rome he saw the corruption of the priesthood there and on his return to England began to speak and write against the pope as the anti-Christ, declaring the papal system unscriptural. In 1377 Gregory XI condemned nineteen points of his writings, but the court protected him against punishment because he was favored by the crown. This made him very bold in his opposition to the pope, and he began to form societies to preach to the poor. His followers were called Lollards. He felt the need to put the Bible into general use and in 1830 translated the first complete Bible into English. As the result of his Bible study he rejected the doctrine of transubstantiation which brought the disfavor of the chancelor of the university upon him. Such opposition caused Wycliffe to speak even more boldly. He put his trust in the Scripture itself and declared, "If there were one-hundred popes and all the friars were turned into cardinals their opinion ought not be acceded to in matters of faith except in so far as they based themselves upon Scripture." The chancelor of the University, however, expelled him from the faculty and a synod at London in 1382 condemned his works. The court protected him from violence and he retired to Lutterworth where he died in 1384. In addition to his emphasis upon the Scripture as the only source of religious authority and rule of conduct, he aroused the animosity of the Catholics by renouncing the use of images, relics, Latin in the services and recognition of festivals. He also opposed private masses and doctrine of extreme unction. He pronounced indulgences and the interdict blasphemous and wholly rejected the doctrine of purgatory. Wycliffe termed the pope anti-Christ and monasticism a monstrous development contrary to the spirit of Christianity. He has been called the "morning star of the Reformation."

Thirty-one years after his death the council of Constance condemned him as a heretic, ordered his bones removed from their tomb, burned and the ashes thrown in the Severn River. This order was carried out in 1428 at papal command. In 1401 the "heresy" of Wycliffe was made a capitol offense in England and those who possessed any of his writings made subject to punishment by death. This action drove the followers of Wycliffe into hiding but many continued to share his sentiments in the years that followed.

II. JOHN HUSS (C. 1373-1415).

The influence of Wycliffe in England soon reached the continent. Students who had gone to England to study brought back to various parts of Western Europe his influence — especially regarding the study of the Bible. John Huss, who later became known as the "John the Baptist of the Reformation," was educated in the University of Prague. He then became a

professor in the University and the leader of a very active reform movement in Bohemia. He was a very powerful preacher
as well as influential teacher. In 1420 he became rector of the
University and through his tremendous influence led the church
of Bohemia in a reformation along the lines that had been set
forth by Wycliffe. After 1409 he became the head of the National Bohemian Party and large numbers reallied under his
leadership in the cause of reformation. He strongly opposed the
doctrine of indulgences and encouraged a return to the study of
Scripture. He was first excommunicated by the archbishop of
Prague and a little later by the pope. He was then summoned
to appear before the council of Constance in defense of his
faith. Hesitant to go, the Emperor Sigismund promised him
safe conduct to and from the council. On the basis of this promise he attended the council and defended his views. The council
condemned him as a heretic and appealed to Sigismund to re-
voke the promise of safe conduct. The Catholic leaders insisted
that Sigismund was not under obligation to keep his word to a
heretic and so John Huss was imprisoned and burned at the
stake on July 6, 1415. His colleague, Jerome of Prague, was
also martyred. These events seemed only to strengthen the
views of their followers. His followers were divided into two
groups, the Taborites and Utraquists. The former could not be
supported by Scripture while the latter opposed only what was
explicitly forbidden. Although the Catholic church destroyed
these reformers, they could not remove the power contained in
their ideas. As a result of their work faithful men in Bohemia
continued to search the Scripture supporting a movement that
resulted in the establishment of the Moravian church whose
members are also referred to as the Bohemian Brethren. It was
out of this movement that some of the great educators arose.
Outstanding among these was John Amost Comenius who
taught for a while in England and became a great influence in
the life of John Wesley. The courage and example of John Huss
was also a great inspiration to Martin Luther when he faced the
German council under similar conditions about a hundred
years later. The council of Constance that burned John Huss
was the same that had the bones of Wycliffe exhumed and
burned. Both Wycliffe and Huss were condemned as heretics
because of their diligent search for the truth and their desire to

reform the church along the lines found in the New Testament.

IV. GIROLAMO SAVONAROLA (1452-1498)

The spirit of reform that was everywhere in the air not only produced outstanding leaders who were willing to die for their faith, but also other reformers who preferred to remain within the Catholic church and try to bring about reform within.

Savonarola, a precocious intellectual student who loved music and poetry, was spurned at the age to twenty by a girl who thought herself above him. This led him to abandon his plan to become a doctor and enter a monastery. He wrote a treatise "On the Contempt for the World" and then wrote his parents saying that "God gave you a son for twenty-two years, now he is to be a Knight of Jesus Christ." Entering a Dominican monastery he studied and wrote, taking his religious life very seriously. In 1482 he went to Florence to preach a series of sermons on Lent but had less than twenty-five people to hear him. This caused him to reconsider his approach and after a more careful study of Scripture he began to preach sermons from the Bible itself and became a very popular preacher. He decided that because of the wealth and sin in the hierarchy the church would have to go through a period of suffering before it could be purified. Accordingly, in 1492 he began to tell of a series of visions in which he saw a hand held out of a cloud over the city of Rome. Swords fell like rain and there was great bloodshed and famine. In another vision he pictured a black cross over the city of Rome and a beautiful cross of light over the city of Jerusalem. He became more bold in his attacks upon the wickedness of the priests and preached a series of sermons on the Ark of Noah in which he stated that a flood was soon to come on the church because of its wickedness. When Charles VIII of France led his army into Italy in 1494 Savonarola welcomed him to the city of Florence and became dictator of the city in 1495. This power gave him opportunity to reform the church within the city after his own thinking. The pope took a hand to stop his criticism of the clergy and offered him the position of cardinal, thinking that increasing his prestige would make him loyal to the hierarchy. Savonarola, however, replied that he preferred a hat of blood to the hat of a cardinal. The pope then demanded that he stop preaching. He refused to

obey and continued his reformatory attempts. He had no intention of leaving the Catholic church, but desired to reorganize
it on a Scriptural basis. Because of his continued opposition
Pope Alexander VI put him under the papal ban in 1497 and
threatened the city of Florence with the interdict. The populace
turned against Savonarola and he was condemned as a heretic.
Being rejected by the adults, Savonarola turned to the young
people and enlisted about four thousand who were twelve to
twenty years of age and sent them throughout the city as active
reformers. They demanded that the women of Florence turn in
their cosmetics and that all people turn to a study of the Scripture and a more devout life. Having become a nuisance in the
eyes of the people of Florence, his monastery was stormed and
he was arrested. During an unfair trial he was tortured for six
days. Under torture he confessed his wrong, but as soon as the
torture was removed he retracted his confession. He was then
hanged and his body burned in 1498.

V. XIMENES (1436-1517)

Another good illustration of attempts to reform the Catholic church from within is found in the work of Ximenes who
made a desperate effort to reform Spain. Ximenes' father, a tax
collector of the lower Spanish nobility, gave his son a good education. His training was in the field of law, but after studying
six years in Rome he decided to give it up and become a Franciscan Monk. Laxity in discipline among the Franciscans made
him desire the life of a hermit, but he had had such outstanding
ability that he was made head of his order. This gave him an
opportunity to change life within the church. He rose to prominence very rapidly and in 1492 was made chief advisor to
Queen Isabella in matters both of church and state. Having obtained favor with the queen, Ximenes was given a free hand to
reform the church throughout the entire realm. His first step
was to purge the church of unworthy personnel, and in carrying out this program he drove more than one thousand corrupt
priests out of Spain. Most of them went to Rome and found
other positions in the church. He next attempted to persuade
the leaders of the church in Spain that the purpose of the
church was to serve the masses of the people rather than ex-
ploit them. He emphasized the idea that the shepherd was to

feed the flock instead of shear it. He set an excellent example by his own frugality, spending very little money on himself and being very liberal with the poor. He believed that the new learning should become a servant of religion, and he, accordingly, began to improve the universities and institute research projects that would improve the text of the Scripture. To this end he authorized the formation of a group of Spanish scholars to undertake a revision of the Greek text of the New Testament. As a result of this there was printed the Complutensian Polyglot. This is an addition of the original text of Scripture with translations placed in parallel columns. It contains the New Testament in Greek and Latin and the Old Testament in Hebrew, Latin (Vulgate), Greek (Septuagint) and Chaldaic. Referred to as the most scientific book of its century it was certainly a most scholarly undertaking. Before it was completed the Spanish government had spent a hundred and twenty-five thousand dollars on the venture. Ximenes accepted every dogma of the Catholic church and limited his reformatory efforts to the purification of the lives and morals of the hierarchy. He put forth every effort to make religion meaningful in the life of the masses.

As long as the papacy maintained its control over the lives and thinking of the people, no real reformation was possible. It is quite clear, however, that many movements were under way which would lead eventually to the Reformation movement. Among those who helped prepare the way for reformation was Erasmus (1466-1536), a Dutch scholar and an unusually brilliant student. He edited a series of studies in the Church Fathers which made available the early history of the departure from the New Testament pattern. He also edited the first printed Greek New Testament and exposed the inadequacy of the Latin Vulgate which had been used as the text of Scripture in the Catholic churches since the time of Jerome. Although Erasmus used ridicule extensively in his criticism of the Catholic church he did not launch out into an energetic program of reformation. He did, however, supply much of the material that other men used. It has been said that Erasmus laid the egg that Luther hatched.

Chapter Twenty-One

Decline of Papal Influence

When one considers the wide spread corruption that pervaded the entire Roman church from 1275 on, it is to be expected that great opposition would develop — opposition destined to overthrow the claims of the strongest popes. There were many factors that favored such opposition. We have noted the rise of a new individualism, renewed interest in nationalism and a loss of spiritual concern which might be called secularization among the common people. There were other factors bearing on the eventual outburst of the Reformation.

I. THE POPES

Boniface VIII (1294-1303) was the last of the strong popes. It is said that he "came in like a fox, ruled like a lion, and died like a dog." The first expression is prompted by the story that in order to secure his predecessor's resignation, he stuck a reed through a crack in the wall and every night after the pope retired he whispered through the reed "it is the Lord's will that thou shouldest resign." Finally, deciding it was the Lord talking to him, he resigned. Boniface then, through bribery, obtained the election. The second expression in the statement suggests the authority he assumed while pope, and the third refers to the unmanly way in which he met his death.

As one third of all the land of Western Europe had fallen into the hands of the church, it was difficult for the secular rulers to find enough taxes to support their government. Accordingly, they began to tax church property. Boniface pronounced an excommunication upon all who demanded taxes from church lands or property. This brought him into direct conflict with the kings of both England and France. Attempting to bring the kings under submission he issued the bull *Unam Sanctum* in 1302, which stated that if the king should err he would be judged by the pope, but the pope could be judged by God alone.[1] And, "furthermore we declare, state, defiine and pronounce that it is altogether necessary to salvation for every human creature to be subject to the Roman pontiff."[2] In opposition Philip of France convened the legislative body of France and due to a new French nationalism the French Knights stood with him against the pope. In the conflict which followed the pope was captured and Italy was brought into submission to Philip. Beaten and humiliated, his mind affected, Boniface died in 1303. Thus the papacy, in conflict with the new feeling of nationalism, was defeated in its claims of supremacy over secular rulers.

After this episode the papacy was dominated by the king of France from 1309 to 1377. The papal court was then moved to Avignon, France, marking the beginning of an era referred to as the "Babylonian Captivity" of the papacy. During this time the papacy was a plaything of the French king. The Italians, of course, disliked losing the pope from Rome and complained that the spiritual aspect of the church was being neglected and that it was becoming more corrupt. In 1377 the Italians were clamoring to bring the pope back to Rome and accordingly produced a council of cardinals that elected a new pope. The events were as follows: In 1377 Pope Gregory XI returned from Avignon to Rome to attempt to regain the prestige of the papacy. He died, however, the next year, and the cardinals were forced by the people of Rome to elect Urban VI as the new pope. Urban immediately showed a lack of respect for the cardinals and feeling that his election had been made under pressure the cardinals reversed their decision and elected Clement VIII as pope. Clement removed the papal court back to Avignon. Both of these men were elected by the same group of cardinals and both claimed to be the legitimate pope and true successor of Peter. In this state of confusion the people were undecided as to which pope should receive their loyalty. As it developed, Northern Italy and most of Germany, Scandinavia and England followed the Roman pope, and France, Spain, Scotland and Southern Italy, Clement VII of Avignon. Thus developed the "Great Schism."

In an attempt to bring order out of this chaos the theologians of the University of Paris suggested that a council be call-

1. Bettenson, p. 162.
2. Ibid., p. 163.

ed to decide the matter. This suggestion was followed, and the
Council of Pisa met in July and August of 1409. At this time
Benedict VIII was pope at Avignon and Gregory XII at Rome.
Each of these popes had excommunicated the other, and the
church was in a state of general confusion. The council deposed both of them and appointed as their successor Alexander
V. The two deposed popes, however, refused to recognize the
decision of the council, and both excommunicated the members
of the council as well as their new pope. Now there were three
popes instead of two. When Alexander V died the following
year, John XXIII was selected to continue his work, claiming
to be rightful pope. Under these conditions John XXIII called
upon Sigsmund, the Emperor of the Holy Roman Empire, to
convoke a council to settle the matter. The council of Constance first met in 1414 and then periodically until 1418. It
succeeded in deposing all three of the men who claimed to be
the true pope and elected Martin V. The unrest, however, continued in France, and until 1449 the French church maintained
a pope at Avignon. During this time they attempted to establish
the French church apart from the power of the Roman pope.
The council of Basel finally acknowledged defeat by dissolving
itself in 1449 which brought an end to the papacy in France.
The attempt of the French church, however, to create a con-
stitutional body without relationship to the Roman pope greatly disturbed the papacy and efforts were made to prohibit such
development in the future. Feeling that the possibility of councils constituted a danger in this respect, Pius II in 1459 issued a
bull called *Execrabilis* which condemned any appeals to future
general councils.

During the Renaissance the popes of the Catholic church
had other things in mind than the welfare of the church itself.
Nicholas V (1447 to 1455) was a cultured and learned scholar
who was interested in literature and art. His driving passion
was to gather together books expressing the culture of the ages.
He founded the Vatican library and put the strength of the
papacy behind the new culture, using the treasury of the Vatican for the purchase of books and buildings. He said that he
would "like to spend all he had on books and buildings." He
did and the church continued in a state of moral decay. Alexander VI who was pope from 1492 to 1503 is one of the out-

standing examples of debauchery in the papacy. He lived a very immoral life, being the father of six children by two women. He served under five popes and bribed twenty-five cardinals to eventually obtain the election. He put his children in prominent church offices but was afraid that his own life might be taken by his son for political reasons. Alexander had outstanding political ability but seemed totally indifferent to the ethical demands of the Christian religion.

Pius II (1458-1464), another example of the Renaissance popes, came from a noble family and was widely traveled, but like most of the men of his day he was not concerned with morality. He was skilled in writing, producing both histories and novels. Present at the Council of Basel, he wrote a history of it. His history, however, was put on the index by the Catholic church because it suggested conciliar rather than papal authority. After his ascension to the papacy his great interest was in outfitting ships and creating an armed force to defend the Empire against the Turks.

Julian II (1503-1513) is referred to as the Warrior Pope because of his love for maintaining an army. He not only raised and supported his own army as pope but delighted to drill the soldiers himself.

In 1513 Leo X was elected to the papacy. He was a member of the wealthy De Medici family of Florence. Being informed that he had received the election, he said to his friends, "God has given us the papacy, let us enjoy it."

In view of these conditions it is not surprising that the church leaders themselves were saying that the church needed a reformation in head and membership. Reaction against the immoral conditions that existed within the church was the direct cause for reform. Any attempts at reformation would be supported by a new nationalism. This, with the support of the new learning which was bringing the study of Scripture into prominence, made success possible. Since the Renaissance found such an important background for undertaking the Reformation, a more detailed look into it is necessary.

II. THE RENAISSANCE

The word Renaissance is of Latin derivation and literally means re-birth. It is used in reference to that rebirth of culture in Western Europe following what is generally referred to as the dark ages. During the medieval period attention had been focused upon the church. Submission to the hierarchy was stressed in order to bring glory to God. The church was the center of life. The power of the pope was felt by all, and every individual felt that the universe was ruled by God, that history had its beginning and end with God and that the church represents God's will on earth. In this arrangement man's life was controlled by institutions. Each individual had an allotted place in society with certain privileges and responsibilities and each had to stay in his place. The Renaissance changed this type of thinking by a rediscovery of the individual. The humanism which developed placed the emphasis upon the fact that each individual was important, and that if it were for the welfare of the individual to move out of the established social order that he should do so.

Another emphasis of the Renaissance was the rediscovery of classical culture. Aristotle and Plato became very popular again, and many persons searched for additional manuscripts of theirs. Writers began not only to rediscover the literature of the past but also to imitate the style of the classical authors, and this brought on an effort to recapture the viewpoint of the ancients. To see life as they saw it resulted in a secularization of thought. Even in some places morals were affected to such an extent that immorality was actually glorified. As a result of this new reverence given to the ancient writers the classics were given a place in the curricula of the schools. This broadened the curriculum of education and produced better methods of study resulting in a more scientific approach to history. This emphasis also brought advances in art and science as well as in literature.

Dante (1265-1321) is a good illustration of the transition that was taking place in medieval thinking. One of his outstanding works, the *Divine Comedy*, depicts the beliefs of the average person of his day. In this composition Dante sets forth in a great religious epic an allegory of Christian thought. It is an encyclopedia of knowledge concerning medieval thought and practices. He pictures Hell, Purgatory and Heaven as having many compartments, each which may furnish the source of later concepts of the after-life. But Dante had other interests as well. He wrote his autobiography entitled *The New Life*. In a work entitled *Concerning the Mother Tongue* Dante pleaded for the use of the *vernacular* language in literary works. Later writers turned from religion to unite on purely secular matters.

III. PETRARCH (1304-1375)

An outstanding example of humanism is to be found in the person and work of Petrarch. In 1323 he gave up the study of law to give himself entirely to the classics. Beginning in 1330 he travelled in search of manuscripts and spent his time writing sonnets. He was so taken by the classical writers of the past that he refused to have the writings of the scholastics in his library, saying that they had no place beside the classics. In 1350 Petrarch met Boccaccio (1313-1375) and encouraged him to take up the study of classical culture. Boccaccio became one of the great humanists and wrote a series of biographies of the Greeks. He wrote romantic novels and became the father of Italian prose. He is the earliest master of the short story, writing the *Decameron* which established a pattern for subsequent short stories.

Humanism in the extreme is a work of Machiavelli entitled *The Prince*. In this manual he stated that the successful prince must set aside all consideration of religion and ethics. It would be proper for him to appear religious and at the same time employ fraud. He might even be ruthless when necessary. There should be two standards of morality — one for the prince and another for the nation. The prince must distrust the masses for they were ungrateful, inconsistent, deceitful and greedy. Accordingly, the prince should not consider himself bound to keep any promises he had made to the people. He emphasized that the state was supreme in power and must be made and kept strong. In this he set forth the principle or totalitarianism. The prince must rely on military force and maintain universal conscription of all over seventeen years of age. The state must be imperialistic, strike suddenly with superior force and do all the injury possible. He further stated that diplomacy should be coordinated with military force in order to advance the state, and that one power should be played against another so that the state would collect from both. Victor Emanuel, who unified Italy in 1870 slept with a copy of *The Prince* under his pillow. Mussolini wrote the dissertation for his doctorate on the "Military Ideas of Machiavelli."

Pico Marandilo (1463-1494), a student of over twenty languages, emphasized the dignity of man, stating that there was nothing more wonderful than a man. He has the power to choose what he wants to do and can either degenerate or develop spiritually as he wills. This emphasis on man's will was a distinct contradiction to the idea held by the medieval church. The Renaissance, emphasizing the dignity of man, laid the foundation for an independence of thought which eventually broke the grip of Catholic theology over the minds of men.

South of the Alps emphasis had been placed on the secular nature of life, but when the Renaissance crossed to the north, it shifted to a study of the Bible in the original languages. The northern humanists shared an interest in the classics to be sure but were more conservative than the Italians, accepting less of paganism.

A number of outstanding scholars, such as John Colet (1467-1519) and Sir Thomas Moore (1478-1535), studied in the better schools of Europe and returned to spread the Renaissance in England.

With the decline of papal influence the effects of the great Schism, the rise of rationalism and a rebirth of learning, the stage was set for successful reformation. There had been many brave reformers in former centuries but conditons had not been favorable for their success. Now the foundation was laid which would insure the triumph of future reformatory efforts.

PART SIX

THE PROTESTANT REFORMATION
1517 - 1800 A.D.

PART SIX

THE PROTESTANT REFORMATION
1517 - 1800 A.D.

Chapter Twenty-Two

The German Reformation

The immediate cause for the reformation in Germany was an arrangement between Pope Leo X and Prince Albert who was Archbisop of two Roman provinces but was also eager to fill the vacant archbishopric of Mainz. Because he needed to raise large sums of money Pope Leo worked with Albert and issued a bill authorizing the sale of indulgences in Germany. Martin Luther, who was a priest at Wittenburg, resented this arrangement and led a movement against the Catholic hierarchy. As we have observed already there were many leaders in the past who had broken with the papacy and attempted to lead reformatory movements, but without success. At this time there were a number of conditions that favored the success of Luther's movement.

The Renaissance had spread to such an extent that through a revival of interest in study of the Scripture many people were aware of the fact that the church of the New Testament was far different from the church in existence in Western Europe. Through the study of the Scripture many people had seen that the sacraments, as dispensed by the hierarchy as the means of obtaining salvation, were not based upon Scriptural authority. Such thinking led these students of Scripture to reexamine the entire basis of faith. As a result of this examination they came to the conclusion that the hierarchy did not stand in a mediatory position and that the system of "work righteousness" was entirely contrary to salvation by grace through faith.

This conclusion, however, had been reached by reformers before. Other factors must be considered in determining the cause of Luther's success. We do not search far until we become increasingly aware of the corruption of the hierarchy in the Roman Catholic church. Selfish priests were buying and selling church offices without restraint. Many such officers would receive the salary for a position in the church but do none of the work. The moral decay was further indicated by the fact that in the church courts "justice" could be purchased for money. For financial considerations an individual also could receive dispensations which would set aside canon law and make an exception in favor of the purchaser. Through this means divorces could be granted or illegal marriages sanctioned. Such moral decay extended to the personal lives of the priests and many of them lived in open sin and kept concubines. Personal religion was neglected and the priests were content to go through the formality of saying masses and proclaiming that through their magic powers they could dispense the grace of God.

The religious and moral corruptions now could be effectively combated because of the intellectual freedom which had been encouraged by the Renaissance. Men began to see in the Scripture that the claims of the clergy were unfounded, and with a new intellectual basis for their criticism, ideas of opposition to the hierarchy spread rapidly.

Secular rulers became willing to support opposition to the hierarchy on religious as well as on economic grounds. At this time in Western Europe the Roman church possessed one third of the land, and the rising middle class as well as the rulers and nobles were eager to obtain these church lands. The rulers had resented the loss of funds that had been siphoned into the papal treasury. The indulgence which aroused Luther's opposition was just another means of bringing additional funds to Rome. Secular rulers were also willing to support the reform leaders out of political considerations. They were supported by a rising nationalism as they opposed the power of this "foreign ruler" of Rome in their territories.

Although these many factors worked together to make the reformation a success the primary motivating force was the desire to return to the purity of New Testament Christianity. The reformers were eager to reform the church in keeping with the New Testament and thus return to the authority of the Bible instead of following the authority of the hierarchy. In rejecting the authority of the hierarchy the reformers of necessity revolted against papal authority. The Catholic church would not allow any divergence from its set pattern of organization and worship. Accordingly, all who attempted real reform were forced out of the Catholic church and treated as heretics.

I. THE SALE OF INDULGENCES

Prince Albert of Brandenburg, at only twenty-three years of age, paid Pope Leo X approximately twenty-five thousand dollars for the dispensation of holding a second bishopric. But being very ambitious, Albert was not satisfied to hold only two high offices in the church. When the Archbishopric of Mainz became vacant, Albert immediately contacted the pope about the purchase of this office. Through papal legates it was arranged that Albert could become Archbishop of Mainz if he would pay approximately $250,000 to the pope as the regular fee and in addition pay another $250,000 for the privilege of holding a third office. It was not expected that Albert would have this much ready cash, and so the legate suggested that Albert could borrow the money from the Fugger banking house in Augsburg. This required collateral, and the pope accordingly issued a bull authorizing the sale of indulgences in certain German states, which would be security to the banking firm that the loan would be repaid. Upon this basis Albert borrowed one hundred thousand dollars cash as a down payment to the pope with the understanding that he would pay another five hundred thousand dollars through the sale of indulgences.

An indulgence grew out of the theory of the sacrament of penance. Because of sin against God or one's neighbor an individual was required to make satisfaction for this offense. It was said that God would forgive sin, but the church must require temporal punishment. The priest was to state the terms upon which the church would forgive sin. Accordingly, it was declared that the individual could not fully atone for his sin on this earth but would have to suffer in purgatory sufficiently to make full atonement. An indulgence was an act of mercy granted by the hierarchy whereby the church, through the power God granted to Peter, could relax the amount of satisfaction required and grant forgiveness for the sin without the required atonement being made. In this way an indulgence would remove all requirements made by the church or by God and obtain full remission. This theory applied not only to the living but extended into purgatory. According to this teaching, living persons could obtain indulgences which would shorten the stay of their relatives in purgatory. To work out all of these details, Alexander of Halles (d. 1245) had explained the existence of a treasury of merits, whereby all of the goodness of Christ and the saints were stored up in a heavenly account and left to the disposal of the pope. Through an indulgence the pope could draw on this extra goodness stored up in the treasury of merits and apply it to any sinner that he so desired.

According to the agreement of Pope Leo X and Albert, John Tetzel was hired as the master salesman. He was to go through Germany and sell certificates for purgatory. Tetzel said that if the living would purchase the certificates for the dead, the very moment he received their money in his big iron chest the soul of the person named on the certificate would be freed from its pain and flit out of purgatory. Tetzel traveled with quite a company of assistants. The Fugger banking company sent along a representative to collect their part out of each day's sales. The indulgences were priced on a scale[1] according to recognized classifications. Then follows a graded schedule of rates. The Kings and Bishops and their families would pay twenty-five Rhenish gold guilders; abbots, counts and barons, etc., were to pay ten; lesser nobles and ecclesiastics and others with incomes of less than five hundred would pay six guilders; and citizens with their own income would pay one guilder and those without regular incomes would pay one-half guilder. Those purchasing these indulgences were guaranteed to receive the full absolution of their sins which was ordinarily reserved to be granted by the pope.

In order to encourage purchasers to buy the instructions stated, "that we also declare that in order to obtain these two most important graces, it is not necessary to make confession, or to visit the churches and altars, but merely to procure the confessional letter."[2] This was interpreted to mean that the purchaser of the indulgence would not have to attend masses or go to confession any further. He had a guarantee that when he died he would skip purgatory. It was this situation which aroused Martin Luther. In the face of such travesty on religion he had to speak.

1. Bettenson, op. cit., 261
2. Ibid., p. 262

II. MARTIN LUTHER

Martin Luther was born in Eisleben, Saxony, in 1483. He
was baptized the day after his birth, and since that was the day
of St. Martin, he was given his name. He was born into a peas-
ant home. His father was a poor miner, and during his early
childhood the family had meager means of livelihood. He had
a godly mother who was interested in bringing him up according to the strict regulations of the hierarchy. Later, the family
moved to Mansfeld where Luther attended a common school
which was entirely in Latin. At fourteen years of age he attended a school maintained by the "Brethren of the Common
Life" and here he came in contact with mysticism and the
humanistic studies. The following year at Eisenach, Luther
studied under John Trebonius, a very able humanist who exchanged letters with Erasmus. Trebonius had a great interest
in the training of young men and to show his faith in education,
he had a habit of taking his hat off to little boys he met on the
street. When asked about this habit he said that he never knew
what great man he might be passing. Trebonius was able to in-
spire Luther to take his studies seriously. In the year 1501 he
entered the University of Erfurt with advanced standing, and
here he specialized in philosophy and began a study of Greek.
In 1502 he received the Bachelors Degree and stood thirtieth
in a class of fifty-seven. His father encouraged him to go into
the study of law, and in 1505 he took his Masters Degree. At
this time he stood second in a class of seventeen. Upon graduation, his father gave him a set of *The Body of Civil Law*.
But at this time, instead of beginning a practice of law, he became more interested in the salvation of his soul and read the
works of Augustine very earnestly. He then decided that he had
been so wicked that he must be among the non-elect but decided to enter a monastery to see if he could purify his soul. In
1505 he entered the Augustinian convent at Erfurt. As a monk
he was very devout and did more than was required by his fellow monks to obtain purity of life. He continually confessed his
sins to his superiors even going beyond the usual requirements.
On one occasion he fasted three weeks and would have died
had not one of the monks, contrary to regulations, entered his
cell to see what was wrong. He found Luther near death but

by careful attention nursed him back to health. In spite of all his confessions, fasting and praying, Luther could not receive satisfaction of heart. He later said that if ever a monk would have gone to heaven by his monkery that he would have gone there. Because of Luther's unhappy spiritual life, Staupitz, an official in the Augustinian Order, suggested that he read the writings of the Apostle Paul. He thought that Paul's letters would give him peace of mind. Accordingly, Luther obtained a copy of the Scripture. His study revealed to him the grace of God, and by the year 1508 he had come to the conclusion that the Catholic church and its system of "work righteousness" was contrary to the teaching of the New Testament.

Luther advanced rapidly in the Augustinian Order. In 1511 he made a trip to Rome on business for his order and was impressed with the immorality there among the clergy. In spite of this he wanted to visit all of the shrines and receive every blessing that could be derived from a trip through the Holy City. He was at the time loyal to the pope. In one church he was shocked when a priest, saying mass in Latin, did not perform the "miracle" of transubstantiation and then gave the bread to the worshippers. The priest later laughed about it to other priests because the people could not tell the difference.

In contrast to his experience in Rome the statement of the Apostle Paul that "the just shall live by faith" began to make a deep impression upon his mind. In 1512 he received his doctor's degree. In 1517 when Tetzel came selling indulgences Luther was holding three jobs. He was teaching in the new University at Wittenburg, giving very popular lectures on the writings of the Apostle Paul and the Psalms. Students came from all over Western Europe to hear his lectures. He was also commissioned by his superiors to serve as parish priest in the church in Wittenburg. And here as a preacher he came to know the lives and problems of the people of the church. He was also an official in the Augustinian Order, being an inspector of monasteries.

Frederick the Wise, Elector of Saxony, knew of the sale of indulgences and determined that in order to hold money within his territory he would not permit Tetzel to enter Saxony. However, Tetzel set up his booth at Juterbock on the border of Saxony and only a few miles from Wittenburg. It was here that many of Luther's parishoners went to purchase indulgences. In opposition to the entire system of selling indulgences Luther nailed on his church door in Wittenburg on October 31, 1517, ninety-five theses in which he set forth his opposition to indulgences and offered to debate any who differed with him. On this same day he sent a copy of the theses to the Archbishop Albert and preached a sermon against indulgences calling attention to his Ninety-five Theses. Such revolt against the hierarchy immediately attracted attention and the Ninety-five Theses within weeks were all over Germany.

John Eck, who was professor of Theology at Ingolstadt, made a review of the Ninety-five Theses and a pamphlet warfare was begun between Luther and Eck. In 1518 there was a meeting of the Augustinian Monks at Heidleberg which Luther attended. There he found that his opposition to indulgences was the center of interest. In explaining his position he found that he had a very strong following among these monks. In this same year news of the theses had reached the pope at Rome and Leo sent a papal legate, Cajetan, to settle the disturbance. Cajetan was an Italian and held the Germans in contempt. In conference with Luther they both lost their tempers and the conference closed with their shouting at each other. Luther then appealed to a general council to consider the situation. In the year 1518 he obtained a very strong supporter in the person of Melanchthon, who began teaching Greek in the University of Wittenburg. In the following year, 1519, the pope in another attempt to settle the disturbance in Germany sent Mililitz who was a German and of mild disposition. In the conference which followed Luther agreed to be silent on the issues if his opponents would stop their criticism of him. John Eck, however, at this time challenged Luther's followers to a debate, and one of the professors of Wittenberg, Carlstadt, who had supported Luther, accepted the challenge from Eck. As Carlstadt was not skillful in argumentation, Luther knew that the debate would go against him and that he would have to defend his position himself. The debate began June 27, 1519, in Leipzig. Carlstadt began but Luther soon took over, and in the discussion which followed he was faced with the necessity of deciding where the final authority in religion resided. Eck contended that the authority was in the church and showed

Luther that he possessed views similar to those of John Huss. Luther rejected the authority of a general council when it differed from Scripture. Eck contended that a great council could not err and that Luther was a heretic.

This re-examination of Luther's position forced him to see the logical conclusion of his position. In defending Scripture, he was proud to defy both councils and hierarchy. In 1520 a bull of excommunication was issued by the pope which stated that unless Luther would recant he would be cast out of the church. To show his contempt for such a document, Luther called together the students of Wittenburg, paraded through the streets and burned the papal bull. For good measure they also threw in a copy of the canon law and some theological treatises of the day.

One reason for the success of the reformation in Germany was Luther's use of the printing press. In the year 1520 he published and gave wide circulation to three tracts. The first one, *An Address to the Christian Nobility of the German Nation,* appealed to the German nobles to take a lead in the reformation of the church. The first part of this tract stated that the pope was hiding behind three walls. The first wall was that the papacy had created a distinction between priest and layman which was not according to Scripture. This placed the spiritual power over the temporal, and in opposition to this Luther asserted the "priesthood of all believers." The second wall was that as head of the church and God's representative on earth the pope had final authority to interpret the Scripture. Luther challenged this principle, declaring that every Christian had the right to interpret the Scripture for himself and that the intelligent Christian could interpret as well as the pope. The third was the fact that only the pope could call a general council. Luther here stated that it was the duty of the Christian princes to call a council. As events developed this proved to be one of Luther's biggest mistakes. For as he began to rely upon secular authority to govern the church, he laid the foundation for national churches and this became a hindrance to future progress toward truth. The second part of this address contains fifty-seven sections in which he discusses individual abuses he found within the church. He mentioned such things as money that was being taken out of Germany to Rome, the size of the Curia that the pope had to support, the corruption of the church trials, the number of pilgrimages that were being required, and suggested that Italian church officials should be kept out of Germany. He also appealed for a reform of education, believing that the writings of Aristotle, since he gave support to Scholastic legalism, should be kept out of the schools.

A second composition of 1520 was *On the Babylonian Captivity of the Church*. This was an examination of the sacremental system. In it Luther examined all seven sacraments of the Catholic church and eliminated them one by one until he had left only the Lord's Supper and baptism as sacraments. He thought there might be some sacramental value to repentance, but not in the idea of penance as developed by the hierarchy.

The third important tract of 1520 was *On the Freedom of the Christian Man*. Luther dedicated this to Pope Leo X. In it he states that he would make peace with the pope if the pope would take over the matter of reformation. He then emphasizes that the Christian man is justified by faith and, accordingly, is free lord of all and servant to none. But the Christian man being justified by faith owes an obligation to every one whom he can serve.

In the following year, 1521, Luther was summoned before the German Diet which met in the town of Worms. Charles V promised Luther safe conduct to and from the Diet. Friends of Luther reminded him that John Huss went to the Council of Constance under the same type of safe conduct and in spite of this was burned at the stake. These friends warned Luther that he would never come away alive. With great courage Luther accepted the invitation and stood trial for his faith. During the council his writings were shown to him, and the Court demanded that he recant his heresy. Luther declared that many things he wrote were true and they would not want him to recant them, but that he would give up anything they showed him to be wrong. He stated that unless he was convinced by Scripture and sound reason that what he wrote was false, he could not recant. Luther regarded the Bible, interpreted by the individual with the aid of reason and the help of the Holy Spirit, as the final authority in religion. He was not willing to bow before the pope or the council or human tradition. He wanted the Diet to debate these principles with him, but they were unwilling to do so. The Diet demanded that Luther give a direct answer to the demand that he recant his heresy. To this Luther replied, "Since then Your Majesty and your lordships desire a simple reply, I will answer without horns and without teeth. Unless I am convicted by Scripture and plain reason — I do not accept the authority of popes and councils, for they have contradicted each other — my conscience is captive to the Word of God. I cannot and I will not recant anything, for to go against conscience is neither right nor safe. God help me. Amen." The earliest printed version added the words: "Here I stand, I cannot do otherwise."[3] The council condemned him as a heretic and asked Charles V to retain him in prison; Charles V, however, kept his word and allowed Luther to leave unmolested. He had 21 days in which to make his decision.

On the way home he was "kidnapped" for his own good by an armed band of friends who escorted him to the castle at Wartburg where he remained in hiding for ten months. While there he spent his time in translating the New Testament into German. The following year, in order to settle the confusion which had developed in the city of Wittenburg, Luther left his hiding, came to Wittenburg and began to preach publicly. Although he was excommunicated by the pope and under imperial ban he was unmolested. Charles V intended to invade Germany and bring the German church into submission to the pope but he had a quarrel with the pope and thought that by waiting he could use the German reformation to get certain concessions from him. He was also kept busy on the borders repulsing the invasions of the Turks, who were threatening to break into the Empire. In addition he had difficulty with the king of France, and being the type man who could not delegate authority he kept postponing his effort to bring Luther into submission. During this period of delay Luther preached boldly, establishing new congregations and organizing the Reformation all over Germany. Graduates from the University of Wittenburg went out in every direction to spread the principle of the Reformation. Many German princes also sponsored Lutheranism in their districts, and with the passing of each week the Lutheran movement was gaining momentum.

3. Roland H. Bainton, **Here I Stand** (Nashville: Abingdon Press, 1950). p. 185.

Luther's writings against Monasticism and life in the convents led many to desert the Monastic life, and on one occasion Luther found himself confronted with a group of young ladies who had been smuggled out of a nunnery. They appealed to him for help and advice. He succeeded in arranging for the marriage of all but one of them to some monk or student. The obstinent young lady was named Katherin von Bora. After suggesting several possible husbands whom Katherine turned down, Luther finally asked her, "Who would you marry?" and she immediately replied "Dr. Luther." She proved a very worthy companion for Luther and with him enjoyed a life of happiness. Into their home were born three sons and two daughters.

As is to be expected in such cases many people began to use the Lutheran Reformation for selfish purposes. The peasants thought they saw in the movement an opportunity to revolt against their lords, and in 1525 there was a revolution known as the Peasants War. Luther had written in favor of the peasants, but when they revolted with violence he took the part of the lords and wrote very strongly against the "murderous, thieving bands of peasants." He said they were like mad dogs and they ought to be treated as such, stating, "Let every one who can, strike, strangle, poison or stab, secretly or in public" these who had rebelled against their lords. This rebellion made Luther question the possibility of relying upon the average man of Germany to bring about reform and he now turned more to the nobility. This conviction resulted later in the development of a State religion.

III. DIET OF SPEIER

In order to consolidate the gains which were being made by the Reformation, the Lutheran nobility of Germany took advantage of a Diet which was called to meet in the town of Speier in 1526. Most of the nobles were Lutheran, and they were able to decree that each German prince had the right to decide which religion would be supported in his principalities. Many princes immediately legalized the Reformation. With this favorable turn of events Luther, Melanchthon and the students of Wittenburg worked desperately to spread the Reformation into the new territory to consolidate their gains. They carried on an extensive correspondence as well as producing many tracts in print. Following this Diet Charles V became disturbed over the increase of Lutheranism and called a second Diet to meet at Speier in the year 1529. At this time the decisions of 1526 were reversed, for the Catholic nobility was in the majority.

During the meeting Lutheran princes immediately protested the reversing of the decision of 1526, and because of this protest, the word "Protestant" was first used in reference to the reformers.

The opposition of Charles led the reformers to realize they would be attacked with physical force and that they would have to organize for armed resistance. Accordingly they formed themselves into what was known as the Schmalkaldic League. By this time the Reformation had spread into Switzerland and the followers of Luther went to Switzerland in an attempt to unite the two movements for greater armed resistence to Charles V. The differences between Luther and Zwingli that prevented a full and complete union of forces will be discussed in the chapter on the Swiss Reformation.

While Charles V was waiting to bring the Lutheran Reformers under submission to the pope they were asked to present a statement of their faith at a Diet which was to meet in Augsburg in 1530. Melanchthon is largely responsible for the composition of this statement which became the Lutheran catechism and is known as the Augsburg Confession. The catechism was condemned by the Diet of Augsburg, and Charles V again expressed his determination to crush the Reformation. He was, however, at this time, having difficulty with the Turks who were trying to come up through the Balkans and he had to turn his attention to them. He told the German princes that within six months he would return and crush Lutheranism. Charles was not, however, able for several years to get his affairs in position to carry out his threat.

Luther died in 1546 of natural causes and was spared the pain of living to see armed conflict. The following year, 1547, Charles did carry out his threat and defeated the German princes in their first encounter. At this time Prince Maurice of France was supporting Charles V. After the first defeat of the reformers Maurice switched sides and the Lutheran reformers rallied under his standard. Charles delayed his second clash until 1552 and at this time the Lutheran army was victorious and the forces of Charles were defeated and forced to withdraw from Germany. In 1555 peace terms were drawn up in the Peace of Augsburg. This document stated that Lutheranism and Catholicism could both be tolerated in the Empire and that each prince could decide which religion would be legal in his territory. It was further stated that if a citizen did not like the decision of his prince he would move without loss of property and take up residence under the prince that he desired. As to the territory held by the church, it was decided that if the Catholic prince in charge of the lands of the church should become a Lutheran that he could not take the church land with him but that it would remain under the control of the Catholic church, but that the priest could not change his religion without molestation.

After the death of Luther, his followers began to quarrel among themselves as to the correct interpretation of certain Scripture. Melanchthon became the leader of the Lutherans but did not have the strength of character sufficient to maintain unity. Many of the Lutheran theologians accused Melanchthon of leaving Luther's doctrine of salvation by faith only as he agreed that man's effort was also necessary. The opposition of the theologians became so strong that Melanchthon was heartsick with internal controversy and when he died in 1560, he made the statement that he thanked God that he could now die and escape the fury of the theologians. The controversy within the church, however, continued and there developed a "Protestant Scholasticism" which was an attempt to crystalize Reformation doctrine very much as the Catholics had crystalized theirs during the period of the Scholastics.

In subsequent years the Augsburg Confession was modified, and through the "Formula of Concord" drawn up in 1580 further attempts at unity were made. This document became a test creed and many Lutherans began to place more emphasis on conformity to the creed than they did upon the study of the Scripture. In this manner the Lutheran movement lost its force. The people looked to the creed with a mere intellectual assent very much as the medieval Catholic had looked to the authority of the Roman Church.

Luther had, however, set a pattern for Reformation that spread over most of Western Europe. He laid down the four basic principles of all Protestantism. (1) Justification by faith; (2) The priesthood of all believers; (3) The right of the individual to interpret the Scripture; and (4) The final authority in religion is the Scripture itself, rather than the authority of the church. These principles were spread in many ways and soon the Reformation had taken foothold in all of the Western European states.

In Sweden the Reformation was adopted as early as 1526. In Denmark it took root in 1539 and in Norway in 1536. The Lutheran church became the state church of these countries. In Bohemia the Lutheran principles were eagerly accepted, but instead of becoming the Lutheran church, Bohemia was influenced by the teaching of John Huss, and the Reformation there strengthened the Moravian church. In Finland Lutheranism was established in 1528 by royal decree, and until today about ninety-seven percent of the people remain Lutheran. The Lutheran movement also spread to America and instead of its being established as a state church, it followed the linguistic stocks which brought it over. In this manner there was established in the United States the Lutheran church in almost every group who came from Europe to America.

From the beginning Luther had not desired separation from the Catholic church, but his principles later forced him into a complete break. The Lutherans at first did not claim to have established any new church. They rather worked to eliminate the unscriptural doctrine and practice of the Catholic church and through Reformation return to the church as it had existed before the development of Romanism. It is on this theory that Lutheran ministers and bishops claim a succession of ordination back through the Catholic hierarchy to the days of the Apostles before the corruption developed.

In looking back over the purposes of the Reformation at its beginning we are caused to regret that the Reformation did not accomplish what its early leaders had hoped. As national churches developed under the secular powers and as creeds were developed to take the place of the Scripture, the Lutheran movement fell short of full truth. Luther was making progress toward a full understanding of New Testament truth until 1529 when he was forced to write his first creed. For after formulating his doctrine in credal form he was forced to spend the rest of his life defending what he had written. If he had not been forced to write his convictions in credal form, he would have continued to pursue his course toward a restoration of the New Testament church. Defending creeds, which at best can only contain partial truth, has constantly been a hindrance to unity and true undenominationalism.

Chapter Twenty-Three

The Swiss Reformation

I. HULDREICH ZWINGLI (1484-1531)

Huldreich Zwingli was born into the family of an influential farmer who was also a chief magistrate in the town of Wildhaus. His uncle, a parish priest who was in good standing with the church, took a great interest in Zwingli and encouraged him to obtain a thorough education. Accordingly, he attended the Universities of Basel and Bern as well as the University of Vienna. He received a B.A. degree in 1504 and an M.A. in 1506. In his education he studied under some of the outstanding humanists of his generation and decided early to devote his life to the humanistic studies. There was, however, the practical problem of how to make a living, and so in 1506 he became parish priest in the town of Glarus. During this time he corresponded with Erasmus, who encouraged him to make a study of the Greek New Testament. Reading the New Testament in the original language developed in him an interest in primitive Christianity and brought to his attention the need for reform. He began his work of reform by criticizing the practice of selling indulgences. At the same time he also opposed the Swiss mercenaries who were selling their services to the kings of Western Europe. He contended that they should give their services only in defense of the papacy. For this the pope granted him a special annual pension.

In 1516 Zwingli was made parish priest at Einsiedeln. Here was located a statue of Mary which was referred to as the "Black Virgin." Pilgrims came annually to this favorite shrine, and there were a number of superstitious stories connected with it. Zwingli began to oppose the blind faith placed in this statue. About this time he also began the study of Hebrew which gave him a better background for a study of the Old Testament. In 1519 he was called to be priest of the church in Zurich and here he adapted a new kind of sermon. Contrary to custom he began to preach a series of sermons on the books of the Bible. It was at this time that he first heard of the work of Martin Luther. He then read with interest everything that Luther wrote. In 1520 he had learned too much to remain a loyal subject to the papacy. He resigned his papal pension and began to criticize publicly the Catholic system. He declared that the tithes being paid to the pope were not of divine authority and that any payment should be on a voluntary basis.

In 1519 he brought into his home a widow, Anna Reinhard, as his wife. There was no marriage ceremony, but this was not uncommon for the priests of his day. There was a public marriage performed for them in 1524. In 1522 he prepared sixty-seven theses in which he differed with the Catholic church. He published them and offered to publicly debate them. At Zurich he became a very popular preacher. In his preaching he broke completely with the past, making his sermons biblical and expository in nature. And in these sermons he condemned many things which had no justification in Scriptures. In challenging the world to debate he called upon the city council to sit as judge. The council agreed to follow the theology of whichever debater proved his point. In 1523 the first of a series of debates was held. The town council decided in favor of Zwingli and one by one, changes began to be made in the worship and organization of the church in Zurich.

Zwingli set forth the idea of justification by faith, condemned the Catholic doctrine of mass and stopped the invoking of the saints. He contended that the clergy ought to marry in order to live holy lives. Church services should be conducted in the language of the people and monastic orders abolished. Being a keen debater, he carried the town council and soon the pictures of idols were removed from church buildings. Organs also were removed from the churches and instrumental music ceased to be used. The Lord's Supper became a memorial institution as the doctrine of transubstantiation was completely repudiated.

After the third debate in 1524 the council asked Zwingli to make any necessary changes that he felt would be in harmony with the Scripture and thus improve the situation in the church. This made Zwingli virtually dictator in the city of Zurich. Having been influenced by Erasmas, Zwingli relied largely on reason in all of his decisions, yet he relied on the Bible as a book of rules. His view of the Scripture would allow in church services only what the Bible approved. Luther would remove only what the Bible condemned, but Zwingli would approve only what he found set forth in Scripture. Zwingli's view was set forth in 1525 in a treatise entitled, "A Commentary on the True and False Religions."

II. MARBURG

As the reforming Protestants were in danger of extermination by the Catholics it was to their interest to unite their forces. Accordingly, representatives from Luther and Zwingli met in the castle of Philip of Hesse in Marburg in 1529 in an effort to work out their differences. These representatives found that the two leading reformers agreed on fourteen out of fifteen points which were considered essential for unity by Luther. The one point upon which they differed was in regard to the Lord's Supper. They both agreed that the priests could not perform a miracle to change the elements into the actual body and blood of Christ, but Luther insisted that the actual body and blood of Christ was present in the elements. The two reformers themselves then met for a discussion of this difference. Luther contended that as an iron was heated until it was red hot, it was still iron, but the heat was within it. He said in this manner there is within the bread and the wine the actual body and blood of Christ. Zwingli contended that the bread and the wine were "representative" of the body and the blood but they were not actually present. Luther took a piece of chalk and wrote on the banquet table, "this is my body" insisting that Jesus meant what He said. Zwingli agreed but argued that when Christ said "this is my body," His flesh was unbroken. He further pointed out that Jesus did not turn the bread into his actual flesh. Zwingli also contended that when Jesus said this cup is my blood He did not mean that it was His literal blood, for after having called it blood He said I will drink henceforth no more of this "fruit of the vine," showing that it was still fruit of the vine — even after he had called it blood. But Luther could not agree with Zwingli. He declared that Zwingli had a different spirit, and he was not willing to fellowship him.

The doctrine of the Lord's Supper as set forth by Luther is known as "consubstantiation" and is still held by modern

Lutheran theologists, who prefer the word "impanation" to "consubstantiation."

In 1529 the break within Switzerland between the Cantons of the Alps which had remained faithful to the pope in opposition to the growing influence of Zwingli, and the reformers came into open conflict. These rural Catholic cantons decided to stop the march of the reformers. To do so they organized the Christians' Union of Catholic cantons and began a warfare against the followers of Zwingli late in 1529. After a very minor conflict they made a peace at Cappel which gave the majority of citizens in each canton the right to decide which form of religion they desired. When the followers of Zwingli, however, continued to expand and made an effort to win Geneva, war broke out again in 1531. At this time Zwingli, as the chaplain, went with the army against the Catholics and was killed in battle. The final result was that each canton was given full control over its internal affairs.

It was not long until John Calvin had come to the front as the leader of the Reformation in Switzerland and the forces of Zwingli merged with the followers of Calvin to create the Reformed Churches of Switzerland. Zwingli had understood much of the teaching of the New Testament, and by accepting the principle that nothing would be permitted in religion that could not be proved by the Scripture, he had gone far toward re-establishing the pure New Testament church. He did not give up the doctrine of predestination, but held to the idea that those who had heard the gospel and rejected it were predestined to eternal condemnation. He had rejected the doctrine of original sin and taught that infants could be saved without baptism. By depending upon the town councils to bring about reformation he was depending upon human authority to reform the whole community. This concept is entirely out of harmony with the New Testament instruction that men are brought to Christ by individual conversion. Yet we are indebted to Zwingli for clarifying many points that were necessary before pure undenominationalism could emerge.

III. JOHN CALVIN (1509-1564)

As Martin Luther made a lasting impression on subsequent generations by his work in Germany so John Calvin in Switzerland became the organizer of a systematic Protestantism and laid down principles which have influenced a large part of the Protestant world until today. The term "Calvinism" is used to designate the system of theology worked out by John Calvin. The term "Reformed" is that generally used to apply to the followers of the Calvinistic Theology. The word "Presbyterian" has also been used to describe the system of government Calvin adopted to guide the church in Switzerland. The Presbyterian Churches are an outgrowth of his movement.

Calvin was born in 1509 of parents in the upper middle class of society. He received a thorough education, entering the University of Paris at fourteen years of age and remaining for five years. Here he studied theology and developed a skill in logic. He then spent two years in the study of law, and as his interest turned to the humanities he spent another two years studying Greek, Hebrew and the Latin Classics. In 1532 he wrote a commentary on "Seneca's Treatise on Mercy" in which he quoted fifty-five Latin authors and twenty-two Greek authors. This indicates that he had a very thorough grounding in the Classics. Calvin's conversion in 1533 was accompanied by a rather violent emotional experience after which he determined to give his life to the spread of Reformation ideas. The University had just selected Nicholas Cop as rector and Calvin helped him prepare his inaugural address. The speech was so filled with Reformatory ideas that it went far beyond what the University was willing to accept causing both Calvin and Cop to involuntarily leave Paris. Calvin wandered about from place to place continuing his studies. In 1536 he published his first edition of the *Institutes of the Christian Religion,* which was the most systematic compendium of religious beliefs produced during the Reformation movement.

In Geneva he met Farel, a preacher of Geneva who pled with Calvin to locate there and encourage the Reformation. Farel set forth his argument so skillfully that Calvin was led to believe it was God's will for him to remain. For the next two years Calvin worked diligently to turn the city of Geneva to the Reformed faith. Since the town council would not go along with Calvin in all of his demands he left the city in 1538. He had so many followers and had created such interest in his program that he was called back in 1541. At this time the town council turned the city over to Calvin and he became dictator of the city.

It was during the time that Calvin was city dictator that the burning of Servetus took place. Servetus was a doctor who had written a treatise on the Trinity, a work with which Calvin disagreed. Calvin persuaded the Catholics at first to apprehend Servetus, which they did. But he was able to persuade them they had the wrong man and escaped from their hands. Later he came through Geneva disguised. Calvin, however, recognized him and had him arrested, tried and burned at the stake in 1553.

Calvin required complete uniformity to his program. The city was so completely organized that a very effective spy system functioned smoothly. The religious leaders pronounced excommunication on all who refused to follow Calvin's theology, and the secular arm carried out the excommunication. Under this system during the period from 1542 to 1546 there were fifty-seven executions and seventy-six banishments from the city of Geneva because of heresy. The life of the individual was very carefully regulated. There were laws that prohibited swearing, requiring even the inn keepers to report any such offense. The inns were required to keep a Bible handy and to allow no dice, cards or gambling. Indecent songs were banned and no one was permitted to be out after nine o'clock at night, except the spies. Calvin officially held no position except membership in the city council of twelve. He was the minister of the church and his religious influence made him master of the city.

In order to spread his Reformation ideas Calvin established a college with Theodore Beza as head. This institution became so popular that students from all over Western Europe came to study. These would later return to their home countries to spread Calvin's ideas.

In many respects Calvin had followed the path of Zwingli. He believed that the Bible was the infallible guide for the church. He, however, believed that the Bible could be properly interpreted only by the elect. He gave the Ten Commandments a very important place in his theology, believing that Christ's re-interpretation of the Ten Commandments contained the heart of Christianity. He taught that the purpose of life was to glorify God instead of seeking pleasure and that man glorifies

260 of THE ETERNAL KINGDOM

God through holiness of life. This caused him to emphasize the idea that a Christian should be free from all luxury. One of the essential principles of his system of theology was human depravity. He accepted the teachings of Augustine that the will of man is depraved, and, accordingly, the doctrine of predestination was a necessary part of this theological system. Whereas Augustine said that God permits people to be damned, Calvin stressed that God "decreed" their condemnation and that the number was definitely established and could not be increased or diminished. For the elect he taught the corollary of predestination and the perseverance of the saints. As has already been suggested he required very strict adherence to his principles. Discipline, with excommunication for those who would not conform, was his rule. He required every member of the church to take communion at least four times a year, but he believed the sacraments of the church were only for the elect. Calvin was weak physically and due to his strenuous responsibilities died in 1564. Theodore Beza took the leadership of the Reformation Movement in Geneva at his death.

Studying the theology of Calvin in the light of the Scripture, we see many serious errors in his teaching. From the viewpoint of the New Testament church we regret that he influenced the thinking of so many people for so long a period of time. However, it should be kept in mind that he was the product of his age and understanding the hardships and handicaps under which he labored, we should be charitable in our judgment of him and grateful that he did make a contribution in bringing to light many of the errors that had come to being through the Catholic church. He made great steps forward, and it is through the efforts of such men as Luther, Zwingli and Calvin that we today can make forward steps toward a fuller understanding of the truth of Scripture.

IV. CALVINISM VERSUS ARMINIANISM

Jacob Arminius (1560-1609) was professor in the University of Leyden. He began to teach that the emphasis of John Calvin upon the bondage of the human will, irresistible grace, predestination and election was not according to Scripture. Among the Reformed Churches of the Netherlands he began to emphasize man's freedom of choice. The Calvinists held that God elects certain persons for salvation and that others are denied salvation no matter how much they desired it or what they did to procure it. This doctrine is called unconditional election. Calvin also taught that for the elect it would be impossible to resist God's grace or to go astray. Accordingly, they would be saved eternally. This was so because God wills it. The Calvinists held that since God had planned it this way it was just. Arminius taught that God would not will to do anything which was contrary to what is right, and thus His will was restricted by justice. He further held that God has foreknowledge and is able to foresee that man will sin of his own free will, but that He does not will nor predestine the man to do so. He emphasized that man's freedom stands in contrast to compulsion or to necessity. He reasoned that freedom exists only where there is a power of alternate choice. The Calvinists taught that the grace of God was available only for the elect and that it could not be resisted. This took salvation out of the realm of human achievement. It also emphasized that a man so predestined could never fall from God's grace. Arminius held that God's grace is not irresistible, but that if a Christian will desire the help of Christ and be active in trying to do His will, Christ will keep him from falling, but if a person rejected Christ, Christ would not hold him by irresistible grace. This conflict between Calvinism and Arminianism was the cause of division then and has continued in the religious world even until now.

Chapter Twenty-Four

The Spread of Reform Ideas in Europe

The movements headed by Martin Luther and Huldreich Zwingli are the two most important of the period. They are not, however, the only reform movements. Springing up almost simultaneously, yet growing out of them, are other movements which differed in many ways. Certain followers of Luther did not agree with him. Luther was willing to retain in church organization and worship anything which was not specifically condemned in the Scripture. This caused many of his followers to leave him and go much further in reformation than he was willing to go. Zwingli wanted to include in church organization and worship only that which the Scripture permitted and authorized, yet a number of his followers did not agree with one conclusion that he reached, and went far beyond that which he himself opposed.

I. ANABAPTISTS

These more radical reformers, who differed widely among themselves, were generally known as Anabaptists. This word suggests the idea of one baptism on top of another and was applied to these, because in general they rejected the validity of infant baptism and contended that in order for baptism to be valid a person had to voluntarily submit to it as a "believer" in Christ. The Anabaptists were persecuted by both Catholics and the followers of Luther and Zwingli. Some of them were very close to the New Testament pattern while others were extremely radical. In general they believed that the church was composed of believers only, rejecting infant baptism and putting church membership on the basis of personal faith and conscious submission to Christ in baptism. They believed that infant baptism was an invention of man and altogether invalid. They did not agree, however, on the method of practicing baptism. Balthasar Hubmaier (1480?-1528), who had been a professor of theology at the University of Ingolstadt and had studied under John Eck, the Catholic theologian, came to the conclusion that the German reformers were not going far enough toward the New Testament pattern and for some time was a staunch supporter of Zwingli. He then disagreed with Zwingli, teaching that only believers' baptism was valid. On Easter Sunday, 1525, he and three hundred other men were baptized out of a milk dish which was filled with water. Sprinkling was commonly practiced by these early Anabaptists, but a little later after further study of the Scripture they, in general, rejected sprinkling in favor of immersion.

Most of the Anabaptists believed in rigid discipline for the members of the church and that the church and state should be entirely separated. They opposed the development of "state churches" as strongly as they had opposed the papacy. Most Anabaptists insisted on liberty of conscience and were willing for all people to have this privilege. Some of them, however, became very intolerant of any who differed with their ideas. Some refused to take an oath in court on the basis of the statement of Jesus that we should "swear not at all." They were persecuted for this but rejoiced that they could suffer, following the teaching of Christ. Certain of the Anabaptists went beyond the teaching of Scripture and began to rely on an "inner light," believing that the Holy Spirit would work apart from the Bible in bringing them to the truth. Most of the Anabaptists rejected the doctrine of predestination and emphasized freedom of the will. A minority group became very radical in stressing an imminent second coming of Christ and thought they knew when and where he would come. Some of this group practiced the community ownership of goods and even went so far to as advocate polygamy. In general the Anabaptists believed in the autonomy of the local congregation and that each church should elect its own officers, ordain its own leaders and conduct its own business affairs.

The Anabaptist movement did not have any one outstanding leader, but a number of highly trained men accepted the teaching either in part or in its entirety. Canrad Grebel (1498-1526) was a well trained theologian who worked with Zwingli from 1520 to 1525. Zwingli had at first accepted the view that infant baptism had no value but later wavered on this point, and when Grebel said that he was not going all the way in restoration of New Testament teaching challenged him to a debate on the baptism of infants. In the discussion Zwingli did very poorly but exerted enough influence with the town council to persuade them to unite against Grebel and the Anabaptists. Grebel and Felix Manz, another well-educated Anabaptist leader, had generated a sizeable following and were holding religious services in Zurich. In 1526 the town council decided to punish all Anabaptists by drowning and many of them fled the city. Hubmaier, whom we have already mentioned, was associated with Grebel in the leadership of the Anabaptists in Switzerland. He, however, had done his earlier work in Germany. These very highly trained men went about over Western Europe organizing churches. Hubmaier was captured and burned at the stake by imperial command on March 10, 1528. His wife was then drowned by the authority of Roman Catholic leaders.

Hans Denck, a German reformer who did not believe that Luther went far enough in reform, became a mystic in his emphasis upon the Holy Spirit's operating directly upon the heart. He was interested in bringing individuals into closer communion with God but had little interest in the outward organization of the church or its ordinances. Casper Schwenckfeld, another German, also accepted the emphasis of the mystical union of the individual with Christ. His followers organized churches throughout Germany, but being severely persecuted along with the other Anabaptists decided to move to Pennsylvania. There the Schwenckfelders became good farmers and reputable members of the community. In recent years they have gathered together the works of Schwenckfeld and remain an independent religious movement.

Melchoir Hoffman became a leader of the radical wing of the Anabaptists. He taught that Christ was going to return and establish the Millennium in 1533 in Strassbourg. Bernt Rothmann had been working in Munster to win over the entire city to Anabaptist principles. When Rothmann became extreme in his views, the Emperor ordered the Bishop of Munster to drive the Anabaptists out of the city. Since Christ did not return to set up His kingdom in Strassbourg, Matthys became the leader of this wing of the movement and decided that the city of Munster would be the location of the new kingdom instead of Strassbourg. In his attempt to take over the city by force he was killed and succeeded by John Leyden who married his widow, along with sixteen other women. Polygamy was approved because there were so many more unmarried women than men in Munster. Anabaptists poured into the city from all over western Europe and the city was soon controlled by them. All who would not accept these views were forced to leave the city. Leyden proclaimed that he was king and would rule until Christ came to take over the kingdom. Under these extreme conditions the Protestants and Catholics united in an effort to stamp the movement out. The city was taken, and the people ruthlessly murdered in 1536. Anabaptists in many places were then drowned or executed in horrible ways. For a time it looked as though the entire movement was doomed for extinction. One man, however, by careful conduct and a more intelligent approach to the study of Scripture, saved the movement from destruction.

II.   MENO SIMONS

In the Netherlands Meno Simons, a Catholic priest, studied the Anabaptist views, turned his back on the priesthood and affiliated himself with the group. Eventually he became the leader of this movement which, in this area, took the name "Brethren" because of widespread hostility to "Anabaptists." The "Brethren" soon adopted the name "Mennonites," however, after the given name of their leader. Simons worked with small groups to bring about a better understanding of Scripture. After the Munster episode he believed that he was called of God to protect the movement from radicals. Simons emphasized church membership upon the basis of personal conversion sealed by adult baptism. He taught against Christians' holding civil offices or bearing arms. Rather, they should be obedient to civil rulers when they were not in opposition to the requirements of God. There should be no state control of the church. Many Dutch Anabaptists moved to America and established the Mennonite Church. Simons also had a decided influence on the Anabaptist movement in England. Many English protestants went to Holland and through various means came in contact with the Anabaptist groups there. In this way John Brown was influenced by Simons and returned to England to establish a new type of congregational worship in England. By

1611 there were many Anabaptists in England. Independent congregations, however, began to call themselves simply "Baptists." The second generation of reformers had not received baptism as children. Accordingly, they refused the name Anabaptist denying that they had been baptized again.

From the influence of Simons' movement congregations were established in Germany and took the name Dunkards or Tunkards. Some of these came to America and brought with them the practice of triune immersion and foot washing. The Quakers, Mennonites, Dunkards and Baptists all had their origin in the Anabaptist movement.

By 1559 the reformed churches under the influence of Calvin numbered probably three hundred thousand in France. In this year they held their first general assembly during which Calvin's ideas were accepted by general agreement. Luther's influence, however, continued to be very strong in France. The upper middle class people of France who were dissatisfied with Catholic corruption almost unanimously adopted some type of reformed teaching. Jacques Lefevre (1455-1536) had translated the Bible into French from 1523-1525. This work was based largely upon the Latin Vulgate, and many felt it to be unsatisfactory. Accordingly, in 1535 Olivetan produced a new translation more acceptable to Protestants, containing a preface by Calvin. In 1559 the first national assembly of French protestants was held in Paris, the Gallican Confession of Faith was adopted and the name Huguenots applied.

The government of France was under the domination of the papacy and by this year began to take action to halt Protestant growth. Civil wars, resulting from religious differences, began in 1559. By 1597 there had been eight such wars in France.

Chapter Twenty-Five

Reformation In England

I. ENGLISH HUMANISM

Preparation for the success of the reformation in England lay in the development of humanism which in turn was a result of the Italian Renaissance.

The humanistic principles first began to reach England during the years of Chaucer. About 1400 Chaucer began a study of the classics and became acquainted with Boccaccio. England at this time, however, was slightly influenced by the Renaissance ideas. Later, Grocyn (1446-1519) brought the humanistic principles into the University of Oxford. He had first studied at Oxford and then went to Italy and for a time was a student at Florence. In 1491 he returned to England where he became a professor at the University of Oxford, and through his influence Greek and a study of the classics was given a place in the curriculum. Thomas Linacre who also was a student at Oxford went to Italy where he studied in a number of Universities and became interested in medicine. He obtained a degree in medicine in 1492 and went back to assist Grocyn at Oxford. Here he translated the Greek work in medicine into English. His translation of the works of Galen stirred research and investigation in the field of medicine. John Colet (1467-1519), the son of a wealthy merchant took a B.A. and an M.A. degree at Oxford and then went to Italy to study Greek, Law and the "Church Fathers." In 1496 he returned to England to teach Greek at Oxford. He did not hold a clerical position in the hierarchy, but he lectured as a layman on the theology of the Apostle Paul. He applied the new learning to an understanding of the Bible. In 1508, upon the death of his father, he inherited a very large estate. This he used to build a school for boys, to develop future leaders for the application of the new learning.

Sir Thomas Moore (1478-1535), a very brilliant student at Oxford, was encouraged by Linacre and financed by the Archbishop of Canterbury to do graduate study. He was especially interested in Plato's *Republic* and Augustine's *City of 'God*. He was deeply religious and thought of becoming a monk. About this time, however, he desired to marry a seventeen-year-old girl and gave up his idea of entering the priesthood. He entered government service under Henry VIII and continued to study and to write. His best known work is *Utopia* which was published in 1516 in Latin. This has been called the most significant contribution in English to Renaissance literature. Sir Thomas Moore remained loyal to the pope, but in this famous work he set forth the idea of a classless society where there would be freedom of thought and of action. This composition did much to prepare the thinking of the English people for a revolt against the authority of the hierarchy.

The influence of the Renaissance in England building upon the background of the New Testament of Wycliffe and Tyndale with the influence of the reformers from the continent conditioned England for a break from papal authority.

The break with the pope under Henry VIII was not effected by the common people but by the crown and was brought about by legal measures. Henry VIII considered himself a well-trained theologian and accepted without question the Catholic church with its sacraments and priesthood. He tolerated heresy in his Empire as a means to bring pressure upon the pope and used the growing reformation in England in political ways in his attempts to gain favor from the pope. But during the life time of Henry VIII and his break with the papacy, the Catholic church remained unchanged. There was a change in authority from the pope to the English crown, but hierarchy, sacraments and ceremonies were traditional.

II. BREAK WITH THE POPE

The difficulty between Henry VIII and the pope developed out of his desire for a divorce from Catherine of Aragon. Henry VII had two sons, Arthur and Henry. Arthur, the elder, was married to Catherine of Aragon while yet a boy and died before the marriage was ever consumated. Henry VII not want-into to return Catherine with her rich dowery to Spain, petitioned the pope for a dispensation to allow his younger son, Henry, to be married to Catherine. Pope Julius II investigated this appeal and granted the dispensation in 1504. Henry was never fond of Catherine but was encouraged out of political reasons to carry out the contract. They lived together in all conjugal tranquillity for eighteen years. Seven children were born to the marriage but only one lived beyond infancy — Mary. Later, when a proposed marriage of Mary to a French prince was prevented because Henry's marriage to his sister-in-law was questioned, he determined to divorce Catherine. Being much older than Henry and in very poor health she was unable to produce a male heir to the throne. Henry then appealed to Clement VII in 1527 to set aside his marriage with Catherine, which he now claimed Julius II had wrongly sanctioned. Clement, however, considered Julius to have made a valid decision and refused to grant the divorce.

It should be kept in mind that Charles V who was Emperor at this time was a nephew of Catherine and was pressing the pope to make the decision favorable to her. When the pope refused to grant the divorce, which would permit Henry to marry Ann Boleyn with whom he had fallen in love, Henry broke with the pope. He then set himself up as head of the Church of England. Many of the priests went along with Henry thinking that it was a temporary step. Thomas Cranmer who had been Henry's chief advocate in attempts to obtain papal recognition of the divorce was made archbishop of Canterbury in 1533. He immediately pronounced Catherine's marriage to Henry void and the marriage with Ann, which had taken place three months before, legal. Cranmer then became the leader of the antipapal movement in England. In 1534 Henry was made "Supreme Head" of the Church of England and the Parliament approved the succession of Ann's children to the throne requiring all to take an oath of loyalty to Ann's children. Sir Thomas Moore and Bishop Fisher refused to acknowledge the break with the pope and the legitimacy of the divorce and, accordingly, were executed. Henry, of course, was excommunicated by the pope and the interdict was brought to bear against England, but these weapons had lost their power as the population of England had become definitely anticlerical. The clergy of England had been abusing the privileges, and the people felt they should be relieved from some of the pressure of papal taxation. The clergy was willing to go along with Henry

in order to be relieved of the exorbitant fees they were having
to send to Rome in the form of annates and other financial obligations imposed by the pope's assistants. There also existed at
this time a general weakness in the clergy. Among the hierarchy very few of them resided in their territories and the holding of several offices was very common. The Archbishop of
York made the statement that he had only twelve priests who
could preach a sermon, and only four bishops resided in their
Sees. The rest of the hierarchy preferred to live near their court
where they could take part in the extravagant living that was
there enjoyed. The landed gentry were willing to support Henry
in his defiance of the pope because of their eagerness to obtain
some of the wealth that had been acquired by the clergy in the
form of rich lands and estates. The authority transferred to
Henry as supreme head on earth of the church in England had
to do with matters of jurisdiction only and did not confer upon
him the powers of ordination. The parliament passed upon all
matters affecting the church only after the religious convocation had passed such measures and then submitted them to the
parliament and the king for ratification. As early as 1531 the
convocation, speaking in the name of the national church, had
suggested to Henry that the subservience of England to the
pope at Rome cease. This decision, however, was not acted
upon until 1534. The reason for Henry's delay was that he had
held out hope that the pope would recognize his divorce and
that he would not have to make a complete break with the
papacy. After Henry decided to make the break with the pope
the convocation declared that "the bishop of Rome hath no
greater jurisdiction conferred on him by God over this country,
than any other foreign bishop." In justifying the break with the
papacy the parliament made it clear that it was not establishing a new precedent but declared the parliament restored the rights and privileges that had been anciently held in
England in regard to self-government within the English
church. They went on to declare that the pope had usurped
these rights that had been traditionally held by the English
church, and that in rejecting the pope they were returning to the
ancient condition within the English church. It was declared
that there was no law, canon, statute or decree on record in all
English history that conferred authority from the English

church to the pope, and that, accordingly, the pope had never had any legal position of authority in England.

During Henry's reign, in order to take over the land of the church and also to establish schools for the study of the new learning, the monasteries were taken over by the crown. First the small ones were broken up, and later laws were passed abolishing the larger ones. By 1539 parliament made all monasteries illegal, and as a result of the confiscation it is estimated Henry received two hundred and fifty million dollars out of the sale of their lands and art treasures.

The biblical reformers of the continent saw opportunities in the English break with the pope to establish a genuine reformation in England. Through their influence parliament drew up in 1536 a statement referred to as the "Ten Articles" in which real concessions were made with the continental reformers. In this statement there is no mention of transubstantiation, and only three sacraments are referred to. Many of the phrases are taken from the Wittenburg Confession of faith; prayers to the saints and prayers for the dead — as well as veneration of the saints — were entirely omitted. Henry seemed not to have realized the direction that the break with the papacy was taking. When it was clearly brought to his attention in 1539 the Ten Articles were revoked and six articles were substituted in their place. These "Six Articles" set forth clearly the doctrine of transubstantiation, communion in one kind only and clerical celibacy, which required all priests and church officials to put away their wives. Thomas Cranmer and other high ranking churchmen were forced to put away the wives that they had taken. The Six Articles also decreed that the vows of monastic celibacy were irrevocable. It set forth the excellency of private mass and the requirement of auricular confession.

These articles offended the reform party, and in Henry's vigor to enforce them, many reformers fled to the continent. This made it clear that Henry did not intend any real reformation within the English church. During his reign there was a cleavage from the papacy, but there was not any official acceptance of Protestantism. The Bibles which had been printed by Tyndale on the continent and smuggled into England were zealously bought up and burned publicly by the bishop of London. Tyndale himself was persecuted and driven out of England. In 1536 he was captured in the Netherlands and burned at the stake. His last words were reported to have been a prayer that the Lord would "open the eyes of the King of England."

III. EDWARD VI

At the death of Henry VIII in 1547 his son Edward, who was nine years old at the time, came to the throne. He ruled through his uncle, the Duke of Somerset, who had very definite Protestant views. During his reign the Church of England was directed toward a genuine reformation. The Duke of Somerset was made lord protector and encourager by Cranmer. Religious life was changed by royal injunction rather than by the act of convocation or by order of the parliament. By order of royal injunction in 1549 there was issued the first prayer book. This was a compromise between the Catholic and the Protestants. It was removed, however, in 1552, and the second prayer book was issued which shows definite Protestant interpretations.

Under the influence of the second prayer book many of the reformers who had fled to the continent during Henry's reign returned to England and began to use their influence to promote true reformation. Edward, however, died in 1553 and Mary, who was the daughter of Catherine of Aragon and who had been brought up a strict Catholic, came to the throne. From Henry's break with the pope until this time, it had been contended that the religion of the ruler should be the religion of the people. Thomas Cranmer had been a strong advocate of this doctrine. When Mary came to the throne, logic would have required that all people of England return as loyal subjects to the pope in obedience to Mary's commands.

Upon being queen Mary sent word to the pope that she desired to bring England back under papal authority. The pope then dispatched Cardinal Pole to England to receive England back into the papal fold. The pope demanded the return of all church property. This created such opposition that Cardinal Pole urged the pope to allow the property to be held by its present owners. He argued that this loss should be considered an expenditure of funds to convert heretics or to do mission work. The pope then agreed to consider it in this light.

During the reign of Edward when Protestant ideas were

promulgated many people had come to a sincere conviction that the papacy, and Catholic teaching on the sacraments, were contrary to Scripture. Accordingly, many could not return conscientiously to the pope. During these six years of Mary's reign, two hundred and eighty-eight persons were martyred because of their refusal to acknowledge the pope as the head of the church. Among those who gave their lives were bishops Ridley and Latimer. Archbishop Cranmer with bishops Latimer and Ridley was imprisoned in Oxford in the fall of 1553. Their execution was postponed and attempts made to force them into a denial of their faith that they might become outstanding examples of Protestants who returned to papal authority. They consistently refused to recognize the pope and on September 30, 1555, Latimer and Ridley were condemned to die together at the stake. They were fastened back to back by a single chain and as the fire was lighted Bishop Latimer cheered Ridley by saying, "Be of good comfort Master Ridley and play the man, we shall this day light such a candle, by God's grace, in England, as I trust shall never be put out."

Cranmer was not put to death until six months later. He was exhorted over and over again by his enemies to believe that a pardon would be granted if he would recant certain messages in his writings and public disputations. The Romanists felt that if the leader of the Reformation could be induced to deny its principles a fatal blow would be struck against all reformation in England. Cranmer weakened to these temptations, and he signed no less than seven different documents of recantation. When the pardon which he was promised did not come he agreed that on Saturday, March 31, 1556, he would make a public recantation in St. Mary's church. When a great assembly of people were present to hear his recantation, Cranmer very courageously denied his former recantations and preached boldly against the papal religion. He was hurriedly led from the church to be burned at the stake. When the flames were kindled Cranmer held his hand in the fire saying, "the hand that sinned the most must burn first," and continuing to repeat, "this unworthy hand," he held it in the fire until it was entirely consumed. The papal bull which condemned Cranmer declared that he was sentenced to be burned "for bringing in the false and heretical doctrines of Wycliffe and Luther." The courage with which Latimer, Ridley and Cranmer faced death, instead of turning the minds of the people back to the pope turned them toward the Reformation. And when Elizabeth came to the throne in 1559, the popular pressure toward reformation was so great that she yielded to it and legalized the Reformed churches.

IV. ELIZABETH

It is said that Elizabeth had learned "the wisdom of caution," and in her efforts to bring peace to Britain she did all she could to satisfy both the Catholics and the Reformers. In her chapel she had a crucifix, burned candles and had private mass, but she pleased the protestants outwardly by making it possible for them to have legal existence. Elizabeth seemed for a time to find a successful compromise which would offend the fewest number of her subjects. She was a trained humanist being able to read both Latin and Greek. Later she was excommunicated by the pope as a Calvinist, but it is difficult to ascertain her religious conviction. As Luther had retained the cross, candle, stained glass, the altar and many outward forms of Romanism, Elizabeth seemed to want to follow this pattern and not offend the Catholics any more than necessary. It is likely that she sincerely desired a middle ground position. In 1559 the Act of Supremacy was passed by which Elizabeth took the title "Supreme Governor of Things Ecclesiastical and Spiritual As Well As Temporal." She took no claim, however, to having the keys to remit sins or to ordain. In the same year was passed an Act of uniformity by which the second prayer book of Edward VI was revived. It was also required that all people must attend church upon the penalty of being fined for non-attendance. After Elizabeth came to the throne there were many Catholic attempts to regain power but all without success.

V. BIBLE TRANSLATIONS INTO ENGLISH

Practical reformation has never been possible without the average person having access to the Scripture itself. Early attempts to translate the Scripture into the English language were made before the year 1000, but the first complete translation was made by John Wycliffe (1320-1384). This work was a great influence in calling attention to the need for reformation.

The defect of this translation was in the fact that it was made from a translation. Wycliffe did not use the original Greek and Hebrew but translated the Latin Vulgate of Jerome into English. This translation, a necessary beginning, was used extensively by the Lollards, the followers of Wycliffe. The work of Wycliffe also influenced in a decided way the Hussite Reformation in Bohemia. Wycliffe made a distinct contribution in emphasizing the Scripture as the authority in religion — rather than the hierarchy.

The first printed English New Testament was that of William Tyndale (1495-1536). He published part of the Old Testament also. Tyndale used the original language as a basis for his work. He translated the New Testament in 1525, the Pentateuch in 1530, the book of Jonah in 1531 and the Psalms in 1534. Tyndale's work was so skillfully done that when the King James Translation was made later by the best Greek-English scholars of the world, about ninety percent of the final translation was still the identical work of Tyndale. Nine-tenths of 1 John is retained in the King James Version from Tyndale and five-sixths of Ephesians. "These proportions are maintained throughout the entire New Testament," Price says in his *Ancestry of our English Bible,* page 251. This accuracy was made possible only because of the critical work which had been done on the text of the Greek New Testament by Erasmus. Tyndale's translation was made from the third edition of the Greek text by Erasmus.

The work of Martin Luther on the continent; the emphasis on scriptural authority made by Wycliffe; the excitement caused by the translation of Tyndale; and the break of Henry VIII with the pope aroused in the English people the desire to have copies of the Scripture. The Bishop of London, however, did all that he could to destroy the printed New Testament of Tyndale. As rapidly as copies were printed on the continent and smuggled into England, the bishop of London would buy them up and burn them publicly. In order to obtain them the bishop had to pay a high price for the copies, and this money in turn financed Tyndale to print that many more copies on the continent.

The demand for a popular translation of the Scripture in English was so great that the convocation pled with the King and the English bishops to make an English translation which would be "authorized" for use by the common people. While there was delay in answering this demand various individuals were bringing forth private versions. The first of these was by Miles Coverdale in 1535 who attempted another translation from Jerome's Latin version. He took much of his phraseology from the work of Wycliffe and Tyndale. While the Coverdale Bible did not receive official sanction, it was allowed to be freely sold and may be considered the first English Bible that was not officially opposed. It was the first complete English Bible to be printed. Two years later the Matthew's Bible was published. This was merely a reprint of Tyndale "with some revision" taken from the work of Coverdale. In 1539 there was issued what is known as the Great Bible. This was ordained to be set up in all of the churches. This is the English version to be "formally authorized" for use in public worship. It was an expensive publication and not many copies reached private hands. This Bible was chained to the pulpit in the churches so that the only opportunity for reading it came by standing in line. The increase in demand led to the decree that only men should have the privilege of reading. They could tell their wives what they read. For a time the lower classes also were prohibited from standing in line.

In order to meet the demand for Bibles by the common people of England the Calvinists on the continent began to help supply the demand. In 1557 there was prepared a New Testament in Geneva. This is the first Bible that divided the chapters into verses. There was also a prologue to each book with summaries and notes throughout. It was translated by Whittingham, a Greek scholar who was the first to use italics to indicate words which were necessary in English to clarify the Greek, but which were not found in the Greek text itself. By 1579 versions were so readily available that the average home was able to afford one. For the next fifty years New Testaments were issued at the rate of more than two versions per year. They were not used in the churches but were commonly found in the homes of England. In 1568 the Bishops Bible, a revision of the Great Bible, was published. It contained no notes but had very elaborate wood cuts and a picture of Queen Elizabeth. It went through twenty-two editions up to 1602 and took the place of the Great Bible in the churches.

Since the common people were obtaining copies of the Scripture the Roman Catholics became disturbed at the number of Bibles containing Protestant notes in the margins. Accordingly they determined to bring out a copy of the Scripture and do for the Catholics what the Protestant leaders had done for their followers. Gregory Martin did the work of translating the New Testament. Since the Council of Trent had decreed that the Latin Vulgate was the official Bible of the Catholic church, Martin translated from the Latin Vulgate and his New Testament was published in 1582. Combined with it was the Douay Old Testament which was published in 1609.

Because of the many versions of the Bible in English with their variant readings (although the differences were slight as far as meaning is concerned) there was a clamor for a unified translation. Accordingly, the Hampton Court Conference in 1604 proposed a retranslation of the Bible. King James immediately named the translation committee which would be composed of the "best learned in both the Universities." The translating committee was divided into six groups, however, two at Westminster, two at Oxford, and two at Cambridge. This committee used the Bishops Bible as their guide and instead of making a retranslation did a moderate revision of the Bishops Bible. It, however, had back of it the very best scholarship that England provided. There were fifty-four translators appointed from the various shades of theological background, but only forty-seven finally did the actual work. This committee set up fifteen rules to guide them in their translation. Some of the more important were: the Bishops Bible was to be followed and as little altered as truth would permit; the old ecclesiastical words were to be retained, and there would be no marginal notes except to explain the Greek or the Hebrew words. The translation was first done by small committees then later approved by the entire group. This version, called the King James Version, soon took the place of the Bishops Bible in the use in the churches and ultimately displaced the Geneva Bible even in home use. From 1615 till 1769 there were many revisions of the King James version in the direction of modernizing the spelling and dropping antequated expressions. During this time there were also private translations that continued to be made. Names of historical significance are in the lists of Bible translators. The more outstanding were William Whiston, Sir Isaac Newton, John Wesley, Archbishop Newcome, Charles Thompson and Noah Webster, who is the author of the dictionary.

After the publication of the King James version a number of events took place demanding its revision. Important Bible manuscripts were being discovered. Codex Alexandrianus was discovered and presented to the King of England. Also, Codex Sinaiticus was discovered by Tischendorf in an old monastery on Mt. Sinai. These and other ancient Greek manuscripts enabled the Greek Bible to undergo minor revision for greater accuracy. It was thought that this more accurate information should be in a revision of the English text. Accordingly, the revision committee of 1870 was established. This committee consisted of both British and American scholars, representing various religious bodies. In 1881 the New Testament was published. There were advanced orders for almost two million copies. Over three million were sold the first year. On May 22, 1881, the entire version was published in the *Chicago Times* and the *Chicago Tribune*. The Revised version was based upon the King James Text with an understanding that it would be changed as little as was necessary for accuracy. The revision committee, however, adopted new paragraphing and punctuation, removed obsolete words and improved the spelling according to modern usage. Altogether, there were more than thirty-six thousand changes from the King James into the Revised Version. These changes, however, in general are very minor but do assist in understanding more accurately the original Greek. In 1901 the American Revision Committee brought out a version which was more in keeping with American usage than the English revision. The English Revision Committee desired to keep certain obsolete words which the American Committee desired to remove. The American Revision Committee made no change in the text of the King James Version except by a two-thirds vote of the committee. Their work did much to clarify the exact meaning expressed in the Greek New Testament. Since the revised version appeared there have been many modern speech translations.

VI. The Rise of Denominations in England

With the religious unrest prevailing throughout Western Europe, it is not surprising that reformers of every type would find their way to England and attempt to set forth their particular views there. A number of these theologians were brought from the continent by Thomas Cranmer and given important positions in educational institutions or other places of prominence. A former Augustinian friar named Peter Matur was given the position of Professor of Divinity at Oxford in 1547. A German by the name of Martin Bucer who had been a dominican friar was given a professorship of Divinity at Cambridge. John A'lasco, a Polish nobleman who had become a reformer, was made superintendent of the refugee communities. Many protestant refugees in England who were meeting for worship in various places were given church buildings for their use. A building was given to the refugees from France and still another to a group from Germany. While protection was given to the more moderate type of reformers who had come under the influence of Luther or Calvin, those that were considered radical were treated with great disrespect. Even Cranmer, who later was to be burned for his faith, approved the burning of at least two Anabaptist leaders in London. He obtained warrants for their execution by charging blasphemy against God and direct denials of the Apostles Creed. Many of these foreign reformers were greatly dissatisfied with the limited extent of the changes that were made by the English church and continually worked for a greater degree of reformation in the direction of New Testament teaching. When it was discovered that a satisfactory reform could not be inaugurated through the Church of England, independent groups began to appear.

VII. The Romanists

The people of England who had remained loyal to the pope continued for a while to worship in the churches as before. During the reign of Queen Elizabeth attempts were made by Roman Catholics to secure churches where their bishops could carry on services. Queen Elizabeth refused to grant this permission claiming that there had been no new faith propagated in England and that no religion had been set up but that which was commanded by Christ, preached by the primitive church and unanimously approved by the ancient fathers. A very significant statement was afterwards made by Lord Chief Justice Coke to the effect that Pope Pius IV had sent a private nuncio to England in 1560 offering to accept the changes which the English church had made in the liturgy, the translation of the Scriptures and the appointment of bishops, if his supremacy would be recognized. This offer was rejected but those loyal to the pope continued to work for papal recognition. In 1570 Pope Pius V, seeing that there was no hope to recover England by diplomacy, published a bull of excommunication against Elizabeth in which he declared the English throne vacant and all Christians, loyal to the pope, absolved from allegiance to the throne. They were commanded to separate themselves from the Church of England. Upon this decree a few loyal papists withdrew from the English churches and formed the English Romanist church. The established Church of England, however, claims that the English Church is not a schism from the church of Rome, but that the English Romanists seceded from the old Church of England. When a papist attempted to nail a copy of the excommunication on the door of the Bishop of London he was executed immediately as a traitor. In 1572 when over twenty thousand protestants in France were massacred at the instigation of Catherine de Medici on the night of St. Bartholomew's Day, and the pope ordered medals to be struck in commemoration of the event, it so increased the bitterness in England that anything connected with papal allegiance was taboo. Several Romanists were executed during the reign of Queen Elizabeth, not so much for their religious beliefs as for their attempt at political disturbance and danger to the throne.

VIII. THE DUTCH REFORM

In 1567 the Duke of Alva began a persecution in the Netherlands of the followers of Calvin and Zwingli as well as the Anabaptists. This drove many Dutchmen to England where they were received with kindness and allowed to worship according to their convictions. This was the beginning of the Dutch Reformed Church. This number was augmented after the St. Bartholomew's Day massacre by many Huguenot families who took refuge in England. Some of these associated themselves with the Dutch Reformed churches and others became Independents. In Norwich Robert Brown became the minister of a large group of Calvinists who had come from Holland. He began his work in 1581 but for a time had to flee to the continent because of opposition from the English hierarchy. His system, however, continued to spread in England and became known as the Congregational Church.

IX. THE PRESBYTERIANS

At the close of 1570 Thomas Cartwright who had been in exile on the continent began to lecture at Cambridge against the Episcopacy. He was expelled from the University and migrated to Antwerp. As parliament was opposing the Romanists and the papal bulls, Cartwright issued pamphlets called "Admonitions to Parliament" in which the Church of England was attacked. These pamphlets were widely circulated and resulted in the formation of the first Presbyterian congregation in England in 1572. They were called Presbyterians because of their opposition to the English Episcopal system of church government and their adoption of the Presbyterian system.

Opposition to ecclesiastical supremacy of the English bishops also gendered great fervor among the Scotch people. John Knox became the leader of the Scotch Reformers. He preached such fiery sermons against image worship that the multitudes were stirred to the point of destroying ornaments, statues and stained glass in most of the churches of Scotland. Civil war broke out involving both England and France. At the conclusion of the conflict, John Knox was effectually the ruler of Scotland. His influence through preaching was so great that the Scotish Parliament proceeded to give statutory effect to the teaching of Knox and abolished the Episcopacy as well. Presbyterianism was established. The success of Presbyterianism in Scotland encouraged the opponents of the English hierarchy. It looked as though the Puritan Congregationalists and Presbyterians in England might obtain greater freedom to work when James VI of Scotland was made ruler in England as James I. He soon held a conference at Hampton Court in January, 1604, at which he presided. He had determined to reestablish the authority of the British King as head over the church with as much uniformity as possible. He stated that Presbyterianism "agreeth as well with Monarchy as God with the Devil." He called the Puritans in this speech schismatics and novelists. James was quite convinced that Presbyterianism and Puritanism were dangerous to the state and should be suppressed. Acts of uniformity were adopted, and Richard Bancroft, who became archbishop in 1604, worked with unyielding persistence to bring outward conformity to the Church of England. All who would not subscribe to the standard procedure were deprived of their offices. The Puritans state that over three hundred clergymen were thus deposed. Archbishop Bancroft, however, stated there were only forty-nine.

The opposition of James I against the papists was of such nature that certain Jesuits conceived the idea of closing up the House of Parliament when James was to make an opening speech. The chief conspirators were Robert Catesby and Sir Edward Digby who provided most of the funds. The conspirators rented a vault under the Parliament house where they stored thirty-six barrels of gun powder. A few days before Parliament assembled a Romanist was warned by anonymous letter from the conspirators not to go to the opening ceremony. The letter was shown to the Prime Minister who in turn laid it before the king and James suspected what was intended. The vaults were searched and the gun powder discovered. They kept their discovery a secret until Guido Sawkes, the conspirator who had volunteered to set the fire, went to the vault to make his final preparation. He was, accordingly, surprised and captured. Although the majority of the Romanists denied having any part in the plot this stirred such hatred against the followers of the pope that more severe measures were passed against them.

James I continued to require uniformity of the Puritans. He said, "I will make them conform or carry them out of the land." This drove many of these devout Christians to America. In 1620 the Mayflower carried a band of Puritans from Leyden, in Holland to America where they landed at Plymouth Rock. From this time forward there was a continual stream of Puritans from the British Isles to the New Colonies in America. These pilgrim fathers, although leaving the continent and England for religious toleration, declined to accept any in the colonies who interpreted the Scriptures differently from themselves. They attempted to make their own Puritanism supreme and exclusive.

X. The Quakers

The Puritans and followers of the pope were not the only ones who were persecuted in the attempts to bring uniformity within the British realm. There were also stern repressive measures enforced against the Unitarians, Anabaptists and Quakers. The Quakers came to be noticed in England about 1650. Their leaders were George Fox and James Nailer. Nailer was described as a half-mad fanatic, and his misdirected zeal brought discredit upon the entire Quaker community. Some of his followers were regarded as public pests, and a contemporary writer described them as "A new sect who show no respect to any man, magistrate or other, and seem a melancholy, proud sort of people and exceedingly ignorant." They are said to have carried on their regular work on Sundays and others of them disturbed congregations during worship by denouncing their preachers as false prophets and lying witnesses. Nailer was at last arrested, whipped and branded. The prisons then were filled with zealots who seemed to follow his lead without question. George Fox, however, repudiated the fanatical tendencies of Nailer. He brought reproach upon himself in his refusal to remove his hat in the presence of magistrates or officials. The followers of Fox, however, developed a deep personal piety. They opposed war and refused to take oaths. In their religious conceptions they objected to sacraments and all ministerial orders. Instead, they relied upon the individual guidance of the Holy Spirit. The Quaker movement in England was a development from within the Anabaptist movement, which in turn, had come out of the Reformation on the continent.

XI. The Baptist Church

The Baptist church in England began as the result of a combination of forces which had their beginning in several streams of religious thought. The Anabaptist movement from the continent was making an impression in English thought. There was also a revival of the principles which had been propagated by Wycliffe and the Lollards. Out of this background emerged two men who are responsible for the beginning of the

Baptist church in England, John Smyth and Thomas Helwys. Due to the opposition of the Church of England to any separate Protestant groups, John Smyth went to Amsterdam in 1608 for conscience sake. Smyth had graduated at Cambridge in 1575 where he had received a fellowship. In 1600 he held the post of Cathedral Preacher in the city of London. In 1602 he was accused of having been appointed "city preacher for life" by fraud. It seems that Mayor Dynnys took the city seal and fixed it to a number of grants contrary to custom, and among them was the appointment of Smyth as city preacher for life. As a result of this action there were law suits and a general municipal uproar. The result was that Smyth found himself out of employment. In 1606 he was in Gainsborough practicing medicine and preaching on Sundays in the absence of the parish priest. This preaching brought Smyth before the officials. He was charged with serving without due authority. He then renounced his Anglican orders and became minister of an Independent congregation. This brought the Anglican persecutors upon the dissenting group and they moved to Holland to find sanctuary. Smyth, along with Helwys and others, began a serious undertaking to rediscover the New Testament church. They accepted the authority of the Scripture and rejected all councils and creeds. In Amsterdam, Smyth found his former tutor at Cambridge, Francis Johnson, preaching for an independent group which was inclined toward a Presbyterian form of government. Smyth entered into controversy with Johnson, and finding they were not able to work together, Smyth started a new Independent church. By this time Smyth had accepted baptism of believers only. He baptized himself by pouring and proceeded to baptize Helwys and others. He thus formed a little congregation that was independent of other movements. Until this time Smyth had associated with the Mennonites in Amsterdam, who were Arminian in thinking, rejected his Calvinism, dismissed the doctrine of original sin and accepted the Pelagian and Arminian view of the fall of man. This led him to accept the idea that infants are born in innocency and are not subject to baptism.

Helwys also accepted Arminianism but broke with Smyth in regard to church organization. Some thirty of his followers decided to unite with the Mennonites who believed in a modified episcopacy. This disagreement resulted in the establishment of other churches. In this state of division, Smyth died and Thomas Helwys returned to England in 1611 and set up what may be regarded as the first Baptist church founded on English soil.

The group under Helwys baptized believers only, but the action was pouring instead of immersion. These general Baptist societies began to multiply, and within ten years they had eleven congregations and by 1644 their number had increased to fifty. The Particular Baptists and Calvinistic Baptists wanted to separate from the General Baptists, and by 1633 there was formed a distinct congregation. Their "mode" of baptism was sprinkling, but seven years later the society rejected sprinkling and accepted immersion only.

At this time none of the members of the Baptist societies had been immersed, and it was a serious problem to decide whether or not an unimmersed brother would be able to Scripturally immerse another. This, however, was the decision reached and all were immersed. By 1641 the Particular Baptists were organized as a society of immersed believers. Within three years their number had increased to seven congregations which were organized into a general association. The Particular Baptists continued to make progress, working together under a loose type of organization. In 1651 the General Baptists numbering thirty societies organized themselves into an association of Western churches and in 1654 held the first general assembly in London. It is evident that the Baptist church was divided in theology between the Calvinistic and the Armenian positions from the very beginning.

XII.   John Wesley and the Methodists

The Established Church of England accepted very few of the principles of the Reformation. It remained largely a system of sacerdotalism, the emphasis being on outward ceremony and the clergy's carrying out its responsibility in a way that tended toward a cold, formal type of religion. Groups not only moved out of the Church of England to establish Protestant organizations, but there was also a movement within the church itself to restore the piety and spiritual zeal found in the reform movements. The personalities behind this effort were John Wesley, his brother Charles and George Whitfield.

John was the fifteenth and Charles the eighteenth child of a family of nineteen children. Their parents were devout Christians who had been brought up in nonconformist homes. However, the parents, Samuel and Suzanna Wesley, had entered the Church of England. John and Charles were given a good education in Oxford. While there Charles influenced two or three other young men to begin with him an attempt to obtain a closer walk with God. They began by going to communion weekly and studying the Scripture. In this way was started what came to be known as the "Holy Club." This group met every night for mutual improvement, Bible study and devotion. John returned to Oxford in 1729 and was given the leadership of the small group. Due to the extreme worldliness of the University campus the little group suffered much ridicule and began to be called "Methodists." This name was given to them because of their insistence upon a "method" of strict observance to all that the prayer book demanded. They contended that a satisfactory life before God required that they follow the method prescribed in the prayer book. They fasted on all appointed days and took communion every Sunday. They denied themselves every luxury and amusement, and saved all of the money possible to pass on to more needy individuals.

In 1735 John and Charles accompanied General Oglethorpe and his party of Moravian emigrants to Georgia. Charles went as the general secretary and John as a missionary under the direction of the "Society For The Propagation Of The Gospel." Their intense emphasis upon keeping the letter of the church ritual made it impossible for them to succeed in missionary activities, and after two years of fruitless effort, they returned to England. Their contact with the Moravians, however, had deepened their piety, and upon returning to London they associated themselves with the Moravian society under the direction of Peter Bohler. It was from Bohler's emphasis upon conversion that they became convinced that each believer ought to be able to point to some definite time and place or circumstance when, where, and by what means the assurance of individual pardon and salvation came to his soul. After several years of devout seeking for God and waiting for such an experience of faith, Wesley's spiritual search was rewarded. He said that at 8:45 on May 24th, 1738, his heart was strangely warmed and God gave him assurance of salvation.

Since the Moravians were a separate group from the Church of England, the Wesleys would not become affiliated with their movement as they determined to remain in the Established Church. John became impressed with the conviction that he ought to go throughout the length and breadth of England reclaiming people from their apathy. Up to 1738 the pulpits of the churches were freely opened to him, but after that date the clergy developed a strong opposition to his work.

When the Wesleys returned from Georgia, George Whitfield decided to do mission work in the New World. He stayed a very short while and returned to England to raise money to carry on his work. Prejudice arose against him, and he began preaching in the open air. His influence was so great that around Bristol audiences assembled that are reputed to be twenty thousand in number, eager to hear his sermons. This was a new type of preaching in England, and many came out of curiosity. Whitfield had a powerful voice and it was reported that he could be heard a mile away. He was very eloquent also.

Wesley joined Whitfield in this "field preaching," and they created a great interest in spiritual revival over all of England. They differed in their theory of salvation. Whitfield accepted the doctrine of the Calvinists and Wesley followed the Armenian doctrine of free will. Soon their movements began to divide into what later came to be known as the Armenian Methodists and the Calvinistic Methodists.

John Wesley was not only a great preacher, but was unusually skilled in organization. As he began to establish study groups and the numbers multiplied rapidly he appointed lay preachers. He did not intend that these preachers should be in competition with the clergy of the Established Church of England, but rather intended that they supplement the Established Church. Mission halls were being opened all over England, and by 1744 the Wesleyan plan was thoroughly organized into a distinct system. Lay preachers began to consider their appointment by Wesley equal to ordination by a bishop. This brought hostility from the regular clergy whose parishes were invaded. Some of the regular clergymen of the Church of England refused to administer communion to members of the Wesleyan Societies. Wesley, however, taught his followers that they should not leave the Established Church but should carry on their work of revivalism on the side. Before Charles died in 1788 he made the statement, "I have lived and I die in the communion of the Church of England, and I will be buried in the yard of my parish church." Just before John's death in 1790 he said, "I hold all the doctrines of the church of England, I love her liturgy and approve her plan of discipline and only wish it could be carried out." After the death of John the Methodist conference which met in 1793 declared, "We are determined in a body to remain in connection with the Church of England." There never was any formal declaration of separation of the Methodist church from the Church of England, but in 1795 the Methodist conference declared that it had power to confer priestly functions upon its ministers which amounted to a declaration of separation from the hierarchy. Wesley himself had difficulty over this matter in regulating the church in America. He ordained Thomas Coke to be superintendent. It is through this connection that the Methodist church in the United States traces its succession of bishops back through Coke and John Wesley into the Church of England and from there back to the papacy. They attempt to point out a succession of bishops all the way back to the Apostles.

John Wesley is an outstanding example of dedication to purpose. He is said to have traveled more than two-hundred and fifty thousand miles on horse back. He made fifty trips to Ireland and ordinarily preached three or four times a day. After he was eighty-five years of age he slowed down to two sermons a day. Throughout most of his ministry he traveled five-thousand miles a year on horse back and preached an average of fifteen sermons a week. Charles was the poet of the evangelical revival of world Methodism and wrote in all more than six-thousand hymns. He has been described as the "great hymn writer of all ages."

Chapter Twenty-Six

Roman Reaction to Reformation

I. BEFORE TRENT

After the Reformation was firmly established and rapidly gaining new territory, the leaders of the Roman church became aware of the seriousness of the Protestant threat to their control. Leo X, pope at the time of Luther's break with the hierarchy, was at first apparently unconcerned with Luther's opposition. Paul III became pope in 1534 believing that God had called him to the papacy to bring about a reform of the Catholic church and to stop the spread of the Reformation.

The corruption of the Catholic church was not imaginary. When the leaders of the Reformation described existing conditions, the people rallied under their leadership and left the Roman church in an attempt to return to purer forms of worship and church organization. In order to check this movement the Roman church would have to purge itself of all immoral practices. If criticisms could not be pinpointed against abuses, it was felt that the traditional organization and worship might withstand Protestant attacks.

Paul III undertook the task of reforming the Catholic church. He decided to follow the pattern set by Ximines in Spain. No plan, however, could be put into operation without the support of strong, loyal assistants. He, accordingly, started with the cardinals and appointed to this position the most learned, devout and loyal men he could find. Among these were Caraffa, a Spaniard who was familiar with the work of reform in his country; Sadoleto, an Italian theologian who exchanged letters with Calvin and, although familiar with Protestant theology, was still loyal to the pope; and Reginald Pole, an Englishman who hoped to return England to the pope.

In the cities there were associations of Catholic humanists eager to reform Catholicism's chief abuses who did not accept the Protestant viewpoint. In Venice there was the "Academy" and in Rome the "Oratory of Divine Love." Out of such groups came strong supporters for the pope's plan. As these groups studied the principles of Luther, Calvin and Zwingli in order to refute them, some were turned from Catholicism. The leader of the Capuchins (a reform group among the Franciscans), Ochino; the Augustinian monk, Peter Martyr; and Pierpaolo Vergerio are outstanding examples of Catholic leaders who started reading the writings of the reformers for the purpose of refutation but ended in agreement with them and left the Catholic church.

Paul III selected nine loyal cardinals to make a survey of the Roman church and report on its true condition. Their report was unsparing in its criticisms. All the reformers had said was true. The Catholic church needed to be reformed in "head and in members." The method to follow was the next problem. There were strong demands for Paul to call a general council, but the pope was afraid of his ability to control the outcome. If the council fell under the influence of the secular rulers or compromised with the protestants his position would be weakened.

While the pope hesitated, the emperor, Charles V, attempted to unite the Catholics and Lutherans in Germany. He called a Diet at Regensburg in 1541. Both sides were willing to make concessions, but when theological differences were discussed it was seen that the two groups were irreconcilable. These differences were in regard to the Lord's Supper and the mediation of the priesthood. The Catholics held that priests could perform the miracles of transubstantiation and grant or withhold divine grace. The Lutherans held to the priesthood of all believers. The tendency on the part of Charles and some Catholic leaders to compromise forced the pope to call a General Council.

II. The Council of Trent

It was felt by many that a general council had authority over the pope. Fearful that the majority of the council might feel that way, the predecessors of Paul III refused to take the chance of losing power to the council. Paul III (1543-1549), however, finally convoked the council to formulate the church's reply to the Protestant Reformation. Because of interruptions, the council actually lasted from December, 1545, to December, 1563. It met in the city of Trent consisting of bishops from all over the world. Italy, Spain, France and Germany sent the largest delegations. The council had before it two major problems: the reformation of morals within the clergy and consideration of doctrinal changes. After a long discussion it was decided that one session would be given over to a discussion of moral improvement and the next to a discussion of doctrine. The council decided to limit itself to an investigation of charges made by Protestants and to singularities of teaching between the two bodies. However, before it adjourned all the distinctive Protestants doctrines of that time had been anathematized. The more important decisions of the council are as follows: (1) Tradition is of equal authority with the Scripture. Protestants had begun to rely solely upon Scripture and had rejected the decisions of the councils and church fathers which they held to be out of harmony with Scriptural principles. The Council of Trent decided that the traditions set forth by the councils and the church fathers constituted authority equal to that of Scripture. It further stated that the hierarchy had the responsibility of determining valid tradition.

(2) The Latin Vulgate, translated by Jerome, was accepted as the authoritative text of the Bible. The Apocrypha thus became a part of the accepted text, being in the Vulgate. (3) The council decreed that the interpretation of Scripture is to be given authoritatively by the church and not the individual. An individual had the right to interpret the Scripture only if his interpretation was not contrary to that of the church. This of course is a meaningless position, for since the church gives the only authoritative interpretation there is no possibility of individual interpretation — certainly not for disagreement. (4) The council further decreed that justification came as a result of both faith and good works. (5) The sacraments of the Catholic church were re-examined, and contrary to Luther, who had rejected all but baptism and the Lord's Supper, the Catholic church reasserted the validity of seven. The council emphasized the purpose of the Mass. The observance involves a repetition of the sacrifice of Christ and benefits the dead as well as the living. In regard to the Lord's Supper the Council reasserted its faith in the miracle of transubstantiation. Stating that a properly ordained priesthood had the power to perform the miracle of the Mass, the council retained the priesthood in a

mediatory position in administering God's grace to mankind. (6) The council restudied the validity of indulgences and declared that the pope held the keys to the treasury of merits and that the goodness of Christ and the saints stored up in heaven was available through the church to individuals who were in need of special grace. It declared that indulgences were to be granted to those who performed some meritorious service to the church but that they were not to be sold. (7) The existence of purgatory was reaffirmed. (8) Images were to be used as aids but not objects of worship. (9) Belief in the mediation of saints was expressed and that it was proper for human beings on earth to invoke the saints for special services.

There were a number of doctrines brought up for discussion that the council rejected. One of these was whether or not mass should be said in the language of the people, and the council decided that it should remain in Latin. Again it was proposed that the laity should receive communion in both kinds, but the council decided that when the average person took of the bread after it had been changed into the actual body of Christ that it contained enough of the blood to suffice for communion. The priests alone were to drink the blood of Christ and the laity receive communion in one kind only. It was also proposed that the clergy should marry as the protestants had insisted. Luther had claimed that the chief reason for the immorality of the clergy was the law of celibacy. He advocated that if each clergyman had his own wife, immorality of the clergy would be eliminated. The council of Trent, however, decided against this. The power of the pope to grant dispensations was discussed at this time also. A dispensation was the setting aside of canon law in order to make exceptions to the general rule. The pope had not previously experienced limitations in this regard but some members of the council felt that certain ones should be made. It was decided, however, in the negative. The council gained no authority over the pope.

The Council of Trent also passed legislation to improve conditions in the church. Among these were provisions which called for a better trained priesthood. Before one could be admitted to the priesthood he would now have to fulfill a six year course of study. Each bishop was required to establish a training school in his bishopric. Before these regulations were enforced the clergy consisted of very poorly trained priests, many of them being illiterate. Since the council they have been well trained.

This convocation also passed regulations requiring supervision of the lives and work of the clergy. Each priest, bishop or archbishop was required to reside in his assigned territory and could not leave without permission from his superior. Legislation was also passed prohibiting an individual from holding two jobs and collecting salaries from both. It was also decreed that bishops and priests prepare themselves to preach. Before this time many of the priests were able to perform the rote duties of the mass but were not able to preach or teach. Each parish priest must now take responsibility in teaching the people of his parish the essentials of the Catholic religion.

In order to check the spread of protestant ideas the council decreed that there should be established an office of censorship to check on published material and decide which works Catholics should read. Since this time all authorized books have carried the imprimatur, which is a stamp of approval for the book in question. Any book not stamped with the imprimatur was to be rejected as reading material for the common people. Since this time the Catholic hierarchy has retained an index of approved books.

In order to check the spread of protestantism the inquisition was reorganized under the control of the pope. To summarize the decisions of the Council of Trent there was prepared and published by the papal authority "The Profession of Tridentine Faith" in 1564. Canon law requires that every paid official of the Catholic church take an oath of loyalty to this creed. It is a clear statement of Catholic faith and gives the official position of that church in regard to doctrine.

III.   THE SOCIETY OF JESUS

We have already seen how the Capuchins lived close to the people and made progress in winning the masses of the people back to Catholicism. There was another order, however, of greater importance in carrying out the decision of the Council of Trent — known as the Society of Jesus. The order was established by Ignatius Loyola, a Spanish nobleman. Loyola was born in 1491 in Northern Spain of a noble family. For a time he served as a page in the court of Ferdinand and Isabella. In 1521 he was wounded in battle as a soldier and while recovering from his injury studied the lives of Christ, St. Dominic and St. Francis which produced in him a determination to devote his life to Christ. In 1522 he entered a Dominican monastery, hung up his armor and said, "from henceforth, I will be a soldier of Jesus." In the monastery Loyola went through a period of spiritual struggle — scourgings, fasting and confession of sins in an attempt to obtain a vision from God. He was seeking assurance of having received God's mercy. In 1523 he went as a missionary to the Holy Lands, but accomplished little due to his lack of preparation. The following year he returned to Spain to prepare himself for more effective work. Entering a preparatory school for boys he disciplined himself severely. He later attended the university of Paris for seven years. Here he attracted a small group of fellow students and schooled them in his ideas. Here he also wrote his "Spiritual Exercises." In 1534 he established the Society of Jesus (though not finally recognized until 1540) when seven young men pledged their lives to serve the church and took the vows of poverty, chastity, obedience and devotion. The order grew very rapidly, and when Loyola died in 1556 it possessed one-hundred and one houses and about a thousand members. Loyola, whose motto was, "For the greater glory of God" offered his order in service to the pope. Paul III officially recognized the order in 1540, and it became a most effective agency in opposition to Protestant development. The order was modeled on military patterns with careful graduation of authority. Every member had to pledge absolute obedience to his superior. In emphasizing the importance of this type of obedience Loyola said that if the church, "shall have defined any thing to be black which to our eyes appears to be white, we ought in like manner to pronounce it to be black."[1] The "general" was elected for life and resided at Rome. He retained six assistants as his general staff. To keep every member of the order functioning efficiently Loyola established an elaborate spy system by which every individual had someone checking on his work. As the order increased in popularity standards were raised for membership and only the very best were admitted. These had to undergo very strict disci-

1. Bettenson, pp. 364-365.

pline and elaborate training. They were to be thoroughly prepared in the study of languages and theology and highly trained as preachers. They, possessing a great interest in education, conceived new educational methods, established colleges and became teachers all over Western Europe. They obtained choice positions as tutors of the children of princes and advisors to the rulers of Europe. Loyola was a man of action and dispensed with the seven hours of daily prayer that was required in other monastic orders. He believed that this time could be better spent in service to others. With this emphasis on labor for Christ orphanages and hospitals were built and extensive missionary activity begun. Consequently Protestantism was suppressed in many parts of Western Europe. From 1565 on the Protestants gained no new territory, but the Catholics retook some of theirs which had been held by the Protestants.

The work of Paul III, the Council of Trent and the Jesuit Order endued Romanism with new life. While the Roman church was strengthened and united under active aggressive leadership the Protestants lost their ablest leaders and divided even more. Among the Lutherans arguments arose over minor points of theology to such an extent that when Melanchthon was on his death bed he thanked God that he could die and escape the fury of the theologians. The Roman system also was better suited to the temperament and ideals of the people of Southern Europe. The rulers of Austria, Spain and France saw in the papacy stronger support for the monarchial system in the coming conflict with democratic ideals.

Chapter Twenty-Seven

The Religious Wars

When Frederick III became the Emperor in 1440, there began a centralization of authority which was destined to continue until Charles V who would become the most powerful ruler that Western Europe had seen. Frederick began this consolidation by marrying his son Maxmillian to Mary of Burgundy thus uniting Germany with Burgundy. Maxmillian and Mary were successful in arranging the marriage of their son Philip to Joanna, who was a daughter of Ferdinand and Isabella of Spain. To this union was born Charles V who was destined to rule over all of Western Europe with the exception of France and the papal states. Although no prince had ever controlled so great or rich an Empire, Charles was defied by a German monk. He apparently was unable to do anything about this revolt. He outlawed Luther as a heretic and wanted to outlaw the entire Reformation, but in spite of threats it continued to grow.

This state of affairs calls for an explanation. Germany was divided into three-hundred and sixty-two feudal states. Each of these was ruled by a prince who was intent on maintaining his independence. This made the territory difficult to control. In addition to this problem Charles was in conflict at various times with the pope over personal matters and he felt that by being slow in dealing with the Protestants he would gain certain privileges from the papacy. He was harrassed by France and felt the continual presence of the Turks as they made trouble along the borders of the Empire. Every time Charles started to unify Germany and crush the Lutheran Reformation, he had to turn aside because of difficulty with either the pope, the Turks or France. The chief explanation, however, of his failure was in the fact that he could not delegate authority. His personality was such that he had to deal with every detail in his own way.

At the second diet of Speier in 1529 Charles let it be

known that he was going to suppress Lutheranism. The protestants in preparation for the coming conflict organized the Schmalkaldic league and worked diligently to spread the Reformation. About the time Charles was ready for action the Turks came up to the Balkans and Charles had to turn his attention to them. He told the German princes that within six months he would come back and crush Lutheranism but at the same time appealed to them to come and help him fight the Turks. From 1530 to 1546 Charles was kept so busy with other things that he was not able to carry out his threats.

Throughout 1545 Luther was in poor health but continued to direct the Reformation with vigor. On a trip to Eisleben Luther fell suddenly ill and died February 18, 1546. He was returned to Wittenburg where he was buried by the side of his pulpit in the church upon the door of which he had nailed his ninety-five theses in 1517. The following year, Charles V came with his army to suppress the Lutheran princes and return Germany to the papacy. After their defeat Prince Maurice of Saxony changed sides, rallied the Protestants around him and made preparation to meet Charles in another battle. Charles delayed his coming until 1522, however, and by this time the Protestants had such military strength that they defeated his army and he had to flee Germany.

It was not until 1555 that peace terms were arranged at Augsburg. In this conference attempts were made to adjust the religious situation in Germany. It was finally agreed that both Lutheranism and Romanism would be tolerated in the Empire and that each prince could decide what the religion was to be in his territory. If a citizen did not accept the decision of the prince, he would be permitted to move so that he could profess a religion acceptable to his conscience, but his lands were to remain under the control of the Catholic church.

The Peace of Augsburg placed Lutheranism on an equality with Catholicism in the Empire. The treaty, however, specified that the Anabaptists and the Calvinists would not be tolerated within its borders. It did not remove the antagonism between the Catholics and Lutherans, and tension continued to grow until war broke out again in 1618 — the Thirty Years War. To add to the growing religious confusion, the Calvinists continued to teach effectively and to gain many followers. The Anabaptists were also increasing in number. The Peace of Augsburg had decreed that the prince had the right to decide which religion would be legal in his territory. On this basis Frederick III after his conversion to Calvinism had a group of theologians draw up a creed known as the Heidleberg Catechism. This was adopted in 1563, and Calvinism was made the official religion in the Palatinate. Since Calvinism had no legal standing in Germany, the Catholics and the Lutherans combined in their protest of this action.

The Lutherans had become so divided in their theological views that the chief leaders of Lutheranism devised a new creed known as the Formula of Concord which was published in 1580. This creed was designed to bring unity within the Lutheran movement. However, as with all human creeds, instead of producing unity it tended to crystalize division. The followers of Melanchthon who were now known as Philippists did not agree with the followers of Luther in regard to original sin and the bondage of the human will. They taught that man had power to cooperate with God in his salvation and emphasized that the actual presence of Christ in flesh and blood did not occur in the Lord's Supper, but that the Supper represented a spiritual presence rather than an actual presence. This branch of Lutheranism turned more and more to the doctrines of Calvin and made great advances in Germany.

All the protestants were thus in a state of confusion and disagreement. Duke Albert V of Bavaria, a Catholic, used the principles of the Peace of Augsburg to expel the protestants from his territory. Encouraged by this, Catholics in 1618 demanded the restoration of all church property confiscated by Protestants since 1555. Although this was properly within the terms of the Peace of Augsburg, such restitution would change districts which for fifty years had been strongly Protestant. As the Catholics became more aggressive, the Protestant princes united for strength. In 1609 the Protestants of Bohemia obtained a charter of toleration from King Rudolf, but he soon died and the Catholics regained power in Bohemia. Protestants were soon denied the right of assembly. The conflict between Catholics and Protestants continued in Bohemia until Ferdinand II became king of Bohemia and Emperor. Ferdinand had been reared a strong Catholic and was trained in a Jesuit college.

While king of Styria, as early as 1598, Ferdinand had begun a persecution of Protestants and showed his determination to oppose them in every way possible. He was so successful in eliminating Protestantism from Styria that upon gaining the position of Emperor the Protestants recognized that their status was threatened seriously. The Protestant nobles of Bohemia revolted and in the opening battle against the Catholics, on November 8, 1620, were defeated. This touched off a war which was to last for thirty years.

The Thirty-years War was an attempt to settle religious questions by military force. As the conflict continued much of Western Europe became involved and political considerations at times overshadowed the religious. The effect of the war was disastrous for much of Germany. Armies of both Catholics and Protestants had marched back and forth across her soil. As in all wars morals were corrupted and the noblest inclinations of men were replaced by hatred, greed and lust. The entire social order was reduced to a semblance of barbarianism, and the population of Germany was reduced by more than one-half.

The futility of bloodshed clearly reflected in the terms of the peace treaty signed at Westphalia on October 27, 1640. These terms almost duplicated the conditions agreed upon in the Treaty of Augsburg, 1555. Each prince was given the right to determine what the religion was to be in his province. There was added, however, a clause protecting the rights of minority groups. Any minority group existing in any province in 1624 was given legal status. During the long war much territory had changed hands. The treaty declared that such property would revert to the side which held it in 1624. The treaty also specified that in case individual citizens were displeased with the religion established by the prince they could sell their property and move to a new district without losses by confiscation.[1]

The Peace of Westphalia was denounced by the pope. Even though no privileges were granted the Protestants in Austria and Bohemia, and the Jesuits were gaining back Poland and Hungary to Catholicism, the pope refused to accept the principle of religious toleration in any land. Religious toleration was won only after the Protestants gained superior numbers and

1. Bettenson, p. 306.

overthrew by force the Pope's armies which had been sent to exterminate them.

In France the Protestants met with great difficulty in their attempts to obtain legal status. The early Protestants felt impelled to resort to radical measures in opposing the pope. In 1535 placards were posted all over Paris denouncing the pope and declaring the mass a perversion of Scripture. Thirty-five of the participants were rounded up and executed.

In Southern France there were thirty villages which embraced the views of Peter Waldo and had been allowed to continue unmolested. When Protestant preachers began to work in their area and were arrested by the Catholics for heresy these Waldensians protested. The Catholics used their protests as a false report to Francis I that they were in revolt. Francis sent an army, under Catholic leadership, which massacred hundreds and destroyed twenty-two towns completely.

Henry II, King of France (1547-59), used strong measures against the Protestants. He required that all officials and all teachers take an oath of loyalty to support the pope. In spite of numerous executions the Hugenots, French Protestants, continued to increase in number. In 1562 the first of the civil wars between Hugenots and Catholics broke out when the Catholics surrounded a barn where Hugenots were meeting and massacred twenty-five persons.

From 1562 until 1598 there were eight civil wars between Catholics and Protestants in France. The most notorious event in the struggle was the massacre of St. Bartholomew, August 24, 1572, in which eight-thousand Huguenots lost their lives in Paris and several times that many in the whole of France. Catherine de Medici, the mother of the French king, had succeeded in marrying her daughter Marguerite to Henry of Navarre, who was nominally a Protestant. All of the important Protestants of France were gathered in Paris to celebrate the marriage. They were encouraged to attend under the belief that toleration was at hand. Catherine, however, had laid a clever plot. She succeeded in making her son think a riot was planned and on a given signal the Catholics killed all of the Protestants who could be found in the city. Word was also sent to all parts of France, and the Paris massacre was duplicated throughout the land.

Henry of Navarre had escaped death by accepting Catholicism, but he apologized to the remaining Protestants and did all he could to assist them. After the death of Henry III, Henry of Navarre was king by right of inheritance, but the Catholics were in command of Paris and would not accept him until he again became a Catholic. He made the statement that "Paris is well worth a mass," went through the formality of Catholic worship and was accepted as legitimate king of France—Henry IV.

In 1598 Henry IV issued the Edict of Nantes which granted religious toleration — under certain restrictions.[2] It gave Protestants the right to hold office and decreed that they should enjoy equal privileges of citizenship, but forbade their conducting religious activities in towns and cities where there were no Protestants.

With this decree it was possible for Protestantism to gain control of France. It came too late, however. The leaders had been killed and the Jesuits were gaining control of education and the reading matter of the people. They were able to close the minds of the people of France to any serious re-examination of the basis of their faith. In spite of these serious handicaps the few remaining Huguenots were true to their convictions and in time they again permeated France. In less than one hundred years the Catholic king, Louis XIV, revoked the Edict of Nantes (1685). This caused over fifty-thousand of the best families of France to flee the country rather than again suffer persecution at the hands of the Catholics.

The early Protestants in the Netherlands were of every persuasion, but as time went on the ideas of Calvin became more dominant. Known as the Dutch Reformed they held their first Synod in 1559. Phillip II of Spain became the ruler of the Netherlands in 1555. He ruled through a regent who made every effort to bring all into conformity to the Catholic church. When Phillip learned of the extent of Protestant progress he determined to force Catholicism upon the Netherlands.

Under the leadership of William of Orange the Protestants organized a league to defend themselves, and many Protestants worked diligently through field preaching to spread their ideas. Some became overly zealous and went through churches break-

2. Bettenson, pp. 304-305.

ing up their images. In retaliation the Catholics who controlled the government condemned Protestants, and hanged its adherents from trees all over the Netherlands. William fled to Germany, organized a government in exile and began making preparation to reconquer the land. After years of conflict in which both England and Spain were involved, the seven northern provinces followed William and became Protestant Holland. The South remained with Spain and became Catholic Belgium.

Chapter Twenty-Eight

Denominationalism Transferred
To America

I. ROMAN CATHOLICISM

The Roman Catholic religion came to America with the first attempts at colonization. Jesuit priests had accompanied the first Spanish expedition to her shores and subsequently established missions in Mexico and the West Indies. By 1510 papal power was being felt throughout South America. Soon Roman Catholicism became the established religion there. The eighteenth century saw its penetration of California well over a century and a half after it had been introduced into Florida at St. Augustine. The French were no less active than the Spanish, evangelizing Louisiana and Canada as well as New York, Maine and Vermont.

There were also Roman Catholics among the emigrants from England who were eager to have a part in the development of America. They were in the minority, however, among many strong anti-Catholic colonies and found their task more than difficult. In 1634 George Calvert founded the colony of Maryland as a refuge for them. The majority of settlers in the new colony were Protestant, however, making the establishment of Roman Catholicism as the state religion impossible. In 1649 the "Toleration Act" was passed by granting religious toleration to all in the colony. By 1692 Maryland was made a royal colony and the Church of England accepted as the established church.

II. THE CHURCH OF ENGLAND

The first permanent colony from England was established at Jamestown, Virginia, in 1607. The English Cavaliers who made up the colony came to the New World for commercial reasons and were all members of the Church of England. The bishop of London appointed the clergymen for the colonies and had the oversight of all religious activities.

The Church of England had thrown off the papal system and replaced it with episcopal form of government. As the colonies broke with England many who had been Anglicans took the name Episcopalian and established the Episcopal church. Their doctrine and organization, however, remained that of the Church of England. These colonists established William and Mary College in 1693 to train ministers. The Church of England remained the established church in Virginia until late in the eighteenth century. North and South Carolina also became exclusively Anglican.

III. PURITANS, SEPARATISTS, CONGREGATIONALISTS

The particular features of doctrine and government set forth by John Calvin and his associates took root in Switzerland, England, Scotland, Ireland, Holland, France and Germany. These ideas were then transferred to America and developed into one hundred and twenty-five distinct denominations. The parent groups were known as Puritans, Independents, Separatists, Presbyterians and Congregationalists.

In England the Reformation developed along three lines: Anglicism, Puritanism and Separatism. The Anglicans became the established church of England. The term Puritans refers to groups and individuals who differed widely in doctrine and organization, but who, in common desired to purify the Church of England of its Romanism. Beginning with the ideas of Luther the Puritan movement gradually accepted the theology of Calvin, emphasizing strict morality and protesting worldly pleasure. Pressed into conformity by Anglican bishops, the Puritans adopted the presbyterian form of church government with congregational autonomy.

In 1581 Robert Browne, with his whole congregation, migrated to Holland from whence he sent his writings back to England in opposition to the Established Church. Five men who distributed his pamphlets were executed for treason. The movement, however, could not be suppressed and found a capable leader in John Robinson. Robinson, an ordained clergyman of the Church of England, had read Brown's writings and turned against the Anglican Church. He led a group of followers to Amsterdam and then to Leyden in 1608. This group sailed to America in 1620 in the Mayflower and established at Plymouth the first Congregational Church in America. The differences that existed in England between the Separatists and Puritans were forgotten in the New World. The number of Puritans coming to America increased rapidly from 1620, and by 1640 there were in England thirty-one strong churches. Soon Congregatlonalism became practically a state religion. Old forms and ceremonies were cast off. The Bible was taken as a code of laws, but interpretations of doubtful passages were not left to the individual. Any who would not accept the general interpretation was banned from the colony. Among the nonconformists who were banished was Roger Williams who had become a Baptist.

After the Revolutionary War the Baptists, Quakers and Episcopalians procurred a measure of religious toleration by opposing taxation as a means of support for Congregational churches.

IV. PRESBYTERIANISM

The historic beginning of the Presbyterian Church is traced to the work of John Calvin in Geneva. The name Presbyterian is taken from the term "presbyter" (a transliteration of the Greek word *presbuteros* — "elder") and is used to designate that form of church organization embracing a group of presbyters as the governing body of several congregations. This type of organization, accompanied by the doctrine of predestination as taught by Calvin, took root in much of Western Europe.

Presbyterianism entered the colonies from England, Wales, Northern Ireland, Scotland, the Netherlands and France. At an early date these various elements combined to become the Presbyterian church in A m e r i c a. Because Presbyterian churches were quite similar to Congregational bodies attempts were made to unite the two groups. These efforts did not prove successful, however.

There are nine major branches in the Presbyterian churches which have retained the same name, and many others have grown out of this movement.

V. THE METHODISTS

The name Methodists, according to John Wesley, first given "by way of reproach" because of the methodical regula-tion of their lives, was soon accepted by the Wesleyans as the name of their movement.

In America, Wesleyan "Societies" sprang up in the midst of Episcopal Churches. Wesley worked diligently to keep these groups from breaking away into separate churches. In 1766 Philip Embury, a Wesleyan preacher from Ireland, landed in New York and began his work. About the same time Robert Strawbridge, also an Irish preacher, assembled a small group in Maryland. Francis Asbury came to Philadelphia in 1771 and became the dominant figure in the growth of the Methodist Episcopal church. John Wesley, his brother Charles and George Whitfield preached throughout the colonies and established their Societies. These Societies had no ordained ministry, however, and had to depend upon the Episcopal clergy to administer the Lord's Supper, Baptism, and Marriage as sacraments and to bury the dead. The young Methodist congregations wanted ordained ministers of their own, but the Bishop of London refused to ordain them. Reluctantly, John Wesley ordained Thomas Coke and gave him authority to ordain other ministers. Wesley instructed Coke to ordain Francis Asbury, which he did, and the two served as joint Superintendents of the "Societies" in America. Thomas Vasey and Richard Whatcoat, ordained by Wesley to serve as elders in America, arrived in America with Coke in November, 1784. On December 24 of that year the "Christmas Conference" assembled in Baltimore, Maryland. Sixty preachers were present as Coke read a letter from Wesley stating that the churches in America were seperated from any connection with either the government or the Church of England, and that Coke and Asbury were to be joint superintendents. At this meeting the name "Methodist Episcopal Church" was adopted, and the Methodist church, as a distinct denomination was formed. Until this conference convened the preachers had been looked upon as lay preachers of the Episcopal Church.

VI. THE BAPTISTS

Historically the Baptist church did not exist until after the Anabaptist movement of the sixteenth century from which its name is derived.

John Smyth, a clergyman of the church of England, became convinced that the only hope for England was a fuller reformation. His principles forced him to become an Independent. Persecuted, he fled to Amsterdam where he affiliated himself in 1608 with other English Separatists. Excommunicated here because of his opposition to infant baptism, he baptized himself by pouring water on his head and then baptized Thomas Helwys and others, thus founding the first Baptist church.

In 1612 Helwys returned to London and founded what seems to have been the first Baptist church in England. "General Baptist" was used of this group to indicate that it was Armenian in theology and had rejected Calvinism.

The first Particular (or Calvinistic) Baptist church began in London, a few years later, 1633, when a group withdrew from a Separatist church, rejected infant baptism and were baptized "again." John Spilsbury was their leader.

The first Baptist church in America was probably established by Roger Williams in Providence, Rhode Island, in 1639.[1]

Roger Williams was banished from the Massachusetts colony because his religious and political views were at variance with those of the Congregationalist church. He moved to Providence, Rhode Island, where he began advocating Baptist views. Here he baptized a fellow believer by affusion who then baptized him. Then others were baptized at this time and became the first Baptist church in America.

The church at Newport, Rhode Island, was begun about this same time apart from the work of Roger Williams. Immersion of penitents was adopted by this church about 1644 and soon became the established practice in most Baptist churches.

Soon many Baptists came to America from Europe and were scattered throughout the colonies. They disagreed among themselves on many points dividing into more than twenty major branches.

VII. OTHER RELIGIOUS BODIES

The Bureau of Census of the United States Department of Commerce gives not only statistics, but the history, doctrine,

1. Robert A. Baker, *A Summary of Christian History* (Nashville: Broadman Press, 1959), p. 273. The author is a professor of Church History at Southwestern Baptist Theological Seminary in Fort Worth, Texas.

organization and work of each religious body in the United States periodically. This report gives information on two hundred and fifty-eight different groups by 1957 and lists fifty-seven other groups with memberships too scattered to obtain statistics.

From the Reformation until 1800 the tendency was to divide into more and more denominations. Since 1800, although many new groups have had their beginning, the trend has been toward unity. About the beginning of the nineteenth century the first movement aiming precisely at unity and undenominational Christianity emerged on the scene of American history. Since this beginning many similar efforts at unity have been made.

VIII. PROPOSED BASIS FOR UNITY

The various proposals to unite believers in Christ may be classified as authoritarian, interdenominational and undenominational. The Authoritarian concept is most clearly seen in the Roman Catholic church. The basis of unity in this concept is agreement with the Roman church. The individual so doing must accept the organization and doctrine developed after the days of inspiration and submit himself to the rule of the Roman hierarchy. He must also maintain a "closed mind" and accept without question such decrees as the traditions of that church may impose. To hope that there can ever be unity of such a basis in this age of enlightenment is unthinkable.

The interdenominational basis for unity rests upon the premise that Christianity contains no divine pattern of organization, doctrine and worship. If this be true one wonders why all Christians could not work out a compromise of their preferences and work and worship together? A cursory acquaintance with the history of the church, however, clearly reveals the futility of such efforts on this proposed basis.

The possibility of all Christians uniting upon the basis of undenominationalism is more than reasonable. This philosophy takes the New Testament as the revealed Will of God and calls upon men to intelligently search its pages in order to find the pattern of organization, doctrine, worship, and work of the New Testament church.

PART SEVEN

THE RESTORATION MOVEMENT

Chapter Twenty-Nine

Early Beginnings Toward Undenominationalism

Undenominationalism has been the goal of sincere Christians in every age. It is entirely presumptuous for anyone to suppose that he alone has attained it. Although historical and Biblical evidence is not available as proof, we have stated earlier the conviction that there have been simple New Testament Christians in every age. We are here chiefly concerned with tracing undenominational efforts in the United States. We have, however, deep respect and appreciation for the unsung heroes of Europe, who, unable to bring the New Testament church into historical prominence, gave their lives rather than compromise with a popular and powerful apostasy.

The early leaders of the Reformation in Europe had no intention of forming denominational churches. Luther told his followers to call themselves Christians — not Lutherans. Yet the followers of these great men crystalized their progress by "institutionalizing" their fellowship. Succeeding generations referred to their interpretations and defended their conclusions. But not all men were so content, for some have emerged to reevaluate the past in the light of Scripture and to stir their generations to continue the search for the ancient order. Often one worked entirely independent of and unaware of the other's activity.

I. JAMES O'KELLEY — METHODIST

Among the first in America to see the need for a restoration of the New Testament church was James O'Kelley. He began preaching in 1775 as a lay preacher in the Episcopal church. His interest in religion was stirred by the writings of John Wesley who exalted the Bible as authoritative and all sufficient for faith and practice. These ideas appealed to O'Kelley, and he deliberately laid his fiddle on the fire, entered the Wesleyan Society and began work as a traveling minister.

It was not Wesley's plan for the Methodist church to be organized on the Episcopal order. In his letter to the brethren in America he stated his conviction that there was no difference in bishops and presbyters. Asbury, however, had other plans. He wanted to head the church and worked toward this end. O'Kelley opposed Asbury and the Episcopal form of government at the "Christmas Conference" in 1784 when the name Methodist Episcopal Church was selected for the Wesleyan Societies. His opposition continued until 1792 when, after failing in the General Conference to prevent what he believed to be unscriptural organization, he planned to withdraw from the Conference and did on December 24, 1793.

A number of preachers followed O'Kelley in his stand and called themselves "Republican Methodists." The following summer, 1794, these brethren met again in Virginia. During the meeting Rice Haggard stood up with a Bible in his hand and pleaded that the Bible itself be accepted as their only creed. Just as the disciples were once called simple Christians, he moved that they be known as Christians only. His motion was accepted and the group then drew up the "Five cardinal Principles of the Christian Church." These were: (1) Christ is the only head of the church, (2) The name Christian is the only acceptable name, (3) The Bible is the only rule of faith, (4) Christian character is the only test of church fellowship and (5) The right of private judgment is the privilege of all.

The first church was established at Chapel Hill, North Carolina, in 1794. The difference between the "Christian Church," thus begun, and the Methodists, was one of organization — not of doctrine. Yet they went to the Bible to learn the Scriptural form of organization. Such an attitude is fundamental to a complete "restoration" in any age.

II. ABNER JONES — BAPTIST

While James O'Kelley was breaking with the Methodists in Virginia, Abner Jones, a Baptist, was reaching similar conclusions in New England. Jones, a doctor in Vermont and a member of the Free Will Baptist church, became convinced toward the close of the eighteenth century that "sectarian names and human creeds should be abandoned, and that true piety alone, and not the externals of it, should be made the test of Christian fellowship and communion." With this conviction he left the Baptist church and established a congregation in Lyndon, Vermont, 1801, which he called the "Christian Church." These Christians took the Bible as their only creed, "Christian" as their only name and made significant strides toward true undenominationalism. Soon, Elias Smith, a Baptist preacher, joined Jones in establishing churches throughout New England. As they worked other preachers gave up denominationalism to have part in this undenominational undertaking.

III. BARTON W. STONE — PRESBYTERIAN

Among the first Presbyterians to see the need of returning to primitive Christianity was Barton W. Stone. Being of serious mind and well educated for his day, he decided to preach. When he was ordained he agreed to support the Westminister Confession of Faith "only so far as it agreed with the Word of God." The doctrines of Calvinism distressed him as he tried to harmonize them with the love of God. He finally rejected the doctrines of total depravity and absolute predestination and began to call upon sinners to accept Christ and turn from their sin.

Over thirty thousand people poured into Cane Ridge, Kentucky, in 1801 for a great revival. Stone was preaching in that area at the time. Methodist and Baptist preachers were invited to assist in the revival. There were a number of preachers in different parts of the camp ground preaching at the same time. Emotional excitement ran through the crowd producing physical reactions of various kinds. Some fell to the ground as though dead, others experienced the "jerks," danced, laughed, ran or sang. This supposedly was a manifestation of the presence of the Holy Spirit.

The preachers from different churches worked together in such a way that Stone was impressed with the value and need of unity. Although desirable, the goal was never reached. When Stone stressed the fact that sinners had the power to turn to Christ a number of strong Calvinistic preachers opposed him. Among those who stood by him, however, were Richard McNemar, John Thompson, John Dunlavy, Robert Marshall and

David Purviance — all of whom joined Stone in forming a new presbytery.

McNemar was charged with heresy in the synod in Lexington. Knowing they would all be suspended, these six preachers sent a statement of withdrawal to the synod. They then organized the "Springfield Presbytery." After renouncing human authority and taking the Bible as their only rule of faith and practice, they started out to establish congregations after the New Testament order. In less than a year they saw that their own organization was unscriptural, and by common consent they dissolved it and determined to be Christians only. The document prepared to dissolve the Springfield Presbytery is unique and is worthy of study by everyone interested in the restoration of New Testament Christianity. We, therefore, give it in its entirety as follows:

IV. "THE LAST WILL AND TESTAMENT OF THE SPRINGFIELD PRESBYTERY"[1]

The Presbytery of Springfield, sitting at Cane Ridge, in the county of Bourbon, being through a gracious Providence, in more than ordinary bodily health, growing in strength and size daily; and in perfect soundness and composure of mind; and knowing that it is appointed for all delegated bodies once to die; and considering that the life of every such body is very uncertain, do make and ordain this our last Will and Testament, in manner and form following, viz.:

Imprimis. We will, that this body die, be dissolved, and sink into union with the Body of Christ at large; for there is but one Body, and one Spirit, even as we are called in one hope of our calling.

Item. We will, that our name of distinction, with its **Reverend** title, be forgotten, that there be but one Lord over God's heritage, and his name One.

Item. We will, that our power of making laws for the government of the church, and executing them by delegated authority, forever cease; that the people may have free course to the Bible, and adopt **the law of the Spirit of life in Christ Jesus.**

Item. We will, that candidates for the Gospel ministry henceforth study the Holy Scriptures with fervent prayer, and obtain license from God to preach the simple Gospel, **with the Holy Ghost sent down from heaven,** without any mixture of philosophy, vain deceit, traditions of men, or the rudiments of the world. And let none henceforth take **this honor to himself, but he that is called of God, as was Aaron.**

1. Winfred E. Garrison and Alfred T. Degroot, **The Disciples of Christ** (St. Louis: The Bethany Press, 1948), pp. 109-110.

Item. We will, that the church of Christ resume her native right of internal government — try her candidates for the ministry, as to their soundness in the faith, acquaintance with experimental religion, gravity and aptness to teach; and admit no other proof of their authority but Christ speaking in them. We will, that the church of Christ look to the Lord of the harvest to send forth laborers into his harvest; and that she resume her primitive right of trying those who say they are apostles and are not.

Item. We will, that each particular church, as a body, actuated by the same spirit, choose her own preacher, and support him by a free will offering, without a written call, or subscription — admit members — remove offences; and never henceforth delegate her right of government to any man or set of men whatever.

Item. We will, that the people henceforth take the Bible as the only sure guide to heaven; and as many as are offended with other books which stand in competition with it, may cast them into the fire if they choose; for it is better to enter into life having one book, than having many to be cast into hell.

Item. We will, that preachers and people, cultivate a spirit of mutual forbearance; pray more and dispute less; and while they behold the signs of the times, look up, and confidently expect that redemption draweth nigh.

Item. We will, that our weak brethren, who may have been wishing to make the Presbytery of Springfield their king, and wot not what is now become of it, betake themselves to the Rock of Ages, and follow Jesus for the future.

Item. We will, that the Synod of Kentucky examine every member, who may be suspected of having departed from the Confession of Faith, and suspend every such suspected heretic immediately; in order that the oppressed may go free, and taste the sweets of gospel liberty.

Item. We will, that Ja————— —————, the author of two letters lately published in Lexington, be encouraged in his zeal to destroy partyism. We will, moreover, that our past conduct be examined into by all who may have correct information; but let foreigners beware of speaking evil of things which they know not.

Item. Finally, we will, that all our sister bodies read their Bibles carefully, that they may see their fate there determined, and prepare for death before it is too late.

Springfield Presbytery   **L.S.**

June 28th, 1804.

Robert Marshall
John Dunlavy
Richard McNemar   —Witnesses
B. W. Stone
John Thompson
David Purviance

The "witnesses" then gave as their reasons for this action a deep concern for unity and the fact that such organizations foster division, are contrary to the teaching of the Scripture and stand as hindrances to the salvation of the lost.

As this movement toward undenominationalism grew, the question of baptism was restudied and immersion accepted. A severe loss was felt when several of its preachers and many members joined the Shakers. Two preachers returned to Presbyterianism.

Stone was sure of the scripturalness of his position and was able to turn many from denominationalism. Churches were founded in Ohio, Kentucky and Tennessee.

V. JOHN WRIGHT — BAPTIST

As the American frontier moved West the principles of undenominationalism moved with it. In 1810 John Wright began to organize Baptist churches in Indiana which were free from human artcles of faith. Soon ten congregations had been formed which were organized into the "Blue River Association." Wright contended for the Word of God as the only rule of faith and opposed all human creeds as heretical. Realizing that the name Baptist was not in the Scripture as a name for the church, and taking the Bible as their only guide "without note or comment," the Association soon dissolved itself. Pleading for Christian union on the basis of Scripture alone, the other Baptist churches of that region united in an undenominational fellowship. Fifteen congregations of German Baptists gave up triune immersion along with other erroneous views and entered into fellowship with the new movement. Since a number of congregations in the area had been started by associates of B. W. Stone, a union was affected with them. The "Silver Creek Baptist Association" had accepted the plea for undenominationalism as set forth by the Campbells and united with Wright's movement. As a result of these efforts more than three thousand people from four distinct religious groups established fellowship as undenominational Christians. This provides clear example of what can be done to eliminate the division that exists in Christendom.

VI. THOMAS CAMPBELL

Because Alexander Campbell aggressively promoted a return to primitive Christianity, many persons have called him the "founder of the Christian Church." Obviously, he was not. The weaknesses of denominationalism and the basic principles necessary to restoring the New Testament church were being preached by many others before Alexander came to America.

Thomas Campbell, father of Alexander, must be given credit for some of the clearest thinking and most important contributions of this period. Thomas was born into an Anglican family. Early in life he showed his independent spirit by refusing to "worship God according to Act of Parliament" and became a member of the Seceder Presbyterian church. Although he preached in the Seceder Churches he reacted against their refusal to fellowship other Presbyterians and made some effort to eliminate such a divisive attitude while still in Ireland.

Being advised to take a journey at sea for his health, he determined to move his family to America. He started out alone, intending for his family to follow as soon as he established himself. When he arrived in America May 13, 1807, he found that the Associate Synod of North America was in session in Philadelphia. Presenting his credentials he was immediately assigned to the Presbytery of Chartiers in Southwest Pennsylvania.

The Seceders were few in number and scattered, but Campbell soon discovered many other Presbyterians and Independents who were without leadership. Some of these people he had known in Ireland, and he included them all in his ministrations as brethren. This was contrary to Seceder practice and evoked criticism. Soon, on a missionary tour with a young Seceder preacher named Wilson, he invited all the pious in the audience, who felt prepared, to participate in the communion service. Many who were not Seceders took advantage of the opportunity as no preacher was conducting regular service in the community. Wilson thought that this act could not be overlooked and at the next meeting of the Presbytery brought several charges against Campbell. In the course of investigation Campbell pleaded for a more Christian attitude toward liberty and fellowship, but the Presbytery found him deserving of censure. Desiring peace among his brethren he submitted to the censure. Spies were sent, however, to his meetings by some who were dissatisfied with his "trial" in an attempt to find grounds for fresh accusations. Campbell soon saw that he could not be true to God and his conscience under such human limitations and after earnest prayer renounced the authority of both Presbytery and Synod. He determined to use his strength to unite all denominations on the basis of Scripture only.

At this time Thomas Campbell was the outstanding preacher in his area. He was highly respected by his denominational neighbors, and the announcement that he was leaving denominationalism made a deep impression in the community. A time was set for a meeting of all who were interested in finding a Scriptural basis for unity. A large company of sincere persons assembled with a common desire to eliminate sects and parties and to seek a closer fellowship.

Campbell addressed the audience by reviewing the events that led up to the meeting. He argued strongly against sectarian division and pled for Christian unity. He then suggested that the basis for unity was the Scripture itself, asking those presence to accept this principle: "Where the Scriptures speak ,we speak; where the Scriptures are silent, we are silent." No one in the audience could find any objection to this fair and clear basis for unity, yet they immediately saw the effect it would have on their doctrine and practice.

After Campbell made this suggestion Andrew Munro arose and said:

"Mr. Campbell, if we adopt that as a basis, then there is an end of infant baptism." This remark, and the conviction it seemed to carry with it, produced a profound sensation. "Of course," said Mr. Campbell in reply, "if infant baptism be not found in Scripture, we can have nothing to do with it." Upon this, Thomas Acheson, of Washington, who was a man of warm impulses, rose, and advancing a short distance, greatly excited, exclaimed, laying his hand upon his heart: "I hope I may never see the day when my heart will renounce that blessed saying of the Scripture, 'Suffer little children to come unto me, and forbid them not, for of such is the kingdom of heaven.' " Upon this saying he was so much affected that he burst into tears, and while a deep sympathetic feeling pervaded the entire assembly, he was about to retire to an adjoined room, when James Foster, not willing that this misapplication of Scripture should pass unchallenged, cried out, "Mr.

Acheson, I would remark that in the portion of Scripture you have quoted **there is no reference, whatever, to infant baptism."** Without offering a reply Mr. Acheson passed out to weep alone; but this incident, while it foreshadowed some of the trials which the future had in store, failed to abate, in the least, the confidence which the majority of those present placed in the principles to which they were committed."[2]

After these preliminary meetings a permanent organization, "The Christian Association of Washington," was formed on August 17, 1809. It was not a church but a study group, organized to discuss the best means of attaining Christian unity. A place to meet was needed, and it was decided that a building should be erected which would meet this need and serve as a schoolhouse for the community also. Accordingly, a log building was constructed in Washington County, Pennsylvania.

The Association prepared a statement of its objectives. The actual writing fell to Thomas Campbell and emerged as "The Declaration and Address of the Christian Association of Washington." Upon presentation to the Association it was unanimously approved and ordered published. This was the outstanding literary production of the period and has been called the "Magna Charta of the Restoration Movement," "the greatest document ever written in the Advocacy of Christian union." It certainly became the basis for serious thought and played its part in the restoration of the New Testament church.

2. Robert Richardson, *Memoirs of Alexander Campbell* (Cincinnati: Standard Publishing Co., 1897), Vol. I, p. 238.

Chapter Thirty

Principles of Undenominationalism

The "Declaration and Address," published by the Christian Association of Washington, Pennsylvania, 1809, and written by Thomas Campbell, was not designed to be the constitution of a church. It was set forth as an intelligent basis upon which Christians could unite. The first section consists of a "Declaration" which gives the purpose and plan of the Association. This is followed by the "Address" which goes into a more detailed statement of conditions existing in the denominational world and calls for a return to New Testament Christianity. This is followed by a frank discussion of principles the acceptance of which Thomas Campbell believed necessary as a basis for unity. The "Declaration" begins as follows:

"From the series of events which have taken place in the churches for many years past, especially in this Western country, as well as from what we know in general of the present state of things in the Christian world, we are persuaded that it is high time for us not only to think, but also to act, for ourselves; to see with our own eyes, and to take all our measures directly and immediately from the Divine standard; to this alone we feel ourselves Divinely bound to be conformed, as by this alone we must be judged. We are also persuaded that as no man can be **judged** for his brother, so no man can **judge** for his brother; every man must be allowed to judge for himself, as every man must bear his own judgment—must give account of himself to God. We are also of opinion that as the Divine word is equally binding upon all, so all lie under an equal obligation to be bound by it, and it alone; and not by any human interpretation of it; and that, therefore, no man has a right to judge his brother, except in so far as he manifestly violates the express letter of the law. That every such judgment is an express violation of the law of Christ, a daring usurpation of his throne, and a gross intrusion upon the rights and liberties of his subjects. We are, therefore, of opinion that we should beware of such things; that we should keep at the utmost distance from everything of this nature; and that, knowing the judgment of God against them that commit such things, we should neither do the same ourselves, nor take pleasure in them that do them. Moreover, being well aware, from sad experience, of the heinous nature and pernicious tendency of religious controversy among Christians; tired and sick of the bitter jarrings and janglings of a party spirit, we would desire to be at rest; and, were it possible, we would also desire to adopt and recommend such measures as would give rest to our brethren throughout all the churches; as would restore unity, peace, and purity to the whole Church of God. This desirable rest, however, we utterly despair either to find for ourselves, or to be able to recommend to our brethren, by continuing amid the diversity and rancor of party contentions, the veering uncertainty and clashings of human opinions: nor, indeed, can we reasonably expect to find it anywhere but in Christ and his simple word, which is the same yesterday, today, and forever. Our desire therefore, for ourselves and our brethren would be, that rejecting human opinions and the inventions of men as of any authority, or as having any place in the Church of God, we might forever cease from further contentions about such things; returning to and holding fast by the original standard; taking the Divine word alone for our rule; the Holy Spirit for our teacher and guide, to lead us into all truth; and Christ alone, as exhibited in the word, for our salvation; that, by so doing, we may be at peace among ourselves, follow peace with all men, and holiness, without which no man shall see the Lord." Impressed with these sentiments, we have resolved as follows."[1]

Campbell then states that the purpose was to form themselves into a religious association called the "Christian Association of Washington" for the sole purpose of promoting simple evangelical Christianity free from all mixture of human opinions and inventions of men. Each member was to give according to his ability to promote the work, and the society was to use all means proper to encourage other groups to do the same. Campbell states that the society was not a church, but a voluntary association created for the purpose of promoting church reform and simple evangelical Christianity. He tells of a standing committee of twenty-one members appointed to carry out the decisions of the association. They were to meet twice a year. Each meeting would include a sermon and a contribution taken for the benefit of the society.

In the second section Campbell describes the existing condition of denominationalism.

It is, to us, a pleasing consideration that all the Churches of Christ which mutually acknowledge each other as such, are not only

1. Young, C. A., Historical Documents Advocating Christian Union (Chicago: The Christian Century Co., 1904), pp. 71-74. Reproduced by The Old Paths Book Club, Box V, Rosemead, Calif., 1955.

agreed in the great doctrines of faith and holiness, but are also
materially agreed as to the positive ordinances of the Gospel institution; so that our differences, at most, are about the things in
which the kingdom of God does not consist, that is, about matters
of private opinion or human invention. What a pity the Kingdom
of God should be divided about such things! Who, then, would not
be the first among us to give up human inventions in the worship
of God, and to cease from imposing his private opinions upon his
brethren, that our breaches might thus be healed?[2]

This is followed by exhortation for the brethren to promote
a genuine reformation which would result in the union of sincere believers. In this appeal he states:

O! that ministers and people would but consider that there are no
divisions in the grave, nor in the world which lies beyond it! there
our divisions must come to an end! we must all unite there! Would
to God we could find in our hearts to put an end to our short
lived divisions here; that so we might leave a blessing behind us;
even a happy and united Church.[3]

When Campbell reaches the point of stating his propositions he begins by saying:

Let none imagine that the subjoined propositions are at all intended as an overture toward a new creed or standard for the Church,
or as in any wise designed to be made a term of communion;
nothing can be further from our intention. They are merely designed for opening up the way, that we may come fairly and firmly to original ground upon clear and certain premises, and take up
things just as the apostles left them; that thus disentangled from
the accruing embarrassments of intervening ages, we may stand
with evidence upon the same ground on which the Church stood at
the beginning. Having said so much to solicit attention and prevent
mistake, we submit as follows:
PROP. 1. That the Church of Christ upon earth is essentially, intentionally and constitutionally one; consisting of all those in every
place that profess their faith in Christ and obedience to him in all
things according to the Scriptures, and that manifest the same by
their tempers and conduct, and of none else; as none else can be
truly and properly called Christians.
    2. That although the Church of Christ upon earth must neces-
sarily exist in particular and distinct societies, locally separate one
from another, yet there ought to be no schisms, no uncharitable
divisions among them. They ought to receive each other as Christ
Jesus hath also received them, to be the glory of God. And for this

2. Ibid., p. 93.
3. Ibid., p. 101.

purpose they ought all to walk by the same rule, to mind and speak the same thing; and to be perfectly joined together in the same mind, and in the same judgment.

3. That in order to do this, nothing ought to be inculcated upon Christians as articles of faith; nor required of them as terms of communion, but what is expressly taught and enjoined upon them in the word of God. Nor ought anything to be admitted, as of Divine obligation, in their Church constitution and managements, but what is expressly enjoined by the authority of our Lord Jesus Christ and his apostles upon the New Testament Church; either in express terms or by approved precedent.

4. That although the Scriptures of the Old and New Testament are inseparably connected, making together but one perfect and entire revelation of the Divine will, for the edification and salvation of the Church, and therefore in that respect cannot be separated; yet as to what directly and properly belongs to their immediate object, the New Testament is as perfect a constitution for the worship, discipline, and government of the New Testament Church, and as perfect a rule for the particular duties of its members, as the Old Testament was for the worship, discipline, and government of the Old Testament Church, and the particular duties of its members.

5. That with respect to the commands and ordinances of our Lord Jesus Christ, where the Scriptures are silent as to the express time or manner of performance, if any such there be, no human authority has power to interfere, in order to supply the supposed deficiency by making laws for the Church; nor can anything more be required of Christians in such cases, but only that they so observe these commands and ordinances as will evidently answer the declared and obvious end of their institution. Much less has any human authority power to impose new commands or ordinances upon the Church, which our Lord Jesus Christ has not enjoined. Nothing ought to be received into the faith or worship of the Church, or be made a term of communion among Christians, that is not as old as the New Testament.

6. That although inferences and deductions from Scripture premises, when fairly inferred, may be truly called the doctrine of God's holy word, yet are they not formally binding upon the consciences of Christians farther than they perceive the connection, and evidently see that they are so; for their faith must not stand in the wisdom of men, but in the power and veracity of God. Therefore, no such deductions can be made terms of communion, but do properly belong to the after and progressive edification of the Church. Hence, it is evident that no such deductions or inferential truths ought to have any place in the Church's confession.

7. That although doctrinal exhibitions of the great system of Divine truths, and defensive testimonies in opposition to prevailing

errors, be highly expedient, and the more full and explicit they be for those purposes, the better; yet, as these must be in a great measure the effect of human reasoning, and of course must contain many inferential truths, they ought not to be made terms of Christian communion; unless we suppose, what is contrary to fact, that none have a right to the communion of the Church but such as possess a very clear and decisive judgment, or are come to a very high degree of doctrinal information; whereas the Church from the beginning did, and ever will, consist of little children and young men, as well as fathers.

8. That as it is not necessary that persons should have a particular knowledge or distinct apprehension of all Divinely revealed truths in order to entitle them to a place in the church; neither should they, for this purpose, be required to make a profession more extensive than their knowledge; but that, on the contrary, their having a due measure of Scriptural self-knowledge respecting their lost and perishing condition by nature and practice, and of the way of salvation through Jesus Christ, accompanied with a profession of their faith in and obedience to him, in all things, according to his word, is all that is absolutely necessary to qualify them for admission into his Church.

9. That all that are enabled through grace to make such a profession, and to manifest the reality of it in their tempers and conduct, should consider each other as the precious saints of God, should love each other as brethren, children, of the same family and Father, temples of the same Spirit, members of the same body, subjects of the same grace, objects of the same Divine love, bought with the same price, and joint-heirs of the same inheritance. Whom God hath thus joined together no man should dare to put asunder.

10. That division among the Christians is a horrid evil, fraught with many evils. It is antichristian, as it destroys the visible unity of the body of Christ; as if he were divided against himself, excluding and excommunicating a part of himself. It is antiscriptural, as being strictly prohibited by his sovereign authority; a direct violation of his express command. It is antinatural, as it excites Christians to condemn, to hate, and oppose one another, who are bound by the highest and most endearing obligations to love each other as brethren, even as Christ has loved them. In a word, it is productive of confusion and of every evil work.

11. That (in some instances) a partial neglect of the expressly revealed will of God, and (in others) an assumed authority for making the approbation of human opinions and human inventions a term of communion, by introducing them into the constitution, faith, or worship of the Church, are and have been, the immediate, obvious, and universally acknowledged causes, of all the corrup-

tions and divisions that ever have taken place in the Church of God.

12. That all that is necessary to the highest state of perfection and purity of the Church upon earth is, first, that none be received as members but such as having that due measure of Scriptural self-knowledge described above, do profess their faith in Christ and obedience to him in all things according to the Scriptures; nor, secondly, that any be retained in her communion longer than they continue to manifest the reality of their profession by their temper and conduct. Thirdly, that her ministers, duly and Scripturally qualified, inculcate none other things than those very articles of faith and holiness expressly revealed and enjoined in the word of God. Lastly, that in all their administration they keep close by the observance of all Divine ordinances, after the example of the primitive Church, exhibited in the New Testament; without any additions whatsoever of human opinions or inventions of men.

13. Lastly. That if any circumstances indispensably necessary to the observance of Divine ordinances be not found upon the page of express revelation, such, and such only, as are absolutely necessary for this purpose should be adopted under the title of human expedients, without any pretense to a more sacred origin, so that any subsequent alteration or difference in the observance of these things might produce no contention nor division in the Church.[4]

These propositions are followed by further exhortation to action. The "Declaration and Address" is signed by Thomas Campbell and Thomas Acheson. In this document are found the basic principles of the Restoration movement. They not only led great multitudes back to New Testament Christianity during the lifetime of Thomas and Alexander Campbell, but they must furnish the basis of every attempt in every age to restore the church that Christ built.

4. Ibid. pp. 107-114.

Chapter Thirty-One

The Restoration Fully Launched

While Thomas Campbell was working out the principles of the Declaration and Address, his son, Alexander, in Glasgow, Scotland, was becoming dissatisfied with the Seceder church. The Campbell family had started for America in September 1808, but had been shipwrecked off the coast of Scotland and decided to spend a year there so Alexander could study in the University in which his father had been educated. In Glasgow Greville Ewing had established an independent congregation that practiced weekly communion. This church interested Alexander. The idea of congregational church government also impressed him as being more Scriptural than that of the Presbyterians. He had become generally dissatisfied with Presbyterianism but had not told his father of his change of views.

The Campbell family again started for America in August, 1809. They arrived in Washington, Pennsylvania, September 29, after a voyage of fifty-four days just as the proof sheets of the Declaration and Address had come from the press. Thomas Campbell was eager for his son to consider it carefully. Alexander told of the occasion in later years.

> On reading the proof-sheets of this "Declaration," as they issued from the press, immediately after my arrival in Washington, Pennsylvania, direct from Scotland, I observed to its author: "Then, sir, you must abandon and give up infant baptism, and some other practices for which it seems to me you cannot produce an express precept or an example in any book of the Christian Scriptures!"
>
> After a considerable pause, his response was to this effect: "To the law and to the testimony" we make our appeal. If not found therein, we, of course, must abandon it.

The Campbells agreed to be guided by this principle. They determined to stand only for that which was "expressly exhibited upon the sacred page," and accept as the constitution, faith and worship of the church only that for which there can be produced a "Thus saith the Lord, either in express terms, or by approved precedent." This principle was to take them farther than they at first realized. Neither of them wanted to give up infant baptism, and they did not foresee that they would also have to give up sprinkling and be immersed.

Alexander was well pleased with the conclusions his father had reached and became an enthusiastic supporter of the new cause. Copies of the Declaration and Address were sent to all of the preachers near Washington with the request that they make any corrections or criticisms they thought necessary. None was received, and no preacher attempted a public reply.

I. THE BRUSH RUN CHURCH

The Christian Association was not planned to be a church in any sense. Thomas Campbell held to this position for some time, but being convinced that the denominations were not going to unite or give fellowship to any who would not accept their creeds, he later became willing to organize the group as a worshipping congregation. In October, 1810, the congregation applied for admission into the Pittsburg Synod of the Presbyterian Church but was refused. In 1811 the Brush Run Church was organized as an independent congregation. Thomas Campbell was appointed elder and Alexander licensed to preach. The following day the church met for worship and celebrated the Lord's Supper for the first time. Determined to follow the Scripture the congregation decided that weekly communion was to be observed since there was "approved precedent" for it.

One member of the new church, Joseph Bryant, refused to partake of the Lord's Supper because he had not been immersed. He also insisted that his baptism follow the New Testament pattern of immersion. In harmony with his desires Thomas Campbell immersed Bryant. This is the first example of immersion in the work of the Campbells.

Thomas at this time held the position that although infant baptism was not found in the Scripture, it yet granted church membership to infants, and they did not need to be "re-baptized." He said:

As for those who are already members of the church and participants of the Lord's Supper, I can see no propriety, even if the scriptural evidence for infant baptism be found deficient, in their unchurching or paganizing themselves, or putting off Christ merely for the sake of making a new profession; thus going out of the church merely for the sake of coming in again."

This view satisfied the church for the present. Baptism was not made a test of fellowship. Circumstances, however, soon arose that forced a restudy of this problem.

On March 12, 1811, Alexander married Miss Margaret Brown, daughter of John Brown of Brooke County, West Virginia. Margaret and her parents were members of the Presbyterian church, and when the first baby, Jane, was born a year later, the question of infant baptism demanded immediate consideration. Alexander read all he could find on the subject both in English and French and was amazed at the weakness of the arguments that had been offered in its defense. Consulting the original language of the New Testament (Greek) he became convinced that immersion alone constituted Scriptural baptism and that it was valid only for a believer. He discussed his findings with his wife who shared his conclusions, and it was decided their infant would not be baptized.

The fact that he rejected infant baptism forced him to conclude that those who had received it were still unbaptized. They had simply experienced a ceremony in their infancy. He further concluded that he could not continue his own ministry and immerse others not having been immersed himself as a believer.

Having reached this conclusion Alexander made a trip of thirty miles to see whether Matthias Luce, a Baptist preacher, would agree to baptize him. On the way he stopped by to tell his father of his convictions and found that his sister Dorthea had reached the same conclusions. Thomas offered no objection to his proposal. In conference with Mr. Luce, Alexander made it clear that the ceremony would have to be performed precisely in accordance with New Testament pattern. There was to be no recitation of a religious experience. The candidates were to be immersed upon the simple confession that "Jesus Christ is the Son of God." Although this was contrary to Baptist custom, Luce agreed to run the risk of censure and perform the rite June 12 (1812) in Buffalo Creek.

Mr. Luce and Henry Spears, who accompanied him, spent the night in the home of Thomas Campbell. The next morning as they were leaving for the site of the baptizing, Thomas Campbell remarked that his wife had brought along a change of clothing for them, and they were also going to be baptized. Upon reaching the creek they found that most of the Brush Run Church and many others had already assembled to witness the event.

Thomas Campbell gave a lengthy explanation of why he decided to be immersed after which Alexander explained how he came to the conclusion that God accepted only a believer's baptism. James Hanen and his wife also decided to be immersed with Thomas Campbell and his wife, their daughter, Dorothea, and Alexander and his wife. A total of seven hours had been involved in the event, and seven people immersed.

During the following week thirteen other members of the Brush Run group were immersed by Thomas Campbell. Others followed. There were some who rejected the necessity of immersion and went back into denominational churches. Immersion eventually became a basis of fellowship in the Brush Run church.

As might be expected this action brought a violent reaction from all those who yet held to infant baptism. On one occasion, for example, while traveling home from an appointment, Alexander was overtaken by a violent storm. He stopped at the home of a member of the Seceder church, asked for shelter, was refused and continued his journey in the storm.

The little congregation, convinced that their course of action was right, rejoiced in their freedom of conscience. They often visited each other to search the Scripture, sing and pray together. They wanted their lives as well as their teaching to be in harmony with that of first century Christians.

II.   ASSOCIATION WITH THE BAPTISTS

The ability of Alexander Campbell as a preacher was soon recognized by all. He was invited to preach for many Baptist congregations whose preachers then urged that the Brush Run church affiliate itself with their Redstone Baptist Association. Although the members of the Brush Run church had accepted immersion there was a wide difference between them and the Baptist churches. They had rejected human creeds and human authority while the Baptist churches accepted the Philadelphia

Confession of Faith. After prayerful consideration, however, application for membership was made. Conditions were laid down in the application that would give complete freedom to the Brush Run group. It was not their desire to become Baptists, but they did hope to achieve a wider scope of influence and fellowship. Mr. Campbell said:

> I had no idea of uniting with the Baptists, more than with the Moravians or the mere Independents. I had unfortunately formed a very unfavorable opinion of the Baptist preachers as then introduced to my acquaintance. . . . The people, however, called Baptists, were much more highly appreciated by me than their ministry. . . . I confess, however, that I was better pleased with the Baptist people than with any other community. . . . I often spoke to the Baptist congregations for sixty miles around. They all pressed us to join their Redstone Association. We laid the matter before the Church in the fall of 1813. We discussed the propriety of the measure. After much discussion and earnest desire to be directed by the wisdom which cometh from above, we finally concluded to make an overture to that effect, and to write out a full view of our sentiments, wishes and determinations on that subject. We did so in some eight or ten pages of large dimensions, exhibiting our remonstrance against all human creeds as bonds of communion or union amongst Christian Churches, and expressing a willingness, upon certain conditions, to cooperate or to unite with that Association, provided always that we should be allowed to teach and preach whatever we learned from the Holy Scriptures, regardless of any creed or formula in christendom. A copy of this document, we regret to say, was not preserved; and, when solicited from the clerk of the Association, was refused.

The proposition was discussed at the Association, and, after much debate, was decided by a considerable majority in favor of our being received. Thus a union was formed.[1]

At this time the Baptist preachers were poorly educated,[2] and there was none in that region who could equal Alexander Campbell as a scholar or popular speaker. This created friction and several opposed him. When the Association met at Cross Creek August 30, 1816, Alexander preached what was later known as his *"Sermon on the Law."* In this famous sermon he exalted the New Testament as God's *final* revelation. He clearly distinguished the Law of Moses from the Gospel of Christ and showed that men were not subject to the Old Testament in the

---

1. Richardson, Memoirs of Alexander Campbell, Vol. I, pp. 438-441.
2. Ibid., p. 439.

Christian dispensation. This is now commonly accepted by Baptists but in 1816 was considered radical. Campbell was charged with upholding "Antinominianism"[3] and became the object of considerable rebuke by Baptist preachers after preaching this sermon.

The next year Alexander was brought to trial before the Association but was acquitted. Opposition, however, increased, and by 1823 his accusers had secured the election of a sufficient number of delegates to insure his conviction. When the Association convened this time all things were in readiness. Delegates to the Association were named by official letter from their congregations. When the letter from the Brush Run Church, giving the names of its delegates was read, his was not among them. He was at the meeting but did not come as an official delegate. Having already forseen the outcome and feeling the need for a new congregation in Wellsburg, thirty-one members of the Brush Run church had withdrawn and started a new congregation with Alexander as their minister. This group was then admitted to the Mahoning Baptist Association; the Redstone Association no longer possessed any authority over Campbell. He was not excluded from the Baptist Church but rather voluntarily changed from an association which *would* have excluded him to another that gave greater independence to its churches. As the restoration proceeded the Mahoning Association dissolved itself so that the churches could become simple New Testament congregations.

III.   THE CAMPBELL-WALKER DEBATE

John Walker, a minister of the Seceder Presbyterian church in Mount Pleasant, Ohio, began a controversy with the local Baptist preacher which led to Walker's challenge to meet any Baptist preacher, in good standing, for a discussion of baptism. The Baptists immediately chose Alexander Campbell to represent them in debate. Although Alexander had a "natural aversion to controversy"[4] he finally accepted the challenge after declining the invitation twice.

The discussion began June 19, 1820, at Mount Pleasant. Large crowds attended with great interest. The topics for dis-

3. i.e., "Against the Law"
4. Garrison and Degroot, **Disciples of Christ**, p. 168.

cussion were the subjects and the action of baptism. Walker was not able to meet Campbell's logic and use of the Greek New Testament, and when they came to the second question, Walker wanted to close the debate after one speech on each side. This sudden change was a surprise to Campbell, but he agreed to close the discussion after two speeches by each debater.

The strength of his own position and the ease with which he refuted error immediately impressed Campbell with the value of debating as a teaching medium. At the close of his last speech he issued a challenge to meet any minister in good standing of any denomination on the subject of infant baptism.

The Presbyterians were not satisfied with Walker's defense and searched for a stronger man to meet Campbell. After the debate Walker was not regarded as highly as he was before. The loss of prestige should not be laid to intellectual weakness, but to the weakness of the position he was trying to defend.

When the debate was published it was read by thousands. The Baptists knew Campbell had defeated Walker, and one even said that "he had done more for the Baptists than any other man." But others doubted his orthodoxy as a Baptist and wondered what his popularity would do to the Baptist church.

IV. THE CAMPBELL-McCALLA DEBATE

The Presbyterians soon arranged for W. L. McCalla of Augusta, Kentucky, to meet Alexander Campbell in debate. McCalla had been a lawyer and was considered one of the greatest of Presbyterian preachers. Arrangements were made for the discussion to be held in Washington, Kentucky, a three hundred mile trip on horseback from Campbell's home. The discusion was held in October, 1823, and lasted seven days. Campbell had carefully re-studied the entire question of baptism and had seen clearly for the first time that the *design* of baptism was significantly related to the remission of sins.

As the debate proceeded it became quite clear that McCalla could not meet the arguments presented by Campbell. The Baptists had so completely identified themselves with Campbell by this time that he felt it necessary to clarify his position with them. On the evening of the fifth day of the discussion he called the most prominent of the Baptist preachers into a room and told them that he disagreed with them as much as he did with the Presbyterians, and that, although they erred in different things, they were about equidistant from the truth of Apostolic Christianity. The preachers were not offended by his criticism but on the contrary seemed to be drawn closer to him. In fact, he was invited to tour their churches and preach for them.

When the debate closed many were convinced that infant baptism was based on human authority, and the Presbyterian cause never recovered from the defeat it had suffered. Campbell was now so fully convinced of the good that could be accomplished by free discussions that he wrote:

> Public discussion is, we are convinced, one of the best means of propagating the truth and of exposing error in doctrine or practice.
> We now reap the benefits of public debates of former times, and we have witnessed the beneficial results of those in our own time. And we are fully persuaded that a week's debating is worth a year's preaching, such as we generally have, for the purpose of disseminating truth and putting error out of countenance. There is nothing like meeting face to face in the presence of many witnesses and "talking the matter over;" and the man that cannot govern his own spirit in the midst of opposition and contradiction, is a poor Christian indeed.[5]

V. THE CHRISTIAN BAPTIST

To provide a wider circulation for the principles of the Restoration Movement, Alexander Campbell began publishing in 1823 a monthly religious paper. He had planned to call it "The Christian," but Walter Scott suggested that he add the word "Baptist," thinking this would give it a wider circulation among the Baptists and would increase its opportunity for doing good. The first issue of "The Christian Baptist" came from the press in August, 1823. In the prospectus he set forth the purpose of the publication as follows:

> THE CHRISTIAN BAPTIST shall espouse the cause of no religious sect, excepting that ancient sect called "CHRISTIANS FIRST AT ANTIOCH." Its sole object shall be the eviction of truth, and the exposure of error in doctrine and practice. The

5. Alexander Campbell, "Debate On Baptism," The Christian Baptist, (Buffaloe, Virginia: By the Author, 1827-29), I, 199. This has been reprinted by the Gospel Advocate Company, Nashville, Tenn., 1955. References hereafter will be made to this six-volume reprint.

editor acknowledging no standard of religious faith or works other than the Old and New Testaments, and the latter as the only standard of the religion of Jesus Christ, will, intentionally at least, oppose nothing which it contains, and recommend nothing which it does not enjoin. Having no worldly interest at stake from the adoption or reprobation of any article of faith or religious practice — having no gift nor religious emolument to blind his eyes or to pervert his judgment, he hopes to manifest that he is an impartial advocate of truth.[6]

The chief purpose of "The Christian Baptist" was to attack every religious idea that Campbell believed to be a hindrance to "the restoration of the ancient order of things." He began by attacking the clergy for perpetuating a clericism more interested in itself than the welfare of the true church. He began with the clergy of the church of Rome but concluded that the Protestant clergy were equally guilty. He attacked synods and legislative organizations, associations, societies and theological institutions. In many cases it was the abuse that he opposed; in others it was an organization that hindered the return to New Testament simplicity. At this time he felt that before positive measures could be adopted successfully it would be necessary to sweep away the traditions and innovations of men. "The Christian Baptist" was the broom he used for this unpleasant task. After seven years of publication, Campbell felt that it had served its purpose and replaced it by a new periodical entitled "Millennial Harbinger." One reason for the change was that followers of his undenominational movement were being nicknamed "Christian Baptists." In his concluding remarks in the last issue he stated, "I am resolved to give them no just occasion for nicknaming advocates of the ancient order of things."[7]

VI. WALTER SCOTT (1796-1861)

Walter Scott was born in Scotland and educated at the University of Edinburgh. At twenty-two years of age he went to America where, at first, he taught in an academy at Long Island. But desiring to go further West, he walked the three hundred miles from New York to Pittsburgh, arriving May 7,

6. Ibid., I, p. iv.
7. Ibid., VII, 309.

1819. Here he obtained a teaching position in an academy conducted by George Forrester.

Forrester had studied with the Haldanes in Scotland and made the Bible his only rule of faith and the absolute authority in all religious matters. Although Scott had adopted Presbyterianism he was yet interested in seeking the truth and began worshipping with a small congregation that Forrester had established. After a few weeks of careful Bible study, he gave up Presbyterianism, renounced infant baptism and was immersed by Forrester. Scott was so effective as a teacher that Forrester soon turned the academy over to him that he might go into full time religious work himself. When Forrester withdrew from the school and shortly thereafter accidently died by drowning, Scott was left with the responsibility of both the school and the church.

In the winter of 1821-22 Walter Scott and Alexander Campbell met for the first time. They were very different in temperament, but immediately became close friends. They were trained in the same religious system and through their own study had reached almost identical convictions. Campbell was inclined to be coldly logical, fearless, self-reliant and firm while Scott was emotional and timid, but gifted with an artistic nature. Alexander could always be expected to present a fine, clear sermon regardless of circumstances, but Walter was easily affected by his audience. Under favorable circumstances, however, his oratory surpassed that of Campbell. On one such occasion with Campbell in the audience, Scott reached such heights that the self-possessed Campbell jumped to his feet in the middle of the sermon and shouted "Glory to God in the Highest!" Scott, however, was not lacking in the ability to do clear, straight thinking. To him the Restoration Movement is indebted for the first clear analysis of the cases of conversion found in the Book of Acts. He was also to become the first really successful evangelist in this Restoration period.

From the time Scott and Campbell became acquainted and found that they shared similar views, they worked together toward the same goals. Scott even wrote occasionally for Campbell's "Christian Baptist."

VII. Extent of Agreement With the Baptists

The influence of his debates and his periodical brought Campbell many invitations from Baptist churches to visit them and preach for them. During 1824 and 1825 he made extensive tours in Kentucky and Virginia speaking in the leading Baptist churches. These tours gave him a personal contact with leading Baptist preachers and an opportunity to set forth clearly the principles of the Restoration Movement.

The association of the Campbells with the Baptist church needs some clarification at this point. The Brush Run church had affiliated itself to some degree already with the Redstone Association, but a segment of the Baptist church continued to oppose the Campbells. Alexander had called to their attention the differences between them during one of his debates when the Baptists began to look upon him as their champion. Among their differences are these:

1. The Baptists accepted the Philadelphia Confession of Faith as their bond of unity and statute of discipline and operated under it. The Campbells rejected all creeds as anti-christian and a hindrance to unity on the basis of the Bible alone.

2. The Baptists stood for Calvinism as set forth in the Confession. The Campbells held Calvinism to be a corruption of Christianity, a curse to the world, a cause of division and a perversion of the truth faith.

3. The Baptists generally had the Lord's Supper every three months and not oftener than once a month. The Campbells taught that the church should break bread every Lord's Day and that monthly communion was a departure from the original order.

4. The Association Baptist church believed that each congregation should have only one elder (or bishop). The Campbells felt that if a congregation did not have a plurality of elders (or bishops) that congregation had digressed from primitive purity.

5. Although it appeared that the Baptists and Campbells agreed on baptism they actually did not. To the Baptists immersion was an ordinance required for church membership but to the Campbells it was done in order to obtain remission of sins. These basic differences indicate that Campbell never truly considered himself a "Baptist." He wrote in May, 1826:

. . . I frankly own, that my full conviction is, that there are many Paido-Baptist congregations (those baptizing infants, J.M.), of whose Christianity, or of whose profession of Christianity, I think as highly as of most Baptist congregations, and with whom I could wish to be on the very same terms of Christian communion on which I stand with the whole Baptist Society.[8]

Although Campbell was not a Baptist he continued to work among them. His explanation for this is of some interest.

If we would heal the sick, we must visit them; if we would restore the lame, we must take them by the hand; if we would correct, inform, or reform erring Christians, we must do as the Savior did; — bear with their weaknesses . . . And the history of the world does not afford one instance of any man, or set of men, reforming, or restoring, or enlightening, or comforting the society from which they separated. . . . The Baptist society exhibits a greater variety than any other society in Christendom. They are a people made up of all religious persuasions; and, generally speaking, their platform is more consonant to the freedom of inquiry, to freedom from ecclesiastical tyranny, to the independence of congregations, than any other. . . . But so long as they will bear reproof, suffer exhortation, and allow us to declare our sentiments without restraint; so long as they manifest a **willingness** to know the whole truth, and any disposition to obey it; so long as they will hear us and cordially have fellowship with us, we will have fellowship with them, we will thus labor for their good, and endeavor to correct what appears to be amiss — commending when praise is due, and censuring when it becomes necessary.[9]

In 1826, Campbell published a revision of the New Testament under the title, *Living Oracles*. It is an excellent translation and was set forth with a wealth of critical information. He did not do the work himself but selected what he believed to be the most accurate translations of his day and published them under one title. He used the gospels as translated by George Campbell, the Epistles by MacKnight and Acts and Revelation by Doddridge. The translation accurately preserves the original meaning of the Greek verb *baptidzo* by giving "immerse" rather than the anglicized "baptize" — a point of considerable discussion then as now. Campbell was sadly disappointed in his anticipations for the new translation. The public was not ready for such a production. It was criticized as an unorthodox tampering with the "sacredness" of the King James Version.

8. Ibid., III, 203, (No. 10, May, 1826).
9. Ibid., 204-205.

The Baptists were especially angry when the wording "John the Baptist" was changed to "John the Immerser," for this eliminated their name from Scripture.

The King James version did need revision and later scholarship has certainly vindicated the work done by Campbell with the *Living Oracles*. The general lack of education among the church members of his day prevented an appreciation of true Biblical scholarship.

VIII. "THE GOSPEL RESTORED"

In 1827, as Campbell was going to attend the annual meeting of the Mahoning Baptist Association at New Lisbon, Ohio, he went by Steubenville to see Walter Scott. Although Scott was not a member of the Association, Campbell prevailed upon him to attend the meeting. The churches of the association were doing very little in the area of evangelism. Among the fourteen churches reporting there had been only thirty-four baptisms, and eleven of them were at Wellsburg, Alexander's home church. Thirteen had been excommunicated, leaving a net gain of sixteen.[10] It had been eighteen years since the publication of the "Declaration and Address," and the Campbells had succeeded in planting only two small congregations. The failure seemed to be a lack of practical application of the principles in evangelistic work. But Walter Scott was destined to remove this difficulty.

During the meeting of the Association Scott was selected as evangelist for the Western Reserve of Ohio. His duties were to travel among the churches and hold meetings wherever he could get a hearing. Due to his own study and hearty acceptance of the plea to return to New Testament purity, he saw that he could not imitate the procedure of denominational evangelists.

The mourners bench system was in common use, and Calvinism had produced a feeling of helplessness. Under this system a sinner was told that he could do nothing to obtain salvation but plead with God in the hope that God would somehow grant his desired election and confirm it to his satisfaction. The evangelists of the day believed they could do no more than exhort a penitent to pray. Scott knew this was not enough, yet he

10. Garrison and Degroot, **History of the Disciples of Christ**, p. 186.

was not sure what they should do. In his perplexity he turned to the book of Acts and studied the teaching and activity of first century preachers. He made a careful analysis of each case of conversion and for the first time saw clearly that there were logical "steps" involved in each sinner's conversion. His synthesis of the New Testament examples of conversion led him to the conclusion that faith, repentance, confession and baptism were necessary to receiving remission of sins and the gift of the Holy Spirit. This teaching he called "The Gospel Restored."

Scott began to preach this "plan of salvation" with the belief that New Testament preaching would bring results similar to those recorded in the New Testament. In this he was not disappointed. There were tremendous responses to Christ's invitation from the very beginning, and he baptized a thousand persons the first year. After that, whole congregations were converted and the number of disciples multiplied greatly.

When the Campbells heard of the success Scott was experiencing they were afraid he was using some kind of sensationalism to draw the people. Thomas Campbell investigated the work of Scott and returned with joy and thanksgiving for the success of the pure gospel Scott was preaching. Scott's contribution to the Restoration Movement was chiefly his putting into practice the principles that the Campbells had already been preaching. Whereas the Campbells had been urging unity among churches, Scott began urging individuals to unite with Christ on the simple terms of the gospel. His was a practical, simple appeal. If all would unite with Christ on New Testament terms they would automatically be united with each other. Unity was a spiritual matter, achieved on the basis of obedience to Christ rather than compromise of religious bodies.

The gospel plan of salvation preached first by Scott was soon adopted by other evangelists with no less stimulating results. There remained, however, but one hindrance to the complete restoration of the church Scott felt. That hindrance was the Mahoning Association to which many churches still belonged.

When the Association met in 1830 Walter Scott worked to dissolve it because it was an unscriptural organization. He had no objection to an annual meeting of disciples on a voluntary

340   THE ETERNAL KINGDOM

basis, but such an organization as the Mahoning Association possessing authority over congregations and consising of elected delegates could not be justified by Scripture he felt. Alexander Campbell was present for the meeting and was in favor of continuing the organization. He did not see why a "Thus saith the Lord" was necessary in such a matter and would have spoken against dissolving the association had Scott not prevailed upon him to remain silent. The motion to dissolve the association passed.

With this achievement congregations became independent in government and the Restoration was fully launched. Accepting the Bible as authoritative, the plan of salvation was restored to the place it occupied in the first century, and congregational matters were placed in the hands of Scripturally authorized elders.

Chapter Thirty-Two

Union of Forces: Stone and Campbell

Strictly speaking, there was no "Union of Forces" among the autonomous congregations of undenominational Christianity — no central controlling headquarters. Yet these various movements that purged the churches of human innovations and encouraged a return to the Bible and the primitive order of things did not remain entirely independent of each other. Their leaders met and exchanged views. They conducted meetings together and broadened their fellowship to include congregations that others had begun. Small churches in the same community united, and individual members from a former "Campbell" congregation, for example, could move membership to a former "Stone" congregation without hesitation or question. This kind of "union" did occur.

The earlier movements begun by James O'Kelley and Abner Jones did not continue long as an organized effort, it seems, though many of their followers merged with the Stone movement. From the earlier efforts ideas had come which motivated individuals to become undenominational in their religious affiliations.

The movement begun by John Wright united with the Stone forces to which amalgamation was added the Silver Creek Baptist Association in 1820. This group had been saturated with the teaching of the Campbells.

While the Campbell movement was associating itself with the Baptists, the movement under Stone was making great progress. By 1820 the Campbells could count only four congregations and less than two-hundred members who had accepted their principles. Stone, however, at this time, had fellowship with five hundred congregations and fifteen thousand members.

Stone's movement, called the "Christian Connection," was in several vital respects quite different from that of the Campbels. Stone was immersed in 1807 as a result of his own conviction that such constituted Scriptural baptism. He, however, did not make immersion a test of fellowship as did the Campbells. He believed that each one should be free to decide the matter for himself. Stone did not observe the Lord's Supper often. It was, perhaps, too sacred to be made a regular part of every worship.

Stone had not seen any definite "plan of salvation" in the Bible. He opposed Calvinism but did not understand just what should be done with sinners who came to Christ. So he retained the mourners bench and encouraged all who seemed to experience any kind of mental relief during a service to consider themselves saved and then receive baptism at their convenience. They could choose the "mode" desired. The preachers among Stone's movement were great exhorters and preached powerfully against sin but did not effectively answer the question "What must I do to be saved?" They opposed sectarianism and brought whole Baptist Associations into their undenominational fold.

Beginning in 1809 there had been steps taken to organize the churches of the Christian Connection. In 1819 the first general conference was held and a central organization formed which began to organize the congregations into a denominational pattern. Stone did not approve of this and in 1826 began the publication of *The Christian Messenger* to oppose the effort. He lost the leadership of the movement, however, to men who were bent on organizing and so was forced to declare himself and a few followers independent of the Christian Connection which later went into Unitarianism and in 1931 was united with the Congregational Church. At this time there were fifty-thousand people in Stone's movement, thirty-thousand of whom were spiritual children of Stone. Only fifteen-thousand of these remained true to their former principles.

While Stone was working to salvage as much of his movement as possible from denominationalism Campbell was working to separate his following from the Baptists. In 1830, feeling that the *Christian Baptist* had accomplished its work, he began a new paper which he called *Millennial Harbinger*. He did not select this name because he was predicting a material reign of Christ upon the earth after His second coming, but chose it rather to suggest the idea that the Kingdom of God on earth

could be realized in its fulness only after a unification of the
children of God. He believed strongly in the unity of God's
people and felt that a restoration of the New Testament church
would provide a practical means of achieving this unity.

With this change in the name of Campbell's paper, the
dissolving of the Mahoning Association the same year and the
publication of a New Testament that omitted the name Baptist,
leaders of Baptist churches felt they had to draw a clear line
of separation between them and the Restoration leaders. The
first "overt acts of separation" were performed by Baptist
churches for what they deemed "not only sufficient but controlling reasons." The Beaver Association of Ohio, about 1829,
issued a circular denouncing the Mahoning Association and
Campbell. It charged them with disbelieving many of the doctrines of Holy Scripture. In the autumn of 1832 the Dover Association of Virginia, after careful deliberation, advised the
churches constituting it to separate from their communion
everyone who was promoting controversy and discord under
the name of "Reformers." This was done on the ground that
the doctrines taught were "not according to godliness, but subversive of the true spirit of the gospel of Jesus Christ, disorgan-
izing and demoralizing in their tendency." Twenty years later,
however, one of the authors of this resolution published a statement of his belief that the report adopted by the Dover Association contained "some unguarded, unnecessarily harsh expressions" and particularly acknowledged that this characteriza-
tion of the doctrines of Campbell as "demoralizing in their tendency" was unjust. After the action of the Dover Association
those who sympathized with Campbell either voluntarily withdrew from the Baptists or were disfellowshipped by them and
within a decade the separation was complete. It was accomplished at a great cost to the Baptist churches, though, for the
denomination was divided in the West and in the South.
Churches were split or completely dissolved. Some churches
even went over as a body to undenominationalism, and a few
entire Associations made the change. Seeds of bitterness and
discord were sown that have borne the fruits of strife for more
than a century.

Meanwhile some degree of unity was being achieved among
Christians. As early as 1826 John T. Johnson had begun work-

ing with Stone to unite the churches in one fellowship. In 1828 Joseph Gaston of the Stone persuasion began holding meetings with Walter Scott. They preached for congregations of both movements. This arrangement, a "Stone man" and a "Campbell man" working together, soon became common.

Yet, as much as all wanted complete unity there were serious difficulties in the way — Campbell's "legalism" and Stone's "emotionalism." Those of Campbell's persuasion were accused of being "all head and no heart" and those of Stone's "all heart and no head." Since Stone had not made immersion a test of fellowship "his" churches admitted the unimmersed to membership and communion. Campbell's followers on the other hand felt that Stone's churches would compromise any doctrine for the sake of union. In spite of such differences a measure of union was being realized: preachers of both groups were working together.

In 1832 the leaders of these movements met in Lexington, Kentucky, to work out a complete union of forces if possible. Preliminary meetings had been held in Georgetown, Kentucky, during December of the preceding year and had been so successful that unity seemed at hand. Many outstanding men from both movements were present, and it was decided that one man from each party should speak. Stone and "Racoon" John Smith were selected. All were opposed to a compromise of principles, but all were eager to see a genuine fulfillment of the prayer of Jesus.

Realizing the importance of the occasion and the fact that union is not necessarily unity, Smith, the first speaker, said with calm dignity:

God has but one people on the earth. He has given to them but one Book, and therein exhorts and commands them to be one family. A union, such as we plead for — a union of God's people on that one Book — must, then, be practicable.

Every Christian desires to stand complete in the whole will of God. The prayer of the Saviour, and the whole tenor of his teaching, clearly show that it is God's will that his children should be united. To the Christian, then, such a union must be desirable.

But an amalgamation of sects is not such a union as Christ prayed for, and God enjoins. To agree to be one upon any system of human inventions would be contrary to his will, and could never be a blessing to the Church or the world; therefore the only union practicable or desirable must be based on the Word of God, as the only rule of faith and practice.

There are certain abstruse or speculative matters — such as the mode of the **Divine Existence,** and the **Ground and Nature of the Atonement** — that have, for centuries, been themes of discussion among Christians. These questions are as far from being settled now as they were in the beginning of the controversy. By a needless and intemperate discussion of them much feeling has been provoked, and divisions have been produced.

For several years past I have tried to speak on such subjects only in the language of inspiration; for it can offend no one to say about those things just what the Lord himself has said. In this scriptural style of speech all Christians should be agreed. . . . I will not linger to build a theory on such texts, and thus encourage a speculative and wrangling spirit among my brethren. I will present these subjects only in the words which the Lord has given to me. I know he will not be displeased if we say just what he has said. Whatever opinions about these and similar subjects I may have reached, in the course of my investigations, if I never distract the church of God with them, or seek to impose them on my brethren, they will never do the world any harm. . . . While there is but one faith, there may be ten thousand opinions; and hence, if Christians are ever to be one, they must be one in faith, and not in opinion. . . . While for the sake of peace and Christian union, I have long since waived the public maintenance of any speculation I may hold, **yet not one Gospel fact, commandment, or promise, will I surrender for the world!**

Let us, then, my brethren, be no longer Campbellites or Stoneites, New Lights or Old Lights, or any other kind of **lights,** but let us all come to the Bible, and to the Bible alone, as the only book in the world that can give us all the Light we need.[1]

When Smith had finished, Stone arose and agreed that Smith had touched upon the real need. If unity was to prevail no one person could press his opinions upon another. He said:

The controversies of the Church sufficiently prove that Christians never can be one in their speculations upon those mysterious and sublime subjects which, while they interest the Christian philosopher, can not edify the Church. After we had given up all creeds and taken the Bible and the Bible alone, as our rule of faith and practice, we met with so much opposition, that by force of circumstances, I was led to deliver some speculative discourses upon those subjects. But I never preached a sermon of that kind that once feasted my heart; I always felt a barrenness of soul afterwards. I

1. John Augustus Williams, **Life of Elder John Smith.** (Cincinnatti: Standard Publishing Co., 1870), pp. 371-373. This work has been reprinted by the Gospel Advocate Company.

perfectly accord with Brother Smith that these speculations should never be taken into the pulpit; but that when compelled to speak of them at all, we should do so in the words of inspiration.

I have not one objection to the ground laid down by him as the true scriptural basis of union among the people of God; and I am willing to give him, now and here, my hand.[2]

At the conclusion of Stone's speech the two shook hands indicating their pledge of fellowship and brotherly love. It was then suggested that all who agreed with the union on this basis give each other a hand of fellowship. This was done as they sang together and the union was ratified.

Neither side gave in to the other, and there was no transfer of loyalties from one leader to another. They all agreed to follow Christ only. The only concession that was made, and it was made by all, was that in regard to differences of opinion they would use the language of Scripture. If the Scripture itself was used no one could object to it; if they refused to separate over speculative matters the union might be permanent.

There were timid souls who feared the outcome. Some were afraid of offending the Baptists. When this was suggested to Smith, he said, "I know not how that may be; but certain I am that the union of Christians, upon a scriptural basis, is right, and that it can never be bad policy to do what is right."[3] Others thought it would be impossible to retain unity without a creed or confession. To this Smith replied, "We have a perfect one, delivered to us from heaven, and confirmed by Jesus and His Apostles — the New Testament."[4] When asked to which party new members would belong Smith replied, "We have no party. It is understood among us that we feel an equal interest in every church of Christ, and we are determined to build up all such churches without regard to their former names."[5]

The ease with which the former "Christians" — the followers of Stone, and the "Reformers" — the followers of Campbell, united, can be understood by the esteem with which these men held each other. After Stone heard Campbell preach he said:

I saw no distinctive feature between the doctrine he preached

2. Ibid., 373.
3. Ibid., 374.
4. Ibid., 375
5. Ibid.

and that which we had preached for many years, except on baptism for remission of sins. Even this I had once received and taught, as before stated, but had strangely let it go from my mind, till brother Campbell revived it afresh. . . .

I will not say, there are no faults in brother Campbell; but that there are fewer, perhaps, in him, than any man I know on earth, and over these few my love would throw a veil, and hide them from view forever. I am constrained, and willingly constrained, to acknowledge him the greatest promoter of this reformation of any man living. The Lord reward him! . . .

The only distinguishing doctrine between us and them was, that they preached baptism for the remission of sins to believing penitents. This doctrine had not generally obtained amongst us, though some few had received it, and practised accordingly. They insisted also upon weekly communion, which we had neglected.[6]

After 1832 the leaders of the two groups worked together as one to make the union complete throughout the country. In 1834 Stone moved to Jacksonville, Illinois, where the movements had not united. Refusing to unite with either until they had united with each other, Stone was able to bring them together.

6. Barton W. Stone, The Biography of Elder Barton Warren Stone (Cincinnati: published for the author by J. A. and U. P. James), pp. 75-77).

Chapter Thirty-Three

The Unfinished Restoration

Although by the nineteenth century restorers did establish New Testament churches, digression soon marred their work. Just as the early followers of Luther and Calvin were soon to find more disagreement among themselves than existed between their leaders, so also the movements of these restorers were unable to retain the measure of unity which they had achieved. For some the "restoration" so nobly begun had ended in "reformation;" union was sought at the expense of unity. Failing to fully realize that men can only be changed by changing their thinking, some of the latter leaders attempted to effect that change through a transfer of organizational affiliation. But the transferring of membership from one church to another was not sufficient to produce a transformation of mind. The only principle upon which all men might unite was soon abandoned. The slogan, "In matters of faith—unity; in matters of opinion—liberty; in all things—love," was forgotten in the heat of controversy. Division was thus inevitable.

The first wedges driven between the disciples were those produced by a departure from the very principle that had originally brought them together: the missionary society and the use of mechanical instruments of music in worship were innovated without precept or example from the New Testament. Alexander Campbell inactively served as the first president of the missionary society which was begun in 1849. L. L. Pinkerton is generally regarded as having introduced the first mechanical instrument of music into the worship of these "restoration" churches at Midway, Kentucky, in 1858 or 1859. Of its use J. W. McGarvey (1829-1911), described by The London *Times* as "in all probability . . . the ripest Bible scholar on earth," made this comment: "It is manifest that we cannot adopt the practice without abandoning the obvious and only ground on which a restoration of Primitive Christianity can be accomplished, or on which the plea for it can be maintained."

(348)

Clearly, the guilt of the division must fall on those who, unwilling to sacrifice their desires for the sake of their brother's conscience, drove these wedges firmly between the disciples on the basis of opinion rather than Scripture. From this historic beginning arose the present day movement known as the Disciples of Christ or First Christian Church, which accepts both innovations — the missionary society and mechanical instruments of music.

The body of Christ has not yet experienced a complete restoration of pure Christianity. It views its own history in many respects with a sense of achievement, but at the same time it is not oblivious to its failures. As the "pillar and ground of the truth" it finds itself still imperfect in doctrine and life; as the "light of the world," still imperfectly reflecting the light which comes from Christ; as "the salt of the earth," still far short of saving the world, as "the body of Christ," often divided, opinionated and prejudiced.

Despite her imperfections, however, the church is the bride of Christ and the object of His love. The restoration of the church to its purity will remain the constant concern of every generation of God-fearing people. It will remain their constant challenge. It cannot be hoped that all men will agree upon every question of religion. It cannot be expected that all men will some day attain to the same degree of understanding. But it is not too much to suggest that all men of every nation, tribe and tongue not only can but must possess a love for truth. Allegiance to parties, persons and creeds must give way to a "hunger and thirst for righteousness" if the world is ever to witness that unity and symmetry of the body of Christ which the Holy Spirit portrays in the New Testament.

The Reformation is unfinished and the Restoration incomplete. Throughout the world devout men are still advocating non-denominational Christianity. The history of Christ's church is still in the making. Voices are everywhere blending themselves into a harmonious anthem to the tune of "Restoration" pleas. "Back to the Bible" and "Let us speak where the Bible speaks and remain silent where the Bible is silent" are phrases echoing from every quarter. The intensity with which undenominationalism is being advocated has attracted the interest of George Cornell, religious writer for the Associated Press. He writes:

> Like the will-o'-the-wisp, their movement, called the "Churches of Christ," is nearly everywhere in the country today, yet nowhere in particular. It has no headquarters. It has no denominational officials. It has no policy-making authority, it has no systematic connections at all. Its only links are strictly spiritual. . . .
>
> The movement, although shunning any over-all planning or structure, has spread like grass seed on a prairie wind. By the best figures available, its membership has more than doubled in 10 years, up from 814,000 to 1,750,000.
>
> This puts it in 11th place among the major Protestant bodies in America.
>
> According to figures in the latest Yearbook of American Churches, the movement now includes 16,500 churches, more than half of them built in the last decade.
>
> Although the movement has no centralized missions bureau, individual congregations support 200 American missionaries abroad. Member contributions also support 16 Christian colleges, 17 children's homes and 10 homes for the aged. (There are congregations in 67 foreign countries. J.M.)
>
> About the source of the movement's vitality . . . "It's going back to the simple teachings of the New Testament and accepting it as the only basis of authority."[1]

The church which Christ built is neither denominational nor Protestant. It possesses no *denominating* creed, name or hierarchy. It was not founded in *protest* to any existing institution. It is not the product of the "Reformation" *or* the "Restoration." But it is, and must be, the full-grown plant which has arisen from the "seed of the kingdom" sown in the hearts of men.[2] Its origin is to be found in the gospel of Christ.[3] It is founded on the apostles and prophets with Christ as the chief corner stone.[4] To date its appearance in history earlier or later than the atonement of Christ is futile, for it is His body[5] and He purchased it with His own blood.[6] By its very nature, the body is exclusive: it is one.[7] There could not conceivably be more

1. **Arkansas Gazette.** April 30, 1960, "Fervent Church of Christ: Independent, Bible-bound."
2. Luke 8:11ff.
3. Acts 2:38, 47; Matt. 28-18-20.
4. Ephesians 2:20.
5. Ephesians 1:22, 23.
6. Acts 20:28; Matt. 26:28.
7. Ephesians 4:4.

than one body as there is but one head.[8] In the presence of a divided Christendom one runs the risk of being misunderstood by suggesting that there is but one church. It is not here suggested that there is but one "denomination." The church of Jesus Christ is neither Jewish, Catholic nor Protestant. It is non-denominational in its origin, worship and organization. It is the body of Christ, functioning according to New Testament directions, organized according to New Testament pattern and worshipping according to New Testament instructions, extensive enough to embrace in its fellowship all who comply with God's requirements and who thus become a part of that body.[9] Moving on through time to its ultimate victory this "stone cut out of the mountain without hands" survives the rise and fall of temporal kingdoms and proves itself to be that which in reality it is — the Eternal Kingdom.

8. Colossians 1:18.
9. Acts 2:47; 1 Corinthians 12:13.